THE PRIVATE PRACTICE MBA

A Step-By-Step Guide to Put
Your Practice on Autopilot

**DR. JEREMY PYLE
& ROBBIE POE**

The Private Practice MBA: A Step-by-Step Guide to Put Your Practice on Autopilot

Copyright © 2023 by Dr. Jeremy Pyle and Robbie Poe

All rights reserved. No part of this publication may be reproduced, stored in a retrieval system, or transmitted in any form by any means, electronic, mechanical, photocopy, recording, or otherwise, without the prior permission of the publisher, except as provided by USA copyright law.

No patent liability is assumed with respect to the use of the information contained herein. Although every precaution has been taken in the preparation of this book, the publisher and author assume no responsibility for errors or omissions. Neither is any liability assumed for damages resulting from the use of the information contained herein.

This book is intended for informational purposes only. It is not intended to be used as the sole basis for financial or investing decisions, nor should it be construed as advice designed to meet the particular needs of an individual's situation.

Published by Forefront Books.
Distributed by Simon & Schuster.

Library of Congress Control Number: 2022923742

Print ISBN: 978-1- 637631485
E-book ISBN: 978-1-637631492

Cover Design by Bruce Gore, Gore Studio, Inc.
Interior Design by Bill Kersey, KerseyGraphics

DEDICATION

JEREMY

For Meg, the Weasel Peanut, Buoy, and the Whale:
You'll always be my favorite things to think, talk, and write about.
For Mom and the OG Dr. Pyle:
Thanks for the roots and wings that gave
me the courage to take this chance.

ROBBIE

For Hazel:
Nothing has revealed more about the importance of
leadership than being a father. This book is for you, baby girl.

TABLE OF CONTENTS

A Note from Jeremy 9

Introduction: Who the Heck Are We? 17

SECTION 1: PUT YOUR BUSINESS ON AUTOPILOT

Chapter 1: The Business of Medicine Is Sick 33

Chapter 2: The Most Powerful Person in the Room:
The Business Owner 51

Chapter 3: The You That You Can't Be: The Business Director . . . 75

Chapter 4: Your Hedge of Protection: The Team Leaders 95

SECTION 2: ALL THINGS MONEY

Chapter 5: Putting Your Cash on Autopilot 113

Chapter 6: The Zero-Based Budget: A Map for Your Money 125

Chapter 7: Staying Connected to Your Cash 145

Chapter 8: The Metrics That Drive Your Internal
and External Accounting............................ 161

Chapter 9: The Ins and Outs of Team Compensation 187

SECTION 3: ALL THINGS SALES AND MARKETING

Chapter 10: Understanding the Patient Journey............. 211

Chapter 11: The Patient Journey Phases 1 and 2:
Awareness and Consideration 231

Chapter 12: The Patient Journey Phase 3: Research.......... 249

Chapter 13: The Patient Journey Phases 4 and 5:
Intent to Buy and Purchase........................ 273

SECTION 4: ALL THINGS OPERATIONS

Chapter 14: Your Operational Ethos....................... 297

Chapter 15: The Power of Checklists...................... 317

Chapter 16: Finding, Prioritizing, and Addressing Issues 335

Chapter 17: Keystone Meetings........................... 351

SECTION 5: ALL THINGS LEADERSHIP

Chapter 18: Aligning Your Team.......................... 381

Chapter 19: Growing Your Team 403

Chapter 20: Leading Your Team 425

Chapter 21: *The Private Practice MBA* **Method in Real Life**..... 447

Recommended Reading............................... 455

Acknowledgments................................... 457

Endnotes 461

A NOTE FROM JEREMY

Before we dig into all the different things we're going to discuss throughout this book, I want to tell you right up front what to expect and explain the different ways you can view and use this resource.

I am a surgeon and a practice owner. So just like you, my mailbox, inbox, and voice mail are full of ads and messages from medical marketing companies and sales consultants making big promises they almost never deliver on. They're always promoting this software or that technique, which will solve all your problems. And they're willing to share it with you for the low, low cost of [fill in the blank].

That's not what this book is about. I'll say right here, right up front that **we do not want your money**. I feel like I have to say that because you and I are always on guard against companies targeting us for a hard sell. I'll talk more about this in a bit. I just wanted to get that out of the way to make sure you don't turn me off too soon.

So what *do* we want?

This book is about function over form. The function we're after is to help providers get their lives back. In the introduction, you'll hear the story of how I pushed my life to the breaking point trying to manage all the demands of being both a surgeon and a business owner. I don't want you to drive your life toward the edge of a cliff at 90 mph like I did. So my business partner and I wrote a book to unpack the plan that pulled me out of the mess my business had become and that literally gave me my life back. The problem with a book that values function over form, though, is that it can be a lot to digest.

That being the case, here's a quick overview of what we're going to cover along with a recommendation for how you might read this book.

THE LEVEL-10 BUSINESS FRAMEWORK

Perhaps the most important thing to know about everything you're about to read is this: *we didn't make any of it up.* In fact, at the core of the accelerated success we've experienced is a powerful triad of principles that are deeply ingrained in virtually every modern, growth-orientated company across the world.

These principles have been given many different titles. Interestingly, many industries don't even give them a formal name simply because they are so widely accepted as best practices. Therefore, it should be comforting to know that much of the information you'll find here isn't the least bit novel, and you can find these principles on a website called The Level-10 Business Framework (www.level10framework.com). It's tried-and-true throughout sector after sector of businesses and across Fortune 50 organizations and small trailblazing companies alike. Giving my team the green light to implement The Level-10 Business Framework eventually changed nearly every facet of my life for the better. But it took a moment.

Early on, when we began implementing The Level-10 Business Framework in our practice, we experienced a mix of the good (in the form of structure and vision) and the bad (of trying to do something, almost anything, really, that isn't already an accepted part of clinical medicine). The Level-10 Business Framework assumes that a business owner is able to work on their business all day long; however, like many small-business participants, physicians simply don't have that luxury.

A NOTE FROM JEREMY

We are busy working in our business all day long, making time to work on our business sparse and always at a cost.

So I had to make a decision. We could either abandon The Level-10 Business Framework altogether, or we could (to our knowledge) do what no one else has ever done—deeply research the powerful Level-10 Business Framework principles and rebuild them from the ground up to work within private medical practices. This book is the result of that labor. More on that soon.

HOW TO READ THIS BOOK

The best way to read this book will depend on what kind of reader you are, what you're hoping to learn, and, frankly, which area of your business is causing you the biggest headaches right now.

The first way to read this book is to start at the beginning and read straight through to the end. This is the ideal way to read it because it will give you a true, 40,000-foot overview of how to successfully implement a business operating system without losing your sanity in the process. You'll see the broad strokes *and* the tiny, yet crucial, details, which will (hopefully) give you the chance to learn from our mistakes and to course-correct much faster and easier than we did.

The second way to read this book is to jump around from section to section or chapter to chapter based on what your biggest needs are at the moment. This is designed to be a go-to, panic-mode resource just as much as a slow-burn, long-game strategy. So once you've read section 1, if you feel the greatest weakness in your practice is your approach to sales and marketing, jump to that section. If your greatest need is to reclaim hundreds of hours per year from the massive ball of red tape you're tangled in, skip to the operations section. If handling such large sums of money makes you nervous, jump to money. If you're an excellent doctor but a terrible leader, skip to leadership. It doesn't matter where you start. In fact, earlier versions of this book and the online course (www.ThePrivatePracticeMBA.com) had these four sections in a totally different order. We kept rearranging them until we finally said, "Screw it. Let the reader decide what they need to read first."

That said, the three roles we discuss in the first four chapters are crucial to understanding what we'll cover in the money, sales and marketing, operations, and leadership sections. You'll see the terms *business owner*, *business director*, and *team leader* throughout the book, and each role has a part to play in each of the systems we'll discuss, so it's worth your time to read those opening chapters before jumping around too much. Even if you *think* you know what we mean by *business director*, for instance, you almost certainly do not—at least not in the way we use the term. Missing that one piece of information alone will throw off how you understand and apply everything else we discuss in the other sections of the book.

Whichever way you choose to work through this book, my guess is you'll read it through a veil of suspicion, waiting for the catch or hidden sales pitch. The information we're handing you could be worth millions in revenue and, more importantly, thousands of hours of reclaimed time, so if we don't deal with this right here, you're likely to read this book with 75 percent attention and 25 percent suspicion. So let's address the elephant in the room: why are we giving this information away (essentially) for free?

WHY WE WROTE THIS FOR YOU

We make our living doing what we love—serving our patients and helping them achieve their goals through aesthetic medicine. I'm a physician, and my coauthor, Robbie Poe, is passionate about business

A NOTE FROM JEREMY

The Level-10 Business Framework

In order to implement the Level-10 Business Framework, the **three foundational pillars** below must be simultaneously established. Then, they will be used to create resources around **twelve critical tenets**. Of these twelve tenets, six focus on external progress and six on internal improvement.

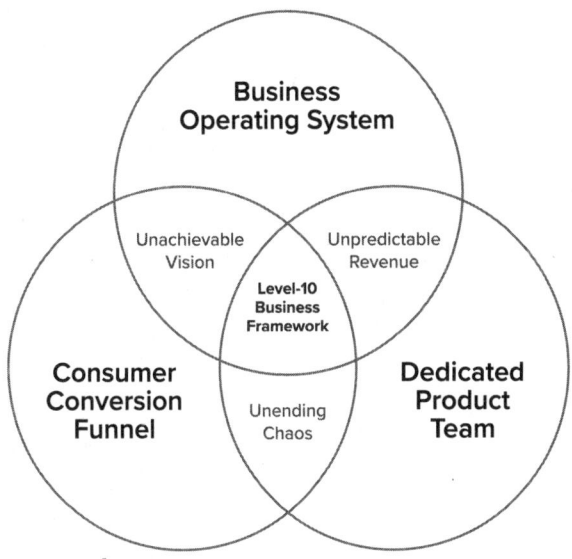

The 12 Tenets

External Progress

Infinite Lead Capture
Corporate and Personal Brand Authority
Psychology-Based Brand Platform
Interrelated Social Platforms
Measurable Ad Strategy
Trusted Marketing Personalities

Internal Improvement

Rapid Iteration on Existing Systems/New Ideas
Amplified Economies of Scale
Teamwide Best Practices Education
Internal-Mentor Business Coaching
Collaborative Communication Platform
Systems-Based Technology Platform

We encourage you to visit Level10Framework.com to learn more.

leadership. It's what we know, it's what we love, and it's how we earn our living. But throughout this book, you'll read about other things Robbie and I are working on to better serve the business side of medicine—for ourselves and for other doctors. You'll hear us mention the software product we provide (for free) to any practice that wants to use it. You'll hear us mention the online video curriculum we provide (for free) that enables us to teach this material in a different format. You'll hear us mention the licensing structure we've developed that allows other surgeons to open and run their own practices using our tools and marketing engine. Depending on when you're reading this, there will likely be a handful of other things out in the marketplace with our names on them. That's because we're passionate about making the practice of medicine better for everyone, doctors and patients alike.

But here's what I want you to hear: *I do not care whether you use all, some, or none of these things.* You're not going to hear a hard sell for anything throughout this book. We'll reference some things because they're important to a story we're telling, an example we're using, or a process we're familiar with. That's it. If you want to follow the link and use it for yourself, go for it. If you don't, that's fine too. We've tried to make this information applicable to you, whether you use the same tools we use or something else altogether.

Our primary goal with this book and the other tools we develop comes down to one word: *freedom*. You'll hear us use that word a lot in this book. Freedom is what I desperately wanted and needed at the low point in my career, and it's the thing I've heard hundreds, maybe thousands of other doctors yearn for (but think they'll never have). It breaks my heart to think about a promising young surgeon who's finishing his training and, because he hasn't been taught any alternative, blindly joins an older surgeon's practice, only to discover his new "mentor" takes strange liberties with his staff, runs the business in the red every month, and slowly gets jealous of the young doctor's burgeoning success. I'm tired of hearing about the academic surgeon nine years into her career who is so frustrated with constant administrative beat downs that she either accepts her "fate" of trudging through another twenty years of misery or faces the less oppressive but more terrifying prospect of opening a private practice.

The reason we put all this stuff out into the world for free (or for the cost of a typical hardback book, not the ridiculous prices we're used to paying for medical books) is that we believe by making your *life* a little better, we can help make *the world* a little better. If that's all we ever get out of this, we'll still call it a success.

AN OFFENSIVE PERSPECTIVE

Now I must say one more thing. I realize this isn't going to be a popular opinion, but I've been in this industry long enough to know that it's true. As physicians, we will never learn to run modern, growth-oriented practices by paying attention to the countless consultants, interactive agencies, or email-spam artists that claim to be "industry experts." The promotion of new ideas is just too much of a gamble for anyone who makes a living convincing doctors to do something. As a result, we get the same, stale, retread advice over and over again. We just do not take risks and these folks know it. (And if you don't believe me, go to any plastic surgeon's website in America. They are all exactly the same. The first photo is of a stock model in amazingly impossible shape, and the next is a picture of the surgeon or surgeons. Every. Single. One. The only variation is that some put the surgeon's photos first.)

There is no medical conference or meeting on the planet that can teach us to scale beyond our personal capacities, and there are especially no "free business development resources" being provided by our vendors that will make any measurable change in our practices.

If we want modern practices... if we want exponential growth... if we want evolution of antiquated, unacceptable business models, then we must lead the charge of systematic, radical change. We must demand the same level of excellence in our business as we demand of ourselves when we cross the threshold of the operating room.

So as you dive in here, just know that there's no catch. The blood, sweat, tears, dirty scrubs, and missed birthday parties that came with adapting The Level-10 Business Framework to our type of work was all done in an attempt to build something bigger than ourselves—something that hopefully can do some good in the world. That's our hope... same as yours.

Dr. Jeremy Pyle
Raleigh, North Carolina

INTRODUCTION
WHO THE HECK ARE WE?

Jeremy: Every doctor and/or practice owner I know is an accidental leader. I sure am. I never really set out to run a big company, lead a bunch of people, or be responsible for growing a brand. I just wanted to be a doctor. I loved the art and science of medicine. I loved the idea of helping people. I loved the challenge of picking a tough, outright intimidating specialty and proving myself in a demanding field. But dealing with P&L statements, budget reviews, marketing, employee performance evaluations, disciplining team members, running meetings, and the daily grind of office management?

Hell, no.

But here we are.

Today I own a successful, growing plastic surgery practice in Raleigh, North Carolina. We have around fifty employees, multiple offices across the country that operate under our brand name, and a couple of side businesses that have grown out of our practice. What started as an interest in medicine and a desire to help people has grown into a huge, eight-arm octopus of a business—and somehow, I'm the one holding the beast's leash. And hey, if you're reading this, my guess is you're in the same boat, either owning a practice already or wanting to someday. How did we get here?

Frankly, I landed in plastic surgery almost by accident. When I was in medical school, several people suggested I choose plastic surgery as a specialty...so I did. I'm embarrassed to say that I honestly didn't put that much thought into it, and it could have gone wrong in a million different ways. But it didn't. It went great—not because I'm a good planner, but because I got lucky.

After fourteen years of postsecondary education, I joined a practice with two surgeons who were at the stage of their careers where they were basically cruising toward retirement. They were not interested in building or growing the business, and they thwarted or ignored every idea I had to do so. So as soon as I could leave that environment, I did. Fortunately, I joined another practice with an older surgeon who was passionate about continually growing his skills and his business. Dr. Glenn Davis ultimately practiced surgery well into his seventies, always questioning, challenging himself, and trying to progress. It's not that he pushed *hard*; he just never *stopped* pushing. I owe a lot to Glenn.

When I became a partner in Glenn's practice, he asked me if I wanted to run the business side of things. Honestly, I didn't know what that meant. If I had known, I would have been too intimidated to say yes. However, ignorance won out, and I jumped at the opportunity. I started off with a lot of enthusiasm and no plan at all. I just assumed that if I was good at my job and kind to the people I worked with, everything would work out. In many ways, I was right. It did work out—but that's not because of my business savvy. It's because the plastic surgery market was booming, and it was incredibly difficult to fail as a plastic surgeon at that point in time.

So instead of failing (which is what my qualifications deserved), our business grew. Quickly. It turns out that being kind to people is strangely uncommon in business and in medicine, and I think that unwittingly became my secret weapon. But what grows an enthusiastic, supportive customer base is not what makes a business great. They are two very different skill sets, and I had one but not the other. A huge piece was missing.

Looking back, I like to describe my business at that point as an impressive-looking ship. The USS *Davis and Pyle Plastic Surgery Practice* looked beautiful. Anyone walking by the dock would have been impressed with its gleaming rails and magnificent sail. But there were cracks in the hull. It could stay afloat just fine in still waters ... but it wasn't ready for a storm. And if there's one absolute in *any* business, it's that there *will* be storms.

At first, the storms were pretty mild: an important employee making a mistake, unpredictable and inconsistent revenue, nominal turnover, and things like that. It was annoying, but I could bail water fast enough to keep the boat afloat. Then it started raining harder. We had a couple of pathological personalities with whom I had put up for years, but as always happens, that festering issue grew into a big problem. They divided the staff into two camps. And when the problematic camp started leaving, they left *en masse*. My desire to grow the business caused me to make some critical hiring failures, and as a result, our boat started taking on water faster than I could bail. For the first time, my failure to invest in the storm-worthiness of our boat put our business in harm's way. I couldn't bail fast enough. It felt as though our boat might sink, and as the captain, I was overcome with the responsibility for all the wonderful people who were still on the boat with me. This wouldn't just be my failure; it would hurt them too.

We got through that season, but it changed me forever. That experience shook my confidence in my ability to lead because of one important reason: it was my fault. The whole ordeal was a series of unforced errors on my part, things I could have prevented if I had approached the business side of the practice with the intentionality that it demanded. It was time for a change. A *lot* of changes.

Fortunately, I had help.

Earlier that year, I made an investment in my practice that most surgeon-owners would have advised me against: I hired an expert COO, Robbie Poe, my coauthor for this book. Robbie came to us from an executive-level position in a $100 million organization (which you're likely familiar with), where he had developed a reputation for brand-building, customer-experience design, and building high-capacity teams. I had met him the previous year when he traveled to Raleigh with one of our patients to be their recovery help. He impressed me enough in our brief interactions that week that I hired him as a business consultant. After working with him for a few months, it became clear to me that *this* was the person who could help me finally get the business side of my practice under control. He came on board and we got to work.

But change takes time.

For a while, no one could see the changes we were implementing in the business—and that was an intentional decision. We knew we had to start by resetting the foundations of the business or, using the boat analogy, patching the cracks in the hull. The long-term goal was to build a new, bigger, better boat, but we couldn't let this one sink in the process. So we focused on things such as leadership development, employee training, and the overall structure of our team. With Robbie's often-forceful encouragement, we stopped focusing on the *urgent-but-not-important* issues for a few months and instead addressed only the *important* issues, whether they were urgent or not. Otherwise, we knew we'd only be playing Whac-A-Mole with our problems.

The problem with *urgent-but-not-important* issues, though, is that they're almost always important to *somebody*. What I had to learn was that an issue that is important to an employee doesn't automatically mean it's important to me as the business owner. In fact, it usually isn't. And because I like to help people, it was hard for me to consciously let those things fall by the wayside. People don't like having what they see as urgent put off, especially by their boss. And they really don't like being made to work on a new system or project that they haven't fully bought into yet. It creates tension. It definitely did for us. In fact, that's what ultimately led to the storm I mentioned, when my team split into two factions—one that resisted the new direction we were heading in and one that had bought into it (or who at least trusted us enough to see it through).

Looking back, it's no wonder why I felt like I was drowning—inside the boat. I had no way of prioritizing what needed my attention. I was spending all day being a surgeon, *doing* my best to *be* my best in the operating room. In there, it was life-and-death. I had to be fully present each and every time I walked through those doors. What I didn't understand back then was that what was happening outside the operating room was life-and-death too—the life and death of my business. And that part of the practice only got my leftovers. Once I left the operating room every evening, I put on my CEO hat and spent all night dealing with the whole day's worth of business decisions that were waiting for me. Calls to return. Employee issues to deal with. Payroll to review. Fires to put out. Interoffice brawls to referee. It was exhausting. And anything I couldn't resolve before passing out for the night made its way into my dreams.

My health took a nosedive, and it showed up in my appearance. People asked me all the time how many hours I was working per week. I lied and told them sixty, but the truth is I was working *all* the hours every week. I never stopped. My brain was always on and always thinking about either my patients or my business. I didn't know any other way to do it. But I did know one thing: This was not sustainable. Something was going to break.

This is, in effect, my recovery story, and every recovery story has a rock bottom. Here's mine: It was a Sunday afternoon, and my parents had come over for dinner with me, my wife, and my children. I had spent the entire weekend at the whiteboard or on the phone with Robbie, trying to figure out how to fill a gap in our leadership plan that was made when a director on our team left unexpectedly. When my parents arrived, I popped out of my home office to greet them before disappearing again until dinner was on the table. We enjoyed a meal I did not help prepare, and then I went back to work, leaving a mess at the table and in the kitchen that I did not help clean up. My parents hung out with my family for the rest of the night as I worked away on my whiteboard.

As my parents prepared to leave, my dad, who has always been my most honest supporter, pulled me aside.

"Jeremy," he said, "it's time to stop."

He wasn't angry. He wasn't judgmental. He was kind. His tone reflected a deep love that any parent would immediately recognize and understand.

"I know you are building something important...but it's not more important than your family and your health. You wife is exhausted. You look terrible. Your kids miss you. Son, it's time to stop."

My guess is you know exactly what I'm talking about. If you don't—maybe you're a resident, or maybe you run your own practice and have not been at this point yet or are not at this point right now—then buckle up, because it's on the horizon. This is something every doctor/practice owner has to deal with, assuming, of course, you want more out of your life than forty years of coasting through your career on your way to retirement. But they didn't teach us how to handle this side of things in medical school, did they? In fact, practically *no one* has come alongside doctors/practice owners to show them how to focus on their medical specialty *and* focus on growing their business.

Until now.

Welcome to *The Private Practice MBA*.

Robbie: OK, so Jeremy just said that he had fourteen years of post-secondary education. I . . . did not. The truth is, I'm a college dropout. I don't have any letters after my name, I don't have a single degree, and most of my professional experience is *outside* the medical world. But wait, don't write me off. While you were nose-deep in medical textbooks and residencies, I was cutting my teeth in marketing, brand-building, customer experience, and leadership within a $100 million company. I've spent most of my life—and certainly all my career—as an entrepreneur who is passionate about business and leadership. I've started and sold multiple businesses, and for the past several years, I've been able to put those passions and my experience to work in the field of aesthetic medicine alongside the man who made me passionate about this industry, Dr. Jeremy Pyle.

Like many people, I grew up with a slanted view of plastic surgery. However, after seeing Dr. Pyle and his team in action up close and personal, I realized how life-changing plastic surgery can be for people—especially when it comes wrapped in a stellar customer service experience. I was so impressed with their level of care and with the results patients were getting that I proposed a consulting engagement. As impressed as I was with the surgical, clinical, and office teams, the business leader in me was able to spot what Jeremy called the "cracks in the hull." I knew his business was demanding far too much from him, and it had far more potential for growth. Additionally, I believe I had the experience and expertise his team was missing. Fortunately, he agreed. That's something I've always been impressed by. One of the hardest things for a leader to do is see his own weaknesses, but Jeremy had the wisdom and humility to recognize his deficiencies and ask for help. If he hadn't reached out for a lifeline, we wouldn't have had a quarter of the success we've had over the past several years. That's on him, and our whole team knows it.

As Jeremy and I were trying to "right the ship" during the traumatic season he mentioned, we continually found ourselves frustrated by the quality of resources that had been created for practices like ours. We always found ourselves saying things such as,

- Why hasn't anyone created business resources for private practices?
- Why is every piece of medical software so terrible?
- Why don't any of these "interactive marketing" companies seem to know what they are talking about?

I bet there's a good chance you've asked one or all of these questions as well. The contrast between what these salespeople promised us and what they were able to deliver was staggering. It was hard not to feel like they were just trying to take advantage of us. Could it be that people in the medical industry's orbit have recognized doctors' inexperience with sales and marketing systems and have tried to push bad solutions to customers who didn't know any better? Perish the thought. Surely *you've* never dealt with a salesperson like that... right?

Maybe we were just talking to the wrong industry partners, but none of these medical marketing or technology companies ever seemed to understand the unique challenges of running a private practice. They were full of advice, and they certainly had plenty of expensive products for us to buy, but they had absolutely no experience doing what you, Jeremy, and I do (or want to do) every day. In fact, I'm certain you've experienced the same thing we did because every other practice we've talked to has been through those sales presentations for products that never lived up to the hype. Is there anything more frustrating than paying good money for the best-available options, and yet none of them is good enough and all of them are way too expensive?

As the COO and business director who was responsible for all these business systems, I finally couldn't take it anymore. I remember sitting across from Jeremy and practically yelling, "Come on! We are in one of the most important industries in the world. We can't keep running our business like a mom-and-pop country store. There are tried-and-true principles that modern organizations have spent billions of dollars testing and perfecting, and we have to start taking them seriously."

Additionally, we had reached a point of such deep frustration with the lack of quality resources for our private practice—especially in areas such as practice management training, patient tracking software, electronic health records, and marketing investments that actually worked. So we decided to do some outside-the-medical-box thinking. I said, "Screw the garbage this industry is trying to push on our business. Let's look at some of our favorite companies like Apple, Tesla, and Nike, and see what we can learn from the way *they* do business." Enter The Level-10 Business Framework.

Like you read in Jeremy's note at the front of this book, we got off to a good start implementing The Level-10 Business Framework, but we quickly hit an impasse because the framework wasn't at all structured to work within private practices. That led us to a make-or-break decision: we could either invest a lot of money into the antiquated business solutions we knew wouldn't work well for us, or we could invest even more money into adapting The Level-10 Business Framework to work within our practice. We took a deep breath and chose the latter.

First, we completely rebuilt the business operating system to take physician owners (the focus of this book) into account, and then we hired over a dozen in-house "skill players." This allowed us to create our own dedicated product team. We hired in-house marketers, graphic designers, product designers, videographers, software developers, machine-learning specialists, and business development experts, which allowed us to take full control over our sales, marketing, technology, and even our analytics. And lastly, we built our own Patient Conversion Funnel from the ground up.

To be blunt, we bet the entire farm on ourselves ... on our ability to run our own marketing, manage our own money, create our own software, design our own websites, and train our own team.

Was it worth it? Well, thank God . . . it worked. Not only did our consultation-to-surgery conversion rate increase by 250 percent, but we tripled our bottom-line profit as well. In fact, the model we created in Raleigh was so successful that we're now in the process of partnering with plastic surgeons all over the United States to open their own Amelia Aesthetics practice.

That success gave us the freedom to focus more on the bigger picture in the industry: the dreadful lack of quality resources *by* practice owners *for* practice owners. We were so excited by the dramatic changes we saw in our business that we wanted to find a way to help other doctors/surgeons who either run their own practice currently or hope to one day. We started with our *The Private Practice MBA* video training course (www.ThePrivatePracticeMBA.com) to help practice owners take their business further, faster while making their lives easier overall. And now we've decided to put all that information—tens of thousands of dollars' worth of training—into one book.

We call our program *The Private Practice MBA* because medical schools don't focus on the skills doctors need to run a medical practice. What you'll read in this book is a plan that should be taught, not something you have to figure out the hard way during the most challenging years of your medical career. Every physician starts their practice by either reinventing the wheel all by themselves or by learning the ropes from another doctor who made it up when they got started. Think about how inefficient that is. It's the business equivalent of every surgeon inventing their own way to perform an appendectomy. Would you trust a friend or family member to a surgeon if that physician simply made up a random way to do a complicated procedure? No way! Then why would you trust your practice—your livelihood and the livelihood of everyone who works for you—to a substandard way of running your business that you made up as you went along?

The fact is, there is zero reason to reinvent the wheel, not when almost all private practice owners face the same top five problems:

1. Stressing out about keeping a steady stream of new patients coming through the door.
2. Having no time to work *on* the business because you're too busy working *in* the business.

3. Feeling forced to sacrifice your hobbies, time with family, and sleep just to create more margin to focus on your business.
4. Banging your head against the wall trying to figure out how to keep growing your business when you're already spending every waking minute working.
5. Lacking the business know-how to identify and fix areas within your practice that are not as healthy as they should be.

Any of these sound familiar? Do *all* of these sound familiar? Trust me, you are not alone. We've heard one or all of these issues from every doctor and practice owner we've talked to. As I've heard the surgeon and author Dr. Atul Gawande say, and I'm paraphrasing, "In medical school and residency, no one teaches you how to think about business, money, or marketing. Yet from the moment you start practicing, you're surrounded by all three."

So isn't it time to learn how to actually do the job you've created for yourself?

In this book, Jeremy and I are going to introduce you to the business operating system we use every day at all our Amelia Aesthetics locations, and we're going to help you avoid all the land mines we survived (sometimes uninjured, sometimes not). We'll cover every area of managing your practice, digging deep into the broad categories of money, day-to-day operations, marketing and sales, and leadership. Everything you're going to learn in this book or in our online course has helped all our Amelia Aesthetics surgeons across the country run some of the most modern, sought out, and profitable practices in the world. Maybe more importantly, every one of them has discovered a new sense of freedom and focus not only in their work, but also in their families and personal lives.

Sound interesting? It is.
Sound easy? It's not.
Sound worth it? Hell yeah, it is.

Jeremy: What Robbie and I have written in this book reflects everything we've learned, practiced, tweaked, and revised over several years of growing our practice. Put simply, it's a plan that works. But this isn't a magic pill for your business. What we experienced in the process did not give us immediate relief. In fact, the old boat sank a little deeper before we got the new one in the water. It was a long, slow, arduous shift from where we were to the one thing I wanted and needed most: freedom. I'm not just talking about financial freedom, freedom of location, or freedom with my time. I'm talking about the freedom to simply take a breath, to take a break with my family when I want to, *and* the freedom to charge a hundred miles per hour toward a new opportunity if I want to do that instead.

That's the whole point of *The Private Practice MBA*: to give doctors and practice owners freedom to focus on ever-more-important and challenging questions by dealing less and less with everything else. We're going to use the phrase *autopilot* a lot in the book, but autopilot doesn't mean cruise control. If you want to push a button and coast through your career and into retirement, I promise, this is not the book for you. You won't like anything we'll talk about, and you almost certainly won't *do* anything we'll talk about. But if you want to build something important—for yourself, your family, your team, your patients, your community, and your industry—then stick with us. We've got work to do.

SECTION 1
PUT YOUR BUSINESS ON AUTOPILOT

CHAPTER 1
THE BUSINESS OF MEDICINE IS SICK

Jeremy: The business of medicine is sick. If you don't believe that, you haven't been paying attention. I don't just mean sick at the patient-experience level, and I don't just mean sick at the bottom line. It is sick for physicians and the businesses we are running. Speaking as a doctor who has been 100 percent guilty of this in the past, practice management is one of the most overlooked and neglected areas of maturation in most private practices. And if we don't treat our businesses with the same care and attention with which we treat our patients, that business—the heartbeat of your career in medicine and the livelihood of every person who works for you—is going to die. The way you manage your business, from financial management to sales and marketing to operations to your basic skills as a leader, needs an infusion of intentionality.

But if there's one thing I know as a physician and surgeon, it's that doctors tend to be extremely slow to change how they do things. We have what's called an *anchoring bias*, the tendency to interpret new information through the lens of what we already know. It's a critical part of medicine so it's something I've lived with throughout my entire career and education. The positive side of this bias is that it enables us to make reasonable judgments quickly. When we hear a list of symptoms, we can pin that set of symptoms to an illness or condition we've studied or treated in the past and have a fairly good idea of what's happening. Of course, we confirm our suspicions through lab work and tests, but we can at least hit the ground running with *some* idea of what the patient is experiencing. In this case, our anchoring bias is working for us.

However, that same bias also causes us to resist dramatic changes to how we do things. We get understandably set in our ways and trust what's always worked for us in the past. When we see a presentation at a medical conference about a new way to perform a procedure, we're skeptical. We tend to assume that "new" means "wrong." After all, if we accept that the new way is better, we are also admitting that the way we've been doing it all this time is wrong or at least not good enough.

As we get into the meat of this material, I'm going to ask you, doctor to doctor, to do something I know will be difficult: set aside your anchoring bias around how you run your practice. There is so much we can learn from other industries, and if we continue to believe that *new* won't work for us because "our situation is different," or "my patients won't like that," or "my team can do it better," then we will continue to fall further and further behind the rest of the world. And as we do, the business of medicine will get sicker and sicker...because we aren't "treating" it with the latest, most appropriate methods.

Much of what we're about to talk about won't feel comfortable to you. It'll be different than what you're doing now, and it'll be different than what your mentors may have taught you. That's OK. This is one time when different and new aren't just *OK*; they're absolutely essential for revitalizing your practice.

YOU NEED AN OPERATING SYSTEM

Robbie: Compared with the most developed countries in the world, according to both patients and providers, the United States ranks last in healthcare system performance and next to last in administrative efficiency.[1] This shouldn't be that shocking, though. As we saw in the introduction, nobody is training doctors how to run their practice as a business. The best, most highly trained and well-respected surgeon could have procedures booked a year in advance with patients traveling in from all over the country and still go out of business. The problem isn't their training and skills as surgeons, and it isn't their bedside manner. The problem usually isn't medical at all; it's business. Vendors paying late. Staff members not knowing what they're doing. Patient records falling into a black hole. Appointments overbooked, underbooked, and never booked. Interoffice conflict. And let's not forget burnout, exhaustion, and potential mental and physical breakdowns from all the pressures of keeping a sinking ship afloat for just one more day ... every day. I need to be blunt here, speaking leader to leader: if *you* are the only thing keeping your business running, then your practice is in serious trouble. Sure, you may be the sole income-generator of your practice, but you absolutely cannot be the sole business leader of your practice. You need help. And that help comes in the form of an operating system.

Abraham Lincoln famously said, "If I only had one hour to chop down a tree, I would spend the first forty-five minutes sharpening my axe." When it comes to running a private practice, you can picture the delivery of medical treatment as cutting down the tree. Everything else in your business is sharpening your axe. Every operational procedure, training session, accounting practice, and employee review—literally *everything else in your business*—should equip your team to operate more efficiently and effectively. The time and effort you spend on mastering these business fundamentals isn't wasted; it's instrumental. And yet our training focuses almost exclusively on using the axe. We aren't even taught how to sharpen it.

Throughout this book, Jeremy and I are going to unpack the operating system we've developed at Amelia Aesthetics. It's called the Autopilot Operating System and it's built on four key areas, each of which will have an entire section dedicated to it. These four areas should be familiar to you because it's literally how every private practice in America operates—even yours.

Four Simple Areas

I'm a car guy. Growing up, one of my favorite pastimes was working on old cars with my grandfather Daddy Bob. He taught me early on that no matter how complex a system is, it can always be reduced to a small handful of components. This is critical because when your car won't start, you need to be able to quickly identify which component is either most affected or responsible. Daddy Bob taught me that pretty much every internal combustion engine can be reduced to three components: air, fuel, and fire. Sure, there are other parts, but the whole system really comes down to those three areas. So when we were diagnosing an engine problem, Daddy Bob would ask, "OK, Robbie, where do you think the problem is: in the air, the fuel, or the fire?" Once we knew that answer, we could move on to fix the problem.

Just like Daddy Bob's engine breakdown, your medical practice can be broken down into its four primary components:

- Money

- Sales and Marketing
- Operations
- Leadership

Continuing the car analogy, you can picture these four areas as the four tires your business is driving on. And just like your car, if one of these tires is underinflated, bald, out of alignment, or completely flat, your business will experience a much rougher ride. The vibrations will be felt across your entire practice, and your journey may come to a sudden, painful stop. If you want to keep your car running smoothly, you've got to keep all four tires in good shape and equally inflated. Business owners who neglect even one part of their organization will put their entire practice in jeopardy.

Let's take a minute to break these four "tires" down at a high level so you know what to expect.

Money

Money is the lifeblood of your practice. Some may balk at that, thinking it sounds too impersonal or greedy, but the fact is your business will be forced *out* of business if the money dries up. When it comes to cash, it doesn't matter how able, available, or affable you are. If you run out of money, you close your doors. It's the cold, hard fact of business.

For that reason, we are going to focus a lot on all things money. But we're not going to bore you with useless financial terms, mysterious accounting practices, or overcomplicated systems. Sure, you need people on your team who understand those things, but that's not the point of this book. In section 2, we're going to teach you, the business owner, the nuts and bolts of how to take care of your money... so your money will take care of you.

Sales and Marketing

Many doctors *hate* the whole arena of sales and marketing. They think that if they're good enough at their job, then the right people will just "find" them. It's hard for them to think of their patients as customers, so they keep business-world concepts such as sales and marketing at arm's length. As a business guy working in the medical industry, I can't stress enough that you cannot afford to ignore sales and marketing. This goes back to the money point: if your patients dry up, your money dries up. And you know what comes next if that happens.

Sales and marketing are not antithetical to health and wellness. You can (and should) be proficient at all of the preceding elements. In section 3, we're going to show you that sales and marketing is simply the intentional, predetermined, step-by-step process of getting the right people to notice your offering, raise their hand to learn more, and take strategically defined steps toward making their life better by purchasing what you're selling. And yes, *selling* is the right word for what your entire team is doing. You're selling ideas. Those ideas lead to procedures, and those procedures lead to incredible life change.

Operations

Operations refers to *how* your private practice provides your offering to the world. It covers everything that happens behind the scenes of your business: defining your operational ethos, identifying and understanding your competition, hiring and firing, which team meetings you need (and, more importantly, which ones you don't), patient experience and feedback, scheduling, managing conflict, mining for problems, implementing technology, and every other pesky detail inherent in running a business. Section 4 really puts the "MBA" in *The Private Practice MBA*!

Leadership

Bestselling author and leadership expert John C. Maxwell famously says, "Everything rises and falls on leadership. But knowing how to lead is only half the battle. Understanding leadership and actually leading are two different activities." We've definitely found this to be true in our practice. Once Jeremy and I became more intentional about how we were leading our team, many of the other pieces fell into place, and many problems suddenly started getting solved without either of us having to lift a finger.

In section 5, we will teach you the most powerful and practical leadership lessons we've learned around things such as vision casting, change management, how to create tight-knit teams, and what to do when you fail as a leader.

We're going to dive deeply into each of these four areas, but don't let it get more complicated in your head than it needs to be. Keep Daddy Bob's simple question in mind: Whenever you're facing a problem in your business, ask yourself, *OK, where is the problem: in the money, the sales and marketing, the operations, or the leadership?* The issue will almost certainly fall into one of these four buckets. With that information, you can start running through the strategies we're going to teach you and the solution should reveal itself fairly easily.

The Power of an Operating System

Practice owners get into trouble when they don't know what to focus on. Because it is impossible to pay consistent attention to every single part of our practice at all times, we, as business owners, naturally gravitate toward two things:

1. What's on fire within our practice
2. What we are personally most interested in within our practice

If we don't have a system in place that consistently puts the *whole* business in front of us and our other leaders, we'll just stick to those two things. That's why so many private practice owners have the same fundamental problems—because we're only looking at what's broken and what's exciting. Everything else will be relegated to the background . . . until it catches fire and demands our attention. You can see the problem here. There is much more to a successful business than these two things, and we've got to figure out a way to keep our eyes on all of it.

Fortunately, there's a proven construct that exists in the business world that helps business leaders like us keep every area of our practice visible. It's called a business operating system, which is simply a collection of principles, rhythms, and technology that keeps your entire organization focused and on track at all times. This is so common in the business world, in fact, that it is still hard for me to believe that physicians are never formally taught the concept of a business operating system. If this was a part of medical education, individual private practice physicians would not have to keep reinventing the same untested, unproven wheels over and over again.

A surgeon, for example, would never simply "make up" their own way of performing an operation without any training whatsoever. They'd spend years studying the best, most-trusted methods, then spend years practicing those procedures under the watchful eye of a more experienced surgeon. Only after developing a solid track record of performing *that* surgical procedure in *that* way under supervision would that surgeon be allowed to operate on their own. Why, then, are doctors expected to "wing it" when it comes to business operations? Not only does it make no sense, it's also expensive, inefficient, and painfully time-consuming.

Eisenhower Matrix

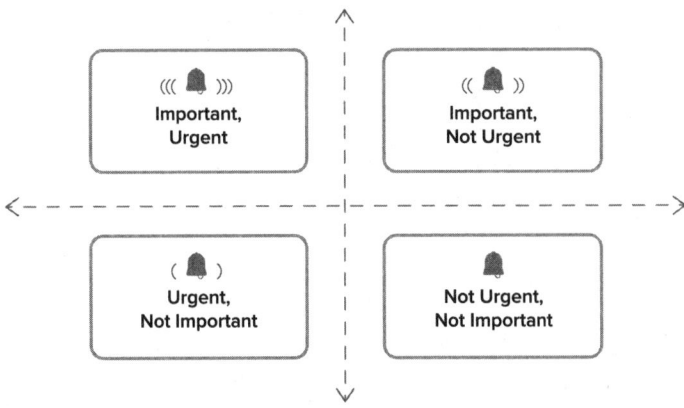

That's why our team has spent years developing the world's first and only business operating system designed for private practices. We call it "Autopilot" because it teaches you why and how to ensure the most important areas of your practice are always running smoothly, even when you aren't able to pay attention to them. This entire system and this book are designed to help you set up a cadence that will put the business of your practice on autopilot, giving you the freedom to focus on your specialty—and your patients—without worrying about everything falling apart when you aren't looking.

Reclaiming Your Attention and Focus

Jeremy: Robbie is kind of a business and process nerd, so he's wired to get a little excited about terms like *business operating system*. I'm wired differently, and I'm also always looking for the *why* behind concepts, processes, and decisions. So it helps me to see these things in the context of the real world. When it came to establishing our business operating system, then, I came to view it through the lens of "important but not urgent." This is a category from the Eisenhower Matrix[2] found in the resources section of Asana.com, which breaks all the things that require a business owner's attention into four clear categories:

- Important and Urgent
- Important but Not Urgent
- Urgent but Not Important
- Not Urgent and Not Important

Implementing a business operating system into our practice has radically changed where, within those four areas, I spend nearly all my time.

For years I spent my precious few hours outside the operating room on the wrong things, the issues that would easily fit into the "Urgent but Not Important" quadrant of the Eisenhower Matrix. I'm sure you could write down ten different things you've done this week that would fit into that category. We all could—*if* we're not paying attention and being, well, *ruthless* with how and where we spend our time as leaders. Using this lens, for the first time in my career, I was able to shift my attention away from the two dozen things I thought needed my attention and toward the two or three things that actually did. This has created a significant change in how I am able to operate as the business owner: the "Urgent but Not Important" stuff never makes it to my desk. I may hear about it secondhand, but no one brings it to me, and our business operating system has given me a reason and the discipline to ignore it even if someone told me.

For example, we recently had a small issue with a chronically late employee. I'm not talking about an hour late; she was just three to five minutes late most mornings. It was enough to need some kind of correction, but it wasn't a big enough deal for the owner of the company to get involved with. Of course, a decade ago, this would have been my problem to handle. Now, however, things are very different. We have a comprehensive business operating system in place that covers things like this. Because of the systems we will discuss in this book, I know this employee has a leader above her who is *empowered* and *expected* to jump in and identify, diagnose, and correct minor issues like this. And because of our reporting structure, I know I'll hear about it later after it's been handled and get the full story.

What happened in this particular situation was especially gratifying for Robbie and me, as we have worked hard to put these systems in place. The employee's leader, Trevor, has learned how I would handle things like this, and I trust him to lead his team in my place. Moreover, he has led his team with consistency for a few years, so they know how *he* would handle issues like this. So when I checked in with Trevor a few days after noticing his team member's tardiness problem, he told me that the situation had already resolved itself—without him! Another member of their team, knowing how Trevor and I both lead, had interceded and said something to the employee with the tardiness problem. And though it may be hard for you to believe, she did so with a positive, loving, encouraging spirit. Her goal was to *help* her teammate rather than call her out for being a "problem." Together, the two of them came up with a plan. Without me. Without Robbie. Without Trevor. This team knew they didn't need me to solve this relatively minor problem so they didn't bring it to me. They handled it themselves...like adults *should* do.

But—and this is a huge *but*—if you are an owner and there is no system in place to teach your team how to handle problems, every problem becomes yours to solve. Whether you realize it or not, you *are* teaching your team how to solve problems: bring them to you. You're teaching them dependency, and they'll just keep bringing you every "Urgent but Not Important" issue because they think that's what you want them to do. You cannot expect them to do otherwise if you have not equipped and empowered them to do otherwise.

This may seem like a minor example of an interoffice problem, but how much of your day (or night) is spent dealing with stuff like this? Multiply this small example by the number of employees you have and the number of "minor" issues they each bring to work, and you can see how all your time can be eaten up by "Urgent but Not Important" distractions. And because you're teaching them dependency, it's only going to get worse as your team and business grow. This is a productivity killer and perhaps the chief sin of a business owner, and it can be completely solved with a quality business operating system. Your goal as the owner should be to make yourself completely unnecessary in the unimportant issues so you can devote your time and effort to the important ones. An operating system is how you do that.

Of course, knowing what to do and how to do it is complicated, especially for men and women like us who spent twenty years in school and yet never had to take a business or management class. That's why we designed *The Private Practice MBA* principles and Autopilot software.[3] So let's talk about them.

THREE COMPONENTS OF A BUSINESS ON AUTOPILOT

Robbie: Diving into business management can feel like drinking out of a fire hose—especially if you are several years into your practice. So in order to give you a simple way to arrange all the information we're going to discuss, I want to introduce three specific components of a business running on autopilot. You can think of these three areas as buckets in which to sort the different parts of the business operating system discussion we'll have throughout this book and in our online resources.

Component #1: Autopilot People

The first component is *Autopilot People*. This represents a set of very specific roles you will need on your team. The good news is that you probably already have most of these people in your business; they may just not be in the right seat with the right set of responsibilities. Of course, it's possible that you are missing a handful of key positions. It's also possible that some of the people on the team today really don't need to be there moving forward. Both situations can cause a great deal of stress for the business owner, but don't worry. We'll talk a lot about hiring, firing, and leading team members later in this book. We will also spend three full chapters (chapters 2–4) unpacking the three different types of Autopilot People you need to identify and/or hire. But by way of introduction, here's a quick recap of the three roles every practice needs.

Role #1: The Business Owner

The first role is obvious: the *business owner*. This is probably you. It's one of the hats you wear, and that's not going to change as long as you own your practice. Sure, there are people, principles, and systems that will make your life easier as a business owner; that's what this whole book is about. But none of that will change the fact that if you own a practice, you're the person at the top. To paraphrase John C. Maxwell, the practice will rise and fall on *you*.

Some businesses call this person the CEO or more "modern" titles like Visionary. Whatever you call it in your practice, the need is the same: your team absolutely must have someone to look to as the heartbeat of the organization. This is the person who believes in the vision and mission of the practice to an unreasonable degree. This was the first person in the organization, and they will be the last person standing at the end of the day. Put simply: this person didn't just *drink* the Kool-Aid; they *made* the Kool-Aid.

The business owner is the person in your organization who inspires, the one who can deliver those Braveheart-like speeches that make everyone else roar with excitement and motivation. The business owner not only communicates where we are going, they also tell us why we are going and make us believe we've got what it takes to get there. In our practice, this person is Dr. Pyle.

Role #2: The Business Director

The second role is what we call the *business director*. Some businesses would call this person the Chief Operating Officer, or COO. The business director is the person who turns the vision of the business owner into reality and who isn't intimidated by however many steps it takes to get there. The business director can nearly match the business owner's energy and commitment levels, they love leading multidisciplinary teams, and they are not the least bit afraid or hesitant to challenge, push, and even argue with the business owner when necessary. That said, the business director is also extraordinarily willing to commit to and take partial ownership of the business owner's direction—even when they disagree.

The business director is the role you will most likely have to hire. Of all the private practices we have worked with, only a rare few already had this person on their team when we started. Of course, most of these organizations have some sort of office manager in place, but that person rarely has the background, experience, or even the desire to take on the responsibilities of a true business director. This is my role on our team so I have a lot of experience with this one.

Role #3: The Team Leaders

The third crucial type of Autopilot People you need on your team are *team leaders*. Depending on the size of your organization, you most likely have pockets of people who represent different teams, such as doctors, nurses, administration, patient coordination, and so on. Within those teams, you can probably identify a person who has a natural influence on the others, even if that person has not formally been given a leadership role. These people *lead with influence*, which is the chief mark of a natural leader. The business owner and business director rely on these team leaders for the day-to-day operations of the practice. You need champions who feel a sense of responsibility for the work, attitudes, and relationships around them.

Component #2: Autopilot Priorities

The second component is *Autopilot Priorities*. This is the big one. This represents the priorities and practices—what you're actually going to *do*—that you'll incorporate into the rhythms of your business. The more of these things you put in place, the more you're going to see the benefits of implementing *The Private Practice MBA* principles. These priorities represent the four "tires" I mentioned earlier:

- Money
- Sales and Marketing
- Operations
- Leadership

The Autopilot Priorities are so important that we'll devote most of this book (sections 2–5) to going through each of these four key areas in detail.

Component #3: Autopilot Practice Management Software
The third and final component is *Autopilot* software. I mentioned in the introduction that Jeremy and I were frustrated at the lack of quality Practice Management (PM) and Electronic Health Record (EHR) software available. None of the ones we tried lived up to the promises of the eager sales reps. So we decided to build our own. Our goal with the *Autopilot Practice Management Software* is to create the most beautiful, simple-to-use PM and EHR software in the world. They are being created especially for private practice physicians who want to run a modern, growth-oriented practice.

Software solutions obviously don't translate well into book form, so we won't be able to cover the *Autopilot* software in-depth in this book. However, you can learn more about it at www.AutopilotOnline.com.

LET'S BE REAL ABOUT WHO AND WHAT WE ARE

Jeremy: As we wrap this chapter up and move into a few chapters about what we call "Autopilot People," I can't help but think about how skewed our perception can be about ourselves as physicians and business owners. Too often, we tend to see ourselves as a one-man show, no matter how many excellent and skilled professionals we have working alongside us. This was never clearer to me than it was several years ago at the end of a huge plastic surgery convention.

Every year, thousands of the world's plastic surgeons converge on one city for the annual meeting of our largest society. I usually do not attend anymore, but early in my career, attending that meeting was exciting. That was where the celebrity plastic surgeons walked among the rest of us. Those were the men and women whose work I followed, whose papers I studied, and whose techniques I tried to emulate. They were stars to me.

One year, the keynote speaker spoke to a packed house, and nearly every person in attendance had more than fifteen years of training and education. As a young plastic surgeon with big dreams, it was hard not to be starstruck—especially by the expert surgeon/speaker who kept us on the edges of our seats throughout his presentation.

The next morning, I was in the airport terminal waiting for my flight home, excitedly writing out a plan for how we were going to use what I had learned that week to create a world-class med spa. I looked up from my computer for a moment and couldn't believe my eyes: the leading plastic surgeon in the world—the celebrity keynote speaker I had just heard the night before—was sitting right across from me in the terminal.

But guess what? He wasn't encased by a heavenly glow like I saw him at the conference. And he wasn't surrounded by a hundred other professionals trying to get a few seconds of his time. He was just sitting there. Alone. With a half-eaten cheeseburger in his lap. Cleaning a ketchup stain off his shirt.

It was jarring to me. Was *this* the superstar I'd been so preoccupied with becoming? It struck me how vast the ocean was between how important I thought that person was to me and how insignificant he was to literally everyone else around us at the time. He was just another guy waiting to catch a flight in the busiest airport in America. That's when I realized that being the most important plastic surgeon in the world doesn't matter. At all. Sure, it matters to him. It matters to his patients and other doctors. But it doesn't *really* matter in the grand scheme of things.

I tell that story because sometimes we tend to view ourselves as doctors and business owners with just a bit too much reverence. We tend to think we are "the only one" who can accomplish something, that we're "special." But 99 percent of the time, that's just not true. That is good news. If we recognize we're not the only one who can accomplish the vision we have for our practice, that means we don't have to make all the decisions. We don't have to do all the work. If we can just find someone we trust to make most decisions 80 percent as well as we would, that's enough. And if we can find a handful of others who can lead, serve, and love our team members nearly as well (if not better) than we can, that's enough too.

There's something no one ever tells you about owning a business: it is lonely as hell. *Braveheart* would have been a much different movie if Mel Gibson had found himself running across the battlefield alone. But he didn't. He had a whole army standing with him to get the job done.

So do you.

As we, then, begin this journey together to revolutionize your business and reclaim your freedom, time, and sanity, let's spend a few chapters talking about the people on the battlefield with you. We'll start in the next chapter by getting crystal clear on *our* role, the role of the business owner.

CHAPTER 2

THE MOST POWERFUL PERSON IN THE ROOM: THE BUSINESS OWNER

Jeremy: Physicians who own and operate their own practice have what I truly believe is one of the most difficult careers in the world—and I'd say that even if I wasn't one myself. Part of what makes it so difficult is that you have two careers at the same time. Most people either work inside a business or they run a business. Physician owners, however, do both. They are typically the people who run the business operations, *and* they are the people who produce all the revenue through an already difficult, time-consuming, and intellectually challenging position. That's a lot.

I am not complaining, though, because leadership evolution in one area can carry over to leadership evolution in the other area. When you are a physician who is leading a medical team, you know the power of your decisions and the power of your words.

Here's what I mean: when you say something needs to be done for a patient, you expect it to be done. We tend to carry that same assumption into the business side of things. When you make a request (or a command) of your office staff, you expect it to be carried out. Aspiring leaders may struggle to develop this kind of confidence, but our medical training and the high stakes of doing what we do have built that into us already.

This is where our advantage ends because when you ask a nurse to put in an IV and start fluid, you stop talking. You don't tell them what gauge needle or what style of dressing to use. You don't tell the nurse what vein to stick or how many times to wipe the skin with alcohol before inserting the needle. Can you imagine a surgeon or emergency room physician stopping to do that every time? It would be insane— *and* it would be incredibly insulting to the nurse, who has spent years learning and perfecting their craft. Instead, you simply make your request and then trust that person to make the appropriate decisions to get the job done. They may not do it exactly as you would, but you trust that the decisions they make will be acceptable. And often, you trust them to make better decisions in that specific situation than you would. Isn't that why you hired them in the first place?

All this means that, as a physician, you have been learning one of the most important aspects of leadership for a long time: your team can do *a lot*. That is true for your clinical team, and it is equally true for your office team.

In this chapter, we are going to talk about the unique position we are in as physicians *and* business owners. As we do, though, I'm going to challenge you to treat your leadership position just like you treat your role as a doctor: make the important decisions, provide important leadership, and then get out of the way and let your team do those things that you either can't do nearly as well or—and this is the hard part—the things you simply don't *need* to do.

THE IMBALANCE OF POWER

Robbie: As the business owner, you have all the power. And if we've learned anything from the endless stream of *Spider-Man* movies over the past twenty years, it's that, "With great power comes

THE MOST POWERFUL PERSON IN THE ROOM: THE BUSINESS OWNER

great responsibility." So what should you do with all that power and responsibility?

As the business owner, you are the one person in the organization who can get involved in anything you want, wherever you want, as often as you want. No matter where you are, who you're with, or what the topic of the day is, you will always be the most powerful person in the room. Stop and think about that for a second. You are the *only one* who can walk into any room, interrupt any conversation, and even change the course of your entire company with a single email. That is a lot of power.

Now, before you start getting a big head about all that power, let me break some bad news to you that your team probably hasn't said out loud—at least in your presence. Yes, you are the only one who *can* walk into any room or break into any conversation . . . but you are also the one person your team probably *doesn't want* to walk into the room or break into the conversation.

I know that sucks to hear, especially if you run a tight-knit team with a fun, family atmosphere. But speaking as the business guy who has spent the last fifteen years standing between the C-suite and the office professionals, I promise this is true 99 percent of the time. The encouraging part of this, though, is that this is actually *good news*. For the business owner, it will never be possible to put your practice on autopilot and grow it beyond your personal capacity to manage if you are still deeply involved in all the tactical, day-to-day operations of your business.

As crazy and counterintuitive as this may sound, we strongly believe it should be your goal to *not* have a crystal clear, minutely detailed understanding of what it takes to keep the day-to-day operations of your practice running. If you, as the business owner, don't find a way to get out of the way and instead focus your time on doing what only you can do, then you will be your business's greatest bottleneck.

If I were you, what I just said would put me back on my heels a bit. Let's be clear: I'm not telling you to shut up, get lost, stay out of the way, or hide in the exam room until a patient walks in. Your team certainly isn't saying that either. What I *am* saying is, as the business owner, you really are the most powerful person in every room—and you must focus that power with laserlike intensity on the handful of things that only you can do and only you should do. You have a distinct, powerful, unique, and highly desirable set of gifts and skills that you are withholding when you're overly occupied with the day-to-day operations. Your team and patients need those gifts. They are what makes your practice uniquely yours. Everyone around you needs you to stop spending every spare moment of your time doing work they could be doing, and they need you to instead show up in the powerful way that only you can.

Your (Frustratingly Intangible) Core Responsibilities

Keeping all this in mind, we'll spend much of this chapter focusing on the core responsibilities of the business owner. These are the things you should be focused on whenever you take off your doctor hat and switch into business-owner mode. Whether you realize it or not, every small-business owner (including you) has three specific gifts that need to be leveraged for the benefit of the entire organization. They are,

- Serving as your organization's heartbeat and True North;
- Casting vision to your entire team on a regular basis; and
- Identifying and cultivating key relationships for the future.

Paying the bills, managing employees' schedules, and dealing with vendors are not on this list. It's not that those things aren't important; it's just that *you* shouldn't be the person responsible for them. Let others handle them so you can focus on your three key roles.

Many personality types may look at these three things and ask, "But what will I actually *create*? True North isn't really something I can write in a procedure manual."

Exactly.

You see, as the business owner—apart from the service role you play to your customers or, in your case, your patients—your most important job is to create the *intangibles* that everyone else in your organization will depend on in order to do their jobs. These are things such as culture, values, feelings, inspiration, and confidence. Even though you cannot see them, they are crucial to the organization. They're the spirit, heart, soul, and backbone. Without them, your business may seem fine on the surface for a while, but it'll be hollow. And a hollow shell will always get crushed when the pressure rises.

Why is it so important that you, as the business owner, create these things? Because if you don't, someone else will. And if someone else sets these fundamental foundations of your business, they're most likely going to get them wrong. You could end up building *your* practice on *someone else's* values and end up feeling like a stranger in your own business. The whole thing can and probably will eventually collapse because it doesn't have a sure footing. The right footing. Your footing.

If you're the kind of person who needs to be able to point at something specific and say, "I made that" or "I did that," let me make a suggestion: Don't worry about "owning" a specific policy, marketing plan, or financial system. Instead, adjust your vision. Pull way back, point at the *whole* business, and then say, "I made that. I did that." Your goal is to "own" the whole business, not the minute details that keep it running every day. If you're doing that, you're doing your job as the business owner.

Now, let's take a deeper dive into each of the three things that only you can do in your practice.

CORE RESPONSIBILITY #1: THE ORGANIZATIONAL HEARTBEAT AND TRUE NORTH

As the business owner, there is no one in your organization who "gets" as much as you do. Regardless of the education level, business background, or personal buy-in of your team members, your personal intuition is a superpower only you possess. Therefore you must trust yourself to lean into it in order to serve as your organization's heartbeat and True North—ensuring you only exercise your full power as the owner to override or veto any decision, something we call the *trump card*—in the most strategic moments.

Practically, here's what that looks like: imagine a situation where a team member comes to the table and makes a really strong case that you would be able to raise your prices by 30 percent and still have plenty of demand. It's a no-brainer, right?

After implementing the price change, you start to notice the clientele you're serving takes a dramatic shift. This starts creating all kinds of problems within the organization because every system and process you've worked so hard to create is no longer meeting the requirements or expectations you're accustomed to experiencing. Simply by changing your prices, you inadvertently changed your entire brand. At this point, you need to decide if keeping the higher prices is worth the fundamental shift it's creating in your business and clientele. You also have to consider if your demand will remain consistent in the brand shift that's been created.

I use this example because the same thing happened to us at Amelia Aesthetics. Our most popular service is typically priced around $7,000 and we discovered we could increase the price of the service to $9,500 and still have plenty of demand. On the surface, this change made a lot of sense and would have resulted in a significant revenue increase. However, Jeremy realized that the demographic our team is passionate about and equipped to serve would be priced out of the market if we were to implement such a steep price increase. He wisely played his trump card and insisted that we keep the procedure within the price range of the demographic we're targeting and built our business around.

And because he's chosen to lean into his role as our chief visionary and has built a practice that reflects *his* values, he took the extra step of using this experience as a learning opportunity for our whole team. In one of our regular staff meetings, he delivered one of his most memorable and powerful talks to our team about who our organization serves and why we've chosen to focus most of our efforts on this particular group. Said differently, he reminded us of why we exist and pointed us back toward our True North.

For you the business owner, the heartbeat of the organization beats in your chest. Your internal, intuitive compass is far more calibrated than anyone else's. In those critically strategic moments, be courageous in playing your trump card, while also balancing the tension of not playing it too often. After all, owners who overplay their veto power undermine their entire team, stripping them of the autonomy and personal buy-in you need them to have.

CORE RESPONSIBILITY #2: CASTING THE VISION FOR THE ENTIRE ORGANIZATION

The second core responsibility you have as the business owner is regularly casting the vision for your organization to your entire team. Does every leader in your organization also have this responsibility? Yes, of course. But first and foremost, they all need to get the vision from the person who also carries the organizational heartbeat. That's you.

Simply put, vision casting is transferring your heart to your team's hearts.

So many business owners I speak with are really intimidated by the concept of vision casting, but remember, you already have this gift. You would never have had the desire to start your own practice if you didn't. It's there; you just have to trust yourself to lean into it. Nevertheless, let me make this just a little easier on you by giving you a construct to follow.

When it comes to vision casting, there are three boxes you'll want to check in order to successfully cast a vision to your team:

- **A Recurring Environment:** Cast the vision to your team at least once per month in a recurring environment. This could be an end-of-week email, a weekly video that hits inboxes at the same time on the same day each week, or a standing agenda item in your weekly staff meeting.
- **A Single Topic:** Once you decide how you're going to deliver the message to your team, select a single topic to cast vision about. As the business owner, you have an infinite amount of subject matter to pull from, such as your vision statement, your mission statement, each of your core values, how your personal story ties into everyone else's, why profit matters,

why you offer the services you do, why you don't offer the services you don't, and so on.
- **A Simple Action Step:** Give one single, simple action step for the team that relates to what you've said to them. Notice I said *one single action step*, not forty-two steps that overwhelm them and not zero steps, which leaves them having to guess what you want them to do with the shared information.

Some of my absolute favorite vision casts that Jeremy has given our team have been around our core values, in which he's shared a personal story and one simple action we can all apply to our day-to-day work to better uphold these shared values.

Remember, the purpose of vision casting is to transfer your heart to your team's hearts. If you do this often enough, you'll be amazed at the radical transformation you'll see in the culture of your business. You will be impressed with how your team improves its decision-making and customer service by simply putting this part of your leadership on autopilot.

Vision casting is one of my favorite topics, and I could go on for days about everything I've learned on the topic from Andy Stanley. For the sake of brevity and clarity, though, I want to share what I think is the most important principle in the world of "visioneering," and that is vision does not *stick*—it *leaks*. Never fall into the trap so many leaders find themselves stuck in, thinking that they only need to say something once or twice before the team adopts it and champions it themselves. That will not happen. People need to hear the vision over and over again. And then they need to hear it some more. As the owner, it's your job to turn *employees* into *champions* for your shared vision, whatever that means for your organization. That will not happen with a once-and-done presentation of your mission and values. It needs to be repeated often if you ever hope for it to stick.

If this is an area that's intimidating or confusing for you, there's no better book on the market for honing your vision-casting skills than Andy Stanley's *Making Vision Stick*. It's a quick read, and I highly recommend it for every leader—especially business owners.

CORE RESPONSIBILITY #3: IDENTIFYING AND CULTIVATING KEY RELATIONSHIPS

The business owner's third core responsibility is all about relationships. Specifically, your team needs you to make space in your day to *identify* and *cultivate* key relationships for the future.

World-famous speaker and author Charlie "Tremendous" Jones dedicated his life to helping others get the most out of life, selling more than two million books along the way. He truly understood the value of key relationships, and he would always say, "Five years from today, you will be the same person that you are today except for the books you read and the people you meet." Of course, this principle isn't just relevant in our everyday lives; it's also a critical factor to the long-term growth of your organization. Every time you genuinely and strategically create a new relationship with someone, you are creating an opportunity for growth somewhere in your business.

Some people may feel awkward about putting too much of a formula around building relationships, especially people who haven't been involved in sales. However, professional salespeople, recruiters, HR professionals, and more know that developing a wide, strong, healthy network of quality people and potential business associates takes, above all else, intentionality. You cannot simply hope to randomly bump into the people you need to grow your business. You need to put some time and effort into *finding* them. That can be intimidating, but it doesn't have to be. Whether you're a natural networker, the idea of networking makes you queasy, or you're anywhere in between, here's a simple plan for developing more than a dozen new, quality contacts per year. And to be crystal clear, I'm not talking about cold-calling for new patients. Growing your customer base is a function of sales and marketing, which we'll discuss at length later in this book. Here we're focused exclusively on expanding your network of professionals who can help you grow your business.

Start by identifying one person—just one person—each month with whom you think you could establish a mutually beneficial relationship. Then contact that person in the format that makes strategic sense, which will usually be either an email or a phone call. In your email, explain to the person why you think a connection between them, you, and your business could be mutually beneficial. Do not be shy! This is not the time to sell yourself short or apologize for interrupting their day. Shyness feels weird, especially over email. Be bold and clear about the benefits of connecting and how your organization could make a positive impact on theirs. As you close your email, ask if they would be willing to schedule a conversation. If they agree, you're in! That's great! Now it's just a matter of setting up fifteen or thirty minutes to have a call or cup of coffee to continue the discussion you started in your email.

Of course, just because you initiated this new relationship, don't assume you personally have to have every conversation with this person on behalf of your organization. Instead, you can pass them to a different member of your team to continue the discussion. You'll still own and guide the relationship, but you can excuse yourself from managing every detail of how your organizations will interact.

The best way to connect your new contact with a member of your team is with an email introduction. In this email, your job is to make both people feel important and to transfer your personal authority between the two parties. Jeremy is a master at this, and I have received hundreds of emails from him connecting me to one of his contacts for follow-up. Here's a real email he wrote to me and Rachel, a physician he had recently connected with:

Hey Rachel,

Also on this email is Robbie Poe. You may have seen Robbie speak at the NCSPS meeting a few years ago, and he's on the schedule for your Senior Resident conference this year.

Robbie is memorable in that he's educated, passionate, and honest when he speaks. It's a strangely uncommon combination at our meetings, so he sticks out. But he has the knowledge and authority to do so as a result of leading our organization for many years now and serving as the Senior Creative Director and business development leader before that with a $100 million organization in Nashville.

Robbie, Rachel is a sixth year/chief resident at Wake Forest. She has a BUNCH of education and is headed to Baltimore next year for a fellowship in breast reconstruction. She is heading to Washington state thereafter and wants to start her own practice. I encouraged her to do so. Rachel and I talked about her finding some time to visit with us. It may not be until the spring because of her schedule, but I would love if you guys could talk for a bit beforehand.

I'll stand down, but I'm here to help in any way I can.

Most sincerely,
Jeremy Pyle

In this example, notice how Jeremy

- builds up the two people who do not yet know each other,
- explains the reason he's connecting them,
- transfers his authority to me so the other person understands I'm acting as his representative and with his authority,
- excuses himself from the conversation, and
- expresses his expectation for the conversation to continue in his absence.

With that, Jeremy can return his focus to his core responsibilities as the physician and business owner while still making sure this new, potentially important business relationship will be taken care of. Of course, he can and should expect updates on whatever Rachel and I talk about and when she will be able to visit, but it shouldn't take much more of his time until or unless he chooses to jump back in.

Though not always "comfortable" for many personality types, establishing and cultivating key relationships is one of the most powerful objectives that any business owner can take upon themselves, and it's one you won't regret putting your time and energies toward.

THE POWER OF YOUR INFLUENCE

Jeremy: I don't like for people to call me "Dr. Pyle."

Of course, I have no judgment for other physicians who prefer everyone calling them "Doctor." I get it. It's just not *me*. I have so much else going on in my life, so many other titles and responsibilities that are more important to me than my role as "Dr. Pyle." I'm a husband, a dad, a son, a business owner, an entrepreneur, a soccer coach, and many other things. I've never considered my role as a physician to be significantly more important than those other roles, so I don't use it as part of my name … most of the time.

There are, of course, some distinct advantages to having earned the title. For example, my wife is also a physician, and we completed our training at the same time. When we started looking for jobs, we had to find a city that could accommodate a plastic surgeon *and* an anesthesiologist. A friend and colleague with many years more experience suggested that I call the CEOs of all the hospitals in the cities we were targeting. I thought she was insane for even suggesting such a crazy idea. After all, we as doctors spend much of our residency being treated like we are not capable of making big decisions and having big conversations. Granted, that's mainly in the world of academia, but I still carried much of that old mindset. Who was I to *dare* to reach out to such high-level professionals?

But I needed a job. And so did my wife. The fear of being a pair of unemployed doctors was a powerful motivator, so I swallowed my intimidation and gave it a shot. I called about fifteen different hospitals, asked to speak to the CEO's office, introduced myself as Dr. Pyle, and left a message for the CEO to return my call.

Every single call was promptly returned by the CEO himself or herself.

I couldn't believe it. If I had called those hospitals as "Jeremy Pyle," I doubt I would have even made it through to the CEO's assistant. I've learned, though, that "Dr. Pyle" *always* gets a return call. That's something I've had to get used to because leading with "Dr. Pyle" still doesn't feel comfortable, even after more than a decade in practice. However, it's a card that I've learned to play when necessary, such as when my team was frustrated that no one at our EHR company would return their calls about an issue that needed urgent attention. After their fifth failed attempt, I decided to give it a try. I guessed at the CEO's email address and sent a note relaying the problem, being sure to sign it "Dr.

Jeremy Pyle." He replied a few hours later, and we had two of their VPs fixing our problem the next day.

The more time I spend in my role as "Jeremy Pyle, CEO," the more strategic I've gotten about when to deploy "Dr. Pyle." I still prefer "Jeremy" most of the time, but I've always got "Dr. Pyle" in my back pocket, ready to get the job done when "Jeremy" can't or shouldn't.

From a strictly pragmatic perspective, you and I have worked exceptionally hard in medicine. We've made sacrifices other people either chose not to make or were, frankly, incapable of making. We've put in the time, effort, forty-eight-hour shifts, missed holidays, and interactions with grumpy patients and grumpier teachers. If all that earned me a subtle benefit such as influence, that's OK. I've learned that having influence isn't something to feel guilty about; *misusing* it is. So I try to be wise and graceful about how, when, where, and why I brandish my influence.

"Jeremy the resident" couldn't imagine that important people would ever want to talk to him about anything. "Jeremy the ten-year vet and business owner" has learned that they do. So I use that influence to create opportunities for growth for my business, for my team, and for the other businesses we interact with. I've learned how to use my influence to open doors, and that is one of the biggest benefits "Dr. Pyle" brings to our practice. It can and should be one of the biggest benefits Dr. You brings to your practice as well.

THE THREE TENSIONS ALWAYS AT PLAY

In addition to the three core responsibilities you and I have as both physicians and business owners, I want to highlight three competing tensions we feel at different times throughout the week:

- The tension that your business needs your revenue to survive and grow.
- The tension that your business needs leadership and guidance from *someone*.
- The tension that there are many decisions to make, many relationships to manage, and many details to attend to every day while directing a business.

Each moment of your work life is likely spent dealing with one of these three tensions. And like it or not, it's practically impossible for anyone to do all three at once. At best, I think we can do *maybe* two—but even then our attention will be split and neither function will get our best work.

What might that look like? What is the reality when we try to personally manage at least two of these tensions at the same time? See if any of these scenarios sound familiar:

- You focus on leading with vision and character while staying stuck in the day-to-day decisions of directing the business.
  But... who is generating the revenue to fund your dream and keep the business alive?
- You focus on directing the day-to-day decisions while seeing patients and generating revenue.
  But... who is zoomed far enough out to lead the business with far-reaching vision for the future?
- You focus on generating as much revenue as you can while leading your business with your vision and character.
  But... who is directing the day-to-day business?

THE MOST POWERFUL PERSON IN THE ROOM: THE BUSINESS OWNER

See the problem? Even if we become masters at keeping two of these three balls in the air, it won't be enough. None of us, standing alone, can do all three. It simply won't happen.

Once we establish that you have a business in which the owner is also the primary revenue generator, then we have to acknowledge *something* must go away in order for your business to be led well. As the owner, you can't really let go of leading the business with your vision and your character. Otherwise, as we've discussed, you'll find yourself effectively working in a practice that looks and feels like someone else's. Your name may or may not be on the door, but it won't really be *your* practice.

As the primary physician in your office, you also can't let go of the revenue generation. Well, I guess you *can* if you hire other doctors and choose to step away from practicing medicine, but my guess is that isn't your favorite option. It definitely wouldn't be mine. So either you do less revenue generating and more managing of the day-to-day minutiae, or you do less managing and more revenue generation. When I got to this point in my business the choice was clear: give up the day-to-day. I love practicing medicine so that's not going anywhere. And I'm personally much more comfortable leading the vision of a team than directing the tiny daily details.

When I work with other practices, the primary pushback I get from physician owners is that people are afraid that if they let go of their unreasonably tight grip of the day-to-day, their business won't be what they want it to be. In my experience, the opposite is true. When we as owners focus on the vision, we are setting a course. We are saying, "This is who we are, and this is where we're going." It's the map. The daily details are just the turn-by-turn directions to get the practice to the destination you, as the owner, set. For example, when I buy plane tickets for a family vacation, I choose the destination. That's me casting a vision for where I want to go. But then I relax and let other professionals (pilots, flight attendants, mechanics, flight crew, ticketing agents, and so on) manage the details of getting us there. If I were to jump in the cockpit and try to micromanage the pilot, I can guarantee the plane and all the passengers would be in more danger than if I simply trust the professionals to do their jobs.

In the language of our practice, I set the vision for how I want the business to look, act, and feel. This isn't dramatically altered by things such as the vendor we use for laundry service and what day they pick up and drop off. I stay out of those decisions. Multiply that by the dozens of other little things that *someone* needs to manage, and I end up with exponentially more time and mental capacity to actually lead the business—all without changing my ability to do the work of revenue generation.

The bottom line with these three tensions is that, as the owner, you get to decide what's important to you. Like Robbie said earlier, you're the most powerful person in the room, and you can choose which rooms, conversations, and duties to jump into. But you cannot do everything. It's a zero-sum game, and the tension between these competing duties is very real. My advice is to choose the long-term vision over the microscopic details. Or in the parlance of medicine, be the heartbeat, not the tiny blood vessels at the end of the chain.

WHAT IF YOUR PRACTICE HAS MULTIPLE OWNERS?

Robbie: One of the most common questions we get around the topic of the business owner role is, "What happens if I'm in a practice with more than one owner?" Multiple-owner businesses are common in medicine and most of those suffer from the same problem: not establishing a clear understanding of who is sitting in the CEO/business owner seat and why.

I understand what a potentially explosive statement this is, but I have to be clear and blunt about this: if you want your business to run successfully on autopilot, only one person can functionally serve in the business owner role we've outlined in this chapter. Anything with more than one head is a monster—and that's exactly what you'll create if you don't clearly communicate and rigidly adopt an organizational structure with a single person who is viewed by all as being ultimately in charge.

I know this is far easier to say than do, but this is a dynamic you simply *must* face head-on with your co-owners. You can either work through the tension of constructively identifying who is in charge or you'll forever live with the pain and inefficiencies of not having the courage and humility to do so.

Who's in Charge?

Jeremy: We've said the business of medicine is sick. Speaking as a plastic surgeon, I feel well qualified to voice an opinion on probably the biggest underlying cause of that sickness: there are too many people who feel entitled to make important decisions, regardless of their skill set, expertise in business, or track record.

We've all seen this at play in hospital settings. You have the doctors and nurses who are doing all the work treating patients, and you have the administrators who are making decisions about *how* the medical staff should treat patients. The result is the one group of people who *aren't* doing medicine are making decisions, and you have the people who *are* doing medicine feeling like they should be the ones making decisions. It's a terrible way to build relationships across an organization and, as a result, we've come up with a million terrible workarounds. Administrators bring in consultants who outline changes that need to be made, and the doctors resist those changes because...well...doctors resist *every* change. This results in a teeter-totter of ideas, none of which can be agreed upon, so any changes the administrators do incorporate are largely ignored.

I'll give you an example that should feel familiar: The administrator decides a certain piece of equipment is "preferred" and requires the medical staff to switch to that device. Some doctors comply, and others resist. Those who resist don't know who made the decision to switch to this new equipment or their reasons for doing so. As a result, the doctors are forced to use a tool they do not like, which is understandably irritating. They then take out their frustrations on the nurses and techs in the room with them, even though those people are just trying to help and had nothing to do with the administrator's decision. Those nurses and techs, then, are stuck having to decide which opposing force to give in to: the doctors making demands *now* or the administrators who will be upset *later*. No one wins, and everyone ends up angry. But no one knows who they should even be angry at.

Hospital medicine is a perfect example of how two people in charge have the same effect as having zero people in charge. Nothing ever changes, grows, or improves; both sides end up pointing fingers and resenting the other; and nobody else in the organization knows who they should really pay attention to. It's a mess.

Those of us in private practice know the same thing happens outside the hospital as well. One person starts a practice, and another person joins and eventually becomes a co-owner. And because these are physicians, not businesspeople, they both either lack the confidence to lead singularly, they lack the humility to let the other person lead, or they lack the time to devote to such a critically important area. The result is a shame: we run multimillion-dollar businesses without a clear leader. Team members have to learn two or more different ways of doing the same tasks so they can be sure not to answer the phone the way Dr. X likes if Dr. Y is within earshot.

No other industry in America conducts ownership, partnership, and decision-making the way we do—and that is not a compliment. Instead, the business world learned a long time ago that every business needs one clear leader in the business owner seat. You can probably name a few companies that have had co-CEOs for a while. It even goes in and out of fashion occasionally when companies are trying to be "edgy." But to my knowledge, no major corporation has ever thrived in the long term in a system where direction is determined by who got there first or who's in charge that day/week/month. In fact, Netflix went to a two-CEO model in 2020 and then experienced its first-ever revenue decline just two years later. Coincidence? Maybe…maybe not.

This gets even more complicated when you throw in our suggestion that the organization's clear number two isn't necessarily the *other* owner but rather the business director, which we will discuss at length in the next chapter. For now, if you are a co-owner of a practice, I just ask that you stick with us as we outline these critical roles. Hopefully, as we go, you'll be convinced of how important it is to establish clear boundaries for you, your co-owner(s), and your business director.

FOCUS ON FEWER THINGS

I have three kids, and they love to play sports. I even get to coach their soccer team now that I've been able to successfully put my business on autopilot. Being a parent is easily the most difficult thing I do—far more difficult than plastic surgery! I don't get it right every time, but one thing I do pretty well is hitting the same fundamental lessons over and over with them. There are a few things I want them to learn and remember for the rest of their lives, so we talk about them—a lot.

One of those cornerstone lessons is the concept of *opportunity cost*, and we talk about it in our home almost every day. When my five-year-old is upset that he can't have two donuts, we talk about excess and the opportunity cost of choosing instant gratification over long-term health. When my eight-year-old wants to play soccer, basketball, and football in the same season, we talk about the concrete limitations of time and how he can't be in two places at the same time. When my ten-year-old wants to do the right thing in a difficult situation but also wants everyone to like her, we talk about the opportunity cost of making the right decision and how you can't always do the right thing while still making everyone happy.

Every decision to do something is simultaneously a decision *not* to do something else. As efficiency expert Michael Hyatt explains:

> If time, and therefore your calendar, is a zero-sum game, we must realize saying yes to one thing means saying no to something else. Even if we hate saying no, we must understand that every yes inherently contains a no ... [and] we're unknowingly saying no all the time—every time we say yes.[4]

For example, I can't have a breakfast meeting with Robbie *and* have breakfast with my family. I can't schedule one person for surgery at 8:00 a.m. if I'm already operating on someone else at 8:00 a.m. Every time I say yes to Option A, I'm actively saying no to Options B–Z. The trick,

THE MOST POWERFUL PERSON IN THE ROOM: THE BUSINESS OWNER

Hyatt argues, is acknowledging the trade-offs and making sure you're saying no to the right people and opportunities.

This is, in my opinion, the most important concept for a young leader to learn, and yet it is the thing most leaders either forget or ignore. The biggest price you pay for doing one thing is that it prevents you from doing something else. So if you spend your time doing the *wrong* things, things that others could do just as well if not better than you, then you've wasted that time. That's right—you *wasted* it. It doesn't matter how much you accomplished or how good a job you did. It doesn't even matter how successful you were. At the end of the day, you just "successfully" wasted your time and robbed your business of the greater value you *could* have added if you had instead spent that time working in your core responsibilities as the business owner.

Time is the most precious resource you have as the business owner. It's the one thing you can't get any more of. That means you have to choose wisely *every time* you decide to spend a chunk of time on something. That's especially true for those of us who are both the source of revenue (the physician) and the business owner because you cannot do both at once. If you teach your team with your words or actions that you need to be involved in every decision, then no decisions can be made while you're in doctor-mode, treating patients, or performing surgery. By the same token, no patients can be served while you're off running the business. Or worse, you'll treat your patients poorly by leaving them alone and frustrated in the exam room for an hour waiting on you while you're sitting in a team meeting.

Unless you're somehow able to clone yourself so you can literally be in two places at the same time, you've got two options:

- You can allow your business growth to be restrained by your inability to do two things at once; or

* You can find and trust other people to do all the things you *could* do but *shouldn't* do, so you can instead spend your time focusing on the handful of things that *only* you can do.

If you're ready to choose the latter, the following two chapters will tell you everything you need to know about the business director and team leaders you need to keep your business running without your day-to-day (micro)management.

CHAPTER 3

THE YOU THAT YOU CAN'T BE: THE BUSINESS DIRECTOR

Jeremy: I could not run my practice without my COO and business director, Robbie Poe. Well, I *could*, but I couldn't run it as well or in the same way we do today. Even if I lose Robbie at some point, there is zero chance that I could ever go back to our old way of doing things. The business has grown far beyond my ability to manage the day-to-day operations. And frankly, I've grown too much as a leader in the business owner role to ever *want* to go back to the way things were. It was a mess back then! Today things are streamlined beyond what I ever imagined. Our business is truly running on autopilot, and so much of that is due to the daily work of our business director.

Robbie's first introduction to our business came through watching us treat another patient. That was back in our "Wild West" days when I was trying to do everything myself. We got a lot wrong back then, but one thing we did well was provide world-class care to our patients. It wasn't about the systems and procedures (which were problematic, to say the least); it was about the love and kindness with which we treated our patients. Showing assurance, comfort, and, above all, respect to patients has always been at our core. It was just common sense. So that value permeated our practice. Apparently, that attitude is rare enough in the field of plastic surgery that it really stands out to our patients—and, it seems, to our patients' friends and family members. That's why I got a call from Robbie out of the blue a few weeks later.

Before coming to work with us at Amelia, he described what he saw in our practice as a "transformative moment" for him. After telling me about his background and experience in leadership and brand building, he asked if I thought there was room for him on our team. After talking a bit more, we both realized the timing wasn't right, but I was impressed enough that I hired Robbie as a business consultant. His experience was impressive, but it was really getting to know him in person that made me comfortable recognizing he was the right person to lead our day-to-day operations. Bringing him on as a consultant was an easy decision. Letting go of control was much harder.

We spent the next year having ninety-minute consulting calls every Friday morning about how we could evolve my business. The calls were definitely useful, but it was evident I didn't need advice as much as I needed someone to come into my practice and actually do the things he and I were discussing over the phone. During that time, I had to choose every day between spending time on my business or spending time with my patients. As we discussed in the previous chapter, this is a tension that every business owner feels if they are also the primary revenue generator. I like to imagine what Amazon would be like today if Jeff Bezos had spent the first seven years personally delivering all the books and products it sold. That's what real life is like for millions of small-business owners—including nearly every physician/practice owner I know.

So when Robbie, my partner Dr. Davis, and I all agreed the time was right to bring him on board full time, the goal was for him to run the day-to-day business and invest in the resources needed to grow the business while my surgeon-partner and I focused on using our trade to generate the revenue to *pay* for those resources. I cannot overstate how difficult this decision was for me. I'm sure you can imagine how hard it would be for you too. On the one hand, I needed help. On the other, accepting help required extraordinary trust. I would have to entrust all the things business owners do not like to share into the hands of someone I had only known primarily over the phone.

It was not an immediate success. We experienced some setbacks, we didn't agree on everything, and there were certainly some tense times between us and among our team members during this transition. It's like climbing Mount Everest: It's a difficult decision to commit to. It's hard to find the right team. The journey from base camp to the top is grueling. You'll almost certainly have some arguments as energy wanes and tempers rise. But then, after all that hard work, you reach the summit. And you know without a doubt that you'd do it all again just to experience the view from the top.

If you're trying to lead your business alone, I know more than anyone that you need help. That's what the business director role is for.

BUSINESS DIRECTOR CORE RESPONSIBILITIES

Robbie: We've mentioned the business director role several times so far, but what exactly is this role? What does this person do?

Imagine you've just boarded a plane, put your luggage in an overhead bin, and got as comfortable as you could squeezed into your seat. Just before you put your earbuds in, the pilot comes over the intercom and says, "Hey folks, unfortunately our copilot couldn't make it today. But never fear, we're going to push off without him and hope for the best!" I don't know about you, but this level of risk and arrogance would prompt me to grab my luggage and exit the plane—quickly. The risk versus the reward wouldn't be worth it.

The very same thing is true in your business. In fact, one of my business owner friends is a pilot, and he assures me that running a business is far more complex than flying an airplane. Trying to run your private practice on your own may be possible, but it carries significant risk and it's going to make it impossible to ever scale your practice beyond your personal capacity. Here, too, the risk versus the reward isn't worth it.

To be clear, when we say *business director*, we are not talking about the $55,000-a-year, run-of-the-mill practice manager typically found within traditional medical practices. No disrespect to the hardworking men and women currently in these positions today, but if your goal is to run a modern, growth-oriented practice, the antiquated position of practice manager is completely useless to you. Instead, when we say business director, we're talking about a highly competent, highly paid natural leader who is deeply passionate and experienced in the areas of business operations and team leadership. This is someone who has a proven track record of strong decision-making, metrics-driven performance, and team-oriented relationship management.

The primary function of this position is simple: This person is there to replace the non-physician piece of you. They are there to be the business leader you *would* be if you *could* be. That means being

- your eyes and ears,
- your face and voice, and
- your hands and feet.

Just as we did for the business leader role, let's break down each of these core responsibilities of the business director.

CORE RESPONSIBILITY #1:
BE YOUR EYES AND EARS

A few years ago, a tree in my backyard was leaning precariously toward my house, and every time there was a storm, it would tip over just a little bit more. An arborist checked it out and told me the tree was rotting from the inside out and needed to be removed before it fell on the house. So I had a tree removal company come out while I was at work one day, and when I got home, the tree was gone. However, I noticed some significant damage to the roofline of my house. I called the tree removal company and asked if it had caused the damage, but the company denied it—until, of course, I sent them the video from my security camera of workers using the crane steering a giant section of the tree trunk right onto my roof line.

You can imagine how quickly their tone changed, and they had it repaired within a few days. How different do you think that would have gone if I hadn't had a security camera set up to keep eyes and ears on my house while I was busy elsewhere?

This is exactly how we see the first core responsibility of the business director: to be the eyes and ears of the business owner, watching over your private practice. Don't misunderstand, though; a business director is far more than a watchdog, as a significant part of their role is to ensure that someone is keeping diligent watch over your practice at all times. Your business director should be giving you regular updates on the day-to-day operations and a thorough weekly report, which summarizes the highs, lows, and rhythms that happened during the practice that week. Practically speaking, this is going to look a little different for each practice; nevertheless, I want to share how we do this at Amelia Aesthetics—just to give you an idea of how it might work for you.

Over the natural course of a business director's day, they should be walking through the entire office on a consistent basis. Like doing rounds in a clinical setting, the business director is intentionally looking for updates from team members and paying close attention to how things are looking and feeling in the practice. During these walks, the business director should try to "bump into" the business owner to give them quick updates about the highs and lows from that day. This is definitely not a meeting; it's more of a quick chat while walking together from one patient appointment to the next or as the owner scrubs his hands and checks his messages between surgeries. Sometimes, for example, if I know Jeremy has a surgical procedure scheduled for 1:30 p.m., I'll hang out near our operating room door a few minutes before to catch him as he walks in. If it's an especially hectic day, a quick end-of-day email or text is better than no update at all.

Additionally, the business directors at our different locations all have a weekly checklist that helps them stay on track with the various goals they are responsible for. While these checklists vary widely in form and structure based on the specific preferences of each business director, its fundamental function remains the same: document, plan, check off each major task that must get completed during the week (often organized by day), and turn it into the business owner at the end of the week along with any clarifying notes.

This process of turning in checklists has been revolutionary at our Amelia Aesthetics locations. As the leadership maxim goes, "You can't *expect* what you don't *inspect*." Well, the checklists make it much easier for the business owner to inspect because they aren't having to wonder, guess, or ask about what's going on in their practice. More importantly, it gives the business director a place to put new recurring tasks that creep up from time to time.

THE YOU THAT YOU CAN'T BE: THE BUSINESS DIRECTOR

And lastly, all the Amelia Aesthetics business directors have a weekly standing meeting with the business owner to do a deep dive on any specific issues, guidance, and updates they feel are especially urgent and/or important. The time and day for these meetings doesn't really matter. One location has them at 6:30 a.m. on Fridays, and another does 5:00 p.m. on Mondays. There really isn't a right answer for when; just make sure you're genuinely connecting with your business director at least weekly in order to stay informed about what's going on in your practice.

Of course, this was just a high-level overview of how the business director can and should serve as your eyes and ears as they "walk the business" every day. We'll talk about checklists and regular meetings in much more detail in later chapters.

You Can't See Everything from the Operating Room

Jeremy: My favorite place in our office is our operating room. That's where I'm at home, where I know I'm doing the job no one else can do, and where I generate the revenue that keeps the business running. It's also where I feel the least amount of stress—not because I'm an especially gifted surgeon, but because that's the room where I truly know what I'm doing. Every time I'm working on a patient, I know all my education and training prepared me for *this* moment. That's a feeling I don't get when I step into a business meeting or look at our accounting. I bet you have a similar experience when you're functioning in your physician role rather than your business owner role.

One reason for my comfort in the operating room is that we've streamlined much of our practice, including my clinical life. As a rule, I only offer six types of operations. I *can* do more, of course, and I *will* do something outside of those six when necessary, but I try my best to stick to my core procedures as much as possible. When I walk into the operating room, I have a *little* anxiety in the pit of my stomach (because I'm human), but I'm not stressed out about the operation I'm about to perform.

The patient on the table, however, is having an entirely different experience. This is probably the first and only time in their life that they are going through this, and they generally have a lot more than "a little" anxiety in the pit of their stomach. Not only do I have an ethical obligation to be mentally present during the procedure, but I also have a selfish reason as well: if I lose my focus and/or stop trying to improve every time I do that particular procedure, the people who come to me for help will be increasingly upset or disappointed. That would make my life drastically harder. The more distracted I am in the operating room, the more likely it is that I'll lose my focus.

But as physicians and business owners, we all know that something urgent, unexpected, and unrelated to patient care will pop up and demand attention. There are distractions running up and down the halls of most practices all day every day. Knowing that's happening "out there" every time I'm in the operating room, two questions immediately come to mind:

- How will I know if something important needs my attention or input?
- Who will solve it out there while I'm busy in here?

I can think of two options here. First, I can pretend that I'll magically be able to find the often-hidden problem lurking *somewhere* inside the organization while also giving 100 percent of my focus to the patients who are paying thousands of dollars and depending on me to be fully present with them as I do my primary job as a surgeon. Or second, I can rely on someone else to find the things, bring them to my attention, and either solve them without me or work with me to find a solution together. Which do you think would be best for the patients, the business, and my sanity?

The business director is my eyes and ears when I'm behind closed doors treating patients. I trust them to walk the halls, talk to the team, check in on everyone's projects, work closely with our team leaders, and bring me the things that *really* need my attention. As our business director, Robbie is the guy chasing down all those distractions that are running around our office. It's his job to spot them and tackle them before they burst through the doors of the operating room and distract me from the surgical work I'm doing. I couldn't do what I need to do on *my* playing field (the operating room) if he wasn't out there doing what I need him to do on *his* turf (the business office).

That doesn't give me permission to totally check out from the business side of things, of course. Robbie and I have an effective system of checking in and tracking his and the team's progress on tasks, which we'll talk more about later in the book.

CORE RESPONSIBILITY #2: BE YOUR FACE AND VOICE

Robbie: One of the business director's most important responsibilities—if not *the* most important responsibility—is to be the business owner's face and voice. That is, a good business director will be the practice's main point of contact for everyone, from team members to patients to vendors. The value of this should be clear to you by now. If everyone is coming to the business director, that means they aren't coming to *you*. This frees you to spend your time on those things only you can or should do.

Speaking as a business director, I can say from experience that this is the most difficult responsibility for a business director to do well . . . because it's the most difficult responsibility for the business owner to *let* them do well. I don't say that flippantly either. I understand how hard it is for the person who started a practice to entrust its operations to someone else. As the owner, it's your practice, your investment, and your reputation on the line. I get how overwhelming the concept of a fully empowered business director must be to you. And yet, to be perfectly candid, empowering your business director to be your face and voice is the only way you, as the business owner, won't become a burdensome bottleneck who severely limits the growth of your organization. If you ever want to put your practice on autopilot and scale beyond your personal capacity, you've got to reach a point where you're willing to hand your personal reputation and authority over to your business director.

Think about how many hours during the business day a busy surgeon is able to be the face and voice of their own practice. In our experience, this is usually about thirty minutes total per day. And that's not even thirty minutes all at once; it's more likely to be fifteen different two-minute, incomplete conversations spread out between patient visits. We can all agree that leading a healthy, growing practice is far too complex for someone who is only able to give it thirty sporadic minutes of attention during business hours each day. There are simply too many patients who need extra attention, team members whose feelings need to be cared for, and vendor relationships that need managing—and those are all things you can't really act on late at night and on weekends when most doctors have time to put on their business-owner hat.

Instead, imagine how much more could be accomplished if someone you trusted were empowered to champion these countless situations on your behalf. It creates a level of freedom, efficiency, and velocity that simply isn't possible otherwise.

Make It Public

It's not enough just to empower your business director to speak on your behalf. To get the biggest ROI out of your business director, you as the owner must *publicly transfer* your authority to them. Everyone must understand that a yes or no from the business director should be taken as a yes or no from you, the owner. Otherwise, the business director will hit roadblock after roadblock in their attempt to oversee your practice and make your vision a reality.

I'm sure you can guess what the most common roadblock would be: people trying to get around the business director and coming straight to you. You cannot let this happen, and you cannot undermine the work your business director is trying to do. If people even *think* they can get a different answer from you than they got from the business director, you'll have a nonstop stream of employees trampling right over the business director on their way to you. This, obviously, only creates more problems and drama in the office, and those are the very things you're trying to eliminate.

Everyone's default position as you begin your transition into *The Private Practice MBA* system will be to bring all their issues to you. That's understandable because, as they say, "It's how we've always done it." Not anymore. That changes today if you really want to grow your practice and create the freedom for yourself that we've described. Handing off so much responsibility and authority will probably feel unnatural at first, so here are some concrete tips for ensuring your business director will get off to a great start and grow into their role appropriately.

First, stand up in front of your entire team and make it clear that they are to go to your business director—not you. First. With anything. At all. Remember, one of your business director's jobs is to protect you and your time, serving as a filter of sorts. You won't believe how much more focused you'll feel when you're only fielding the mission-critical questions that the business director filters up to you in this process.

Second, after the initial public handoff, remind the team regularly what you told them initially. Don't allow anyone to slip into old patterns of bringing things straight to you. And if or when they do, always redirect them to the business director and do not give them your opinion on the matter without first checking with the business director yourself. It's possible that some team members will try to play you and the business director off each other like a manipulative teenager. If they don't like the answer they got from the business director, they may try to get a different answer from you. If a team member comes to you for something via email, reply to them and copy the business director on the email, asking them to get together to work it out. If you don't shut down these attempts to skirt the system early and often, you'll be sending mixed messages and, worse, knocking the business director's legs out from under them.

Third, make sure everyone sees you—visibly *sees* you—meeting with your business director on a regular basis. They need to see you two working closely together. That visual reinforcement will help solidify their understanding that the business director really does speak as the voice of the owner. It also reinforces the fact that you, as the owner, are still plugged into the operations of the business and that the business director isn't running the business without you.

Fourth and last, when it comes to working with partners and vendors, introduce your business director as the person who runs your practice. Be sure to mention the fact that you don't have a standard practice manager and that your business director is fully capable of running with the conversation on your behalf. Naturally, you should be kept in the loop, but you're there to be the clean-up hitter. Let your business director get the bases loaded for you.

I know handing off this much authority is a challenge, but it is a crucial step to freeing yourself of all the daily chores that have been eating away at your time up to this point.

Short, Clear, and Concise

Jeremy: Whenever Robbie catches me in the hall when I'm running from one appointment to another or when he catches me between surgeries, I know he's going to have a question, an update, or both. We have a standing meeting every Friday, so these quick chats and check-ins throughout the day are usually about something urgent, something that can't wait until our meeting. That means I need to be careful in my response to him. This isn't the time to have a long, detailed discussion. There's no chance I'm going to get the big picture and all the details on the matter in the precious minute or two that we'll have. I have to trust that he's giving me the key details I need, and I have to be ready to give him a response that is short, clear, and concise.

Giving clear and concise answers *on the spot*—often with very little context—has always come naturally to me. I stumbled in this area when Robbie and I first started working together. I was used to those quick answers solving immediate problems, but it wasn't creating any real solutions. It took a while for me to go from "solve the problem" to "give my opinion and let him take it from there." Learning how to receive information, digest it, formulate an opinion, and communicate that opinion in just one or two minutes isn't easy. And like anything else that's new and difficult, it will take some time and effort. You're essentially working a muscle that's never been used before, so expect it to be weak, to struggle, to fail, and to get sore for a while.

Of course, there are some questions that you simply will not be able to answer quickly. If I'm coming out of a challenging three-hour surgery and heading into another one, my brain is already busy trying to put the surgery I just completed aside and switching tracks over to a different patient and an entirely different procedure. That's probably not the best time for me to come up with a thorough response to a million-dollar issue. In those moments, I have to have the discipline to table the issue until our weekly meeting or, if necessary, until later that day when I have some time and space to think. It will take some time for you and your business director to learn each other's rhythms and thought processes, so don't be surprised if your director occasionally brings you big things at the wrong times at first. It's all part of figuring out your new working relationship.

The goal, though, should be to get to the point where your business director can bring you an appropriate issue at the appropriate time and you can give your perspective in a clear and concise way. That way, you're still plugged in, and you still have a voice, but the business isn't grinding to a halt while everyone waits for you to come down from the mountain with a final answer.

CORE RESPONSIBILITY #3:
BE YOUR HANDS AND FEET

Robbie: The third core responsibility of the business director is likely to be your favorite because it's going to allow the business side of your practice to continue running full steam ahead—even when you're completely wrapped up in patient care.

We will dive deeply into the specific ways your business director will serve as your hands and feet in the Money, Sales and Marketing, Operations, and Leadership sections of this book. For now, though, I want to caution you about one of the biggest mistakes a business owner can make when implementing *The Private Practice MBA* system: skipping the first two business director's responsibilities we covered and jumping right into having them *do* something. I understand this temptation. After spending years being stretched too thin, it's easy to get excited about bringing on a business director who will eventually take all that mission-critical business work off your desk. But stop. Take a breath. Dumping all that sensitive work on them before they've had a chance to get to know you, your way of thinking, your leadership style, and your intentions for the practice carries unnecessary risk.

When you bring a business director on board, spend your first few weeks focusing on equipping them to be your eyes, ears, face, and voice. Once you are confident that they truly *know* you and are ready to act on your behalf, you can then set them loose to do all the work you hired them to do. Being the hands and feet of the business owner requires a lot of heavy lifting; don't overburden them with tasks and projects until you're sure they're ready to run with the load you're putting on them.

THE BUSINESS DIRECTOR AS YOUR CHIEF RESIDENT

Jeremy: Think back to your residency training. You'll remember that the first part of training is mostly about gathering data and then doing *what* someone else says to do and *how* they say to do it. Then you advance to the next phase, which is more about understanding how that data is utilized and following the guidance of more senior doctors to determine what to do with it. Finally, you reach the point where you feel more empowered and equipped to implement what you know the attendings you have spent years with would want you to do. The whole thing is a process of maturing into a fully formed, self-sufficient physician under the watchful eye of an attending physician.

Right up to the very last day before you complete your residency, though, every decision you make must be sent up the chain. The big difference is that, early on, you run it up the chain and then make the decision. Near the end, the reverse is true: you make a decision and then you run it up the chain after the fact.

In *The Private Practice MBA* system, you can think of your business director as an exceptional chief resident. Eventually, *after the training period*, you'll be able to trust them to speak and act on your behalf, saying and doing things just as you would if you were there. But just like in residency, this doesn't happen on the first day. They need time to get their bearings and learn your way of doing things before they're ready to get to work, making decisions and taking action without you and filling you in later.

Of course, there are going to be times when things aren't going in the direction you want. That's when you'll need to know how to play your trump card.

HOW AND WHEN TO PLAY YOUR TRUMP CARD

Robbie: Working alongside a business director is always going to have different tensions to manage, but you have an ace up your sleeve that no one else in the organization has: you as the owner always have a trump card to overrule whatever decisions you want. You may hear that and think, *Heck, yeah, I have a trump card. I'm the owner. This is*

THE YOU THAT YOU CAN'T BE: THE BUSINESS DIRECTOR

my *business, and I'll do* what *I want,* when *I want!* Others may think, *I really don't want to step on any toes by undermining my business director.* Maybe you're somewhere in between these two extremes. Regardless of where you fall on this spectrum, there are a couple things you absolutely must know about your trump card.

First, if you play it too often, you'll only be undermining yourself. A properly empowered business director is very connected to your business, and they are much closer to most of the problems than you will be. Oftentimes they may make much better decisions than you will—and if you're consistently playing your trump card, not only are you undermining your entire practice, but you're going to undermine and demoralize your business director. A business owner who overplays their trump card will never feel the value of putting their business on autopilot because they're always waiting in the wings and looking for a chance to jump in and shake things up.

Second, *never* playing your trump card is also dangerous. If you never jump in, your team will drift further and further from your vision for the organization. Remember, your entire team (including your business director) is busy leading, growing, and maturing the day-to-day operations of your business. They are stuck in the weeds, so it's easy for them to lose sight of the forest, your greater vision for the business.

It is important to remember that whenever you play your trump card, you're almost always going to disrupt your team. Playing your trump card is like pulling the emergency brake on a moving car. It's going to catch people off guard, and it might even upset your business director or other team members who are involved. So only play that card in moments when your team can voice their opinions about your decision. Even if you know for certain that you are right and that no one else will be able to change your mind, you should still give them a platform to disagree. Grown women and men want to be heard before they fully get behind an idea. And in my experience, most team members are very willing to disagree yet commit as long as they have an opportunity to weigh in on your decision.

The agreement you need to make with your team is "I will allow you to *weigh in*, so you can *buy in*." And the agreement your team needs to make with you is "We will *disagree* yet *commit*." This is how adults function within a healthy team, and this is how a trump card is effectively used.

But what about a business with more than one owner? How does the trump card work then? Does every owner have a trump card? Well, yes... *but*...

I strongly recommend that all owners make a commitment to each other to run every trump card decision through the person sitting in the CEO/business owner role. Otherwise, your team will never feel the freedom to take risks and innovate. Instead, you will train them to play it safe and keep their heads down, which will all but ensure that you never put your business on autopilot.

THE HIGHEST HURDLE

Jeremy: I know we've covered a lot here, and I know as a business owner that this can be a touchy subject—this whole concept of trusting your business operations to someone else. But here's the deal: if I had been unwilling to find someone with real business acumen to come in and help me back away from the day-to-day of my business... if I had been unwilling to pay that person drastically more than the going rate for a typical practice manager... if I had been unwilling to trust that this person with more than a decade of high-level leadership and business development experience would

THE YOU THAT YOU CAN'T BE: THE BUSINESS DIRECTOR

be better at running the day-to-day details of my business than I was...well, then, today I would still be where I was back then, right where most private practice owners end up.

I would pick "here" over "there" any day—and not because of our business success or the increased revenue and profit we've gained. I would pick here over there *because my life is better.*

When Robbie joined our team, two things happened. First, as our business director, he pushed our business forward further and faster than I could have done. Second, the fact that *he* was doing that instead of me meant that I progressively reclaimed more of my time—and my life. I was slowly freed to do other things, the things I had wanted to do for years but could never make time for, such as coaching my kids' soccer teams or spending the weekends with my family instead of trying to solve staffing problems. Without a business director, every decision in my organization would fall on my shoulders. I wouldn't just *get* to make all the decisions; I'd *have* to make all the decisions.

I know this is controversial, this idea that someone else should make most of your day-to-day decisions. I know we are taught to scrap and fight for every measure of control we can. I think in a hospital system, that's probably true. But in a private practice, the opportunity costs are just too high.

Earlier in this book, I told you about my rock-bottom moment, the Sunday night my father challenged me to choose between my business and my family. Without a business director, I would have chosen my business. I'm not proud of that. It actually makes me really sad. But it's the truth. I didn't have the discipline to lay my work responsibilities down for the sake of my family.

Because I had a competent, skilled, well-paid business director to fall back on, I didn't have to choose between my business and my family.

I discovered I could have both—but it required me to place my trust fully in Robbie's leadership and decision-making. Once I did, some amazing things began to happen. I get to weigh in, give feedback, and set a big vision, such as adding 20 percent more surgery time without sacrificing patient experience. And then I walk away, get back to surgery, and leave it to my business director to figure out how to make it happen. Our open positions are filled by wonderful new team members, whom I often meet for the first time on their first day of work. I say things like, "I think our social media would be better if we actively replied to more comments," and then I disappear back into the operating room while the business director leads the charge to get it done. In short, I get to walk away from practically everything that used to eat up all my free time, nights, and weekends—the things that *aren't* surgery and the things I felt wholly unqualified to handle—and I get to spend more time doing what I love, whether that's performing surgery or spending more time with my family. And the best part is, my business is better, bigger, stronger, and more successful than it would be otherwise.

For many doctors and business owners, finding and then handing control over to a business director is the highest hurdle to jump in *The Private Practice MBA* system. But as with many things in life, the biggest challenge is also the most rewarding.

CHAPTER 4

YOUR HEDGE OF PROTECTION: THE TEAM LEADERS

Jeremy: "Don't bring your personal drama to work."

That was the attitude of pretty much every previous generation of professionals—especially in medicine. The prevailing thought in our industry was that our work is too important—lives are literally hanging in the balance—and no one has time to wait around for a nurse who's running late because she had to take her child to school or an anesthesiologist who is distracted by the fight he had with his spouse as he left that morning. Business owners of past generations expected their employees to leave their personal selves at home, as though it were as easy as flipping a switch from "home me" to "work me."

That is actually the premise of the Apple TV+ series *Severance*. The premise is that a tech company develops a medical procedure to separate their employees' personal memories from their work memories. So when they come to work, there actually *is* a switch they can flip that removes every trace of their personal lives from their minds. They are, in effect, completely devoted to the company because during working hours, there is nothing else in their minds. For some business owners I know, this sounds like a dream. As much as I wish the *personal* didn't bleed over into the *professional* so often and easily, though, it sounds like a total nightmare. It doesn't turn out so well in the show either.

Science fiction notwithstanding, the days of keeping home at home and work at work are gone. And if you're still leading your team with that mindset, all your employees will be gone soon as well. This is the age of the integrated self, and employers have to get used to seeing the *whole* person whenever they look at their team members.

Honestly, this makes me extremely uncomfortable. I don't *want* it to be true. I'd much rather have everyone keep their personal lives personal and their professional lives professional. But I have to admit that if our business discounted the personal lives and struggles of our employees, I probably would not still be working with all the incredible people I get to work with every day. Instead, I would have "had" to fire them.

Everyone has hard times and bad days. That's why most jobs offer personal time. Everyone gets sick a few times a year. That's why we offer our team members sick time. If they have they flu, they stay home. It's only a few days a year, so it's no big deal. It isn't that complicated. At least it wasn't—until the spring of 2020. Once COVID-19 hit, though, the traditional understanding of sick time went out the window. The rules changed overnight, and businesses were forced to adapt. Fast.

Our clinical director, Renee, leads our four clinical teams (RNs, MAs, surgical techs, and anesthesia). Without a doubt, Renee had the most difficult job in our office throughout the pandemic. No one on any of her teams could work from home, and every single one of them was vital to our day-to-day operations. So when even one member of her finely tuned team was out, she felt it. And as I'm sure you remember, people were out *a lot* during COVID. One might be out because she was sick herself. Another could be out because her child was sick. Yet another could be out because she'd been exposed and had to quarantine. On and on the list went.

The old-school rules say that if someone can't *do* the job or *show up* for the job, then they *lose* the job. If we had followed that way of thinking, we would have fired everyone. Instead, we had *less* turnover during those two years than we normally have. This was definitely not the industry norm at the time. Instead, we kept seeing article after article revealing clinical providers were leaving their jobs—unhappily and *en masse*—while we were experiencing the opposite.

Why? How did we get so "lucky" when our competitors were losing their entire teams?

It's because we act and lead with empathy. We get to know the whole person, not just their professional skill set. We break our large staff up into smaller teams, and each team has a team leader who digs in and develops strong, binding relationships with the people under them. We value the emotional intelligence of our team leaders, and we strive to help every team member understand how valuable they are to our organization—both for what they do and, maybe more importantly, for who they are.

We're going to talk about the responsibilities of the team leader role throughout this chapter, but as we do, don't lose sight of the power of *emotional intelligence*. Prioritizing interpersonal connections with each team member is vital to building an organization full of happy, long-term, committed, sold-out champions for your business.

TEAM LEADER CORE RESOPNSIBILITIES

Robbie: The role of team leader is one of my favorite parts of our whole *The Private Practice MBA* system. This is where the concept of putting your business on autopilot really gets going. Remember, the goal should not just be to put *your* nonmedical responsibilities on autopilot but to put the entire business on autopilot. To do that, you need more people than just the business owner and business director. You need a team, and those team members need quality team leaders.

When we say team leaders, we're referring to an individual who is being held accountable for the performance, attitudes, and communication of three to five other team members—almost always within their same area of discipline. For example, this could be a member of your front-of-house team who leads the rest of the front-of-house team. Or it could be a medspa injector who leads the rest of the medspa providers. These people aren't just excellent at their specific skill, they're also gifted at and willing to accept additional leadership responsibilities beyond their daily skill tasks.

When to Add Team Leaders

We're often asked when the right time to implement team leaders is for an organization, and here's what we've found: As long as your practice is fewer than five or six people, the entire team can and should report to your business director. When your practice grows any larger—more than six people—it's time to implement team leaders. Obviously, this will change your organizational chart because you're adding a new level of leadership. At that point, your business director will no longer personally lead the entire team. Instead, your business director will lead your team leaders, and each team leader will be responsible for their own direct reports.

In most practices, this initial split will likely happen between the office staff and the clinical team. Once you get, say, three office workers and four or five clinical staff members, it becomes too much for the business director to personally manage. So you formally create a clinical team and an office or administrative team, and your business director appoints a team leader for each. That ensures everyone, including the business director, has a small, tight, manageable team.

The logic here is based on multiple studies that have found even the highest-capacity leaders struggle to lead more than four or five people well. Anytime a leader's team grows beyond five people, they end up giving more attention to the *problematic* team members and less attention to the most dedicated and loyal team members. That's obviously a huge problem where your best and brightest aren't getting the recognition and opportunities they deserve. This, in turn, makes *keeping* your best team members nearly impossible.

When implemented well, team leaders serve a vital function to the business and the business director. They hold a linchpin role in making sure the entire team is doing their jobs with excellence, happy in their roles, hearing their peers, listening to their leaders, and sharing their personal opinions. Specifically, they have three key responsibilities we want to highlight in this chapter. Team leaders will

- Oversee execution,
- Create joy and fulfillment, and
- Ensure 360° communication.

As we've done for the business owner and business director roles, let's dig deeper into these key responsibilities of team leaders.

CORE RESPONSIBILITY #1: OVERSEE EXECUTION

As a business owner, we worry about every altitude in our business—everything from the ten-year vision to the way the phone is answered. However, it's completely unrealistic to think that you'll ever scale your practice beyond your own capacity if you are holding yourself personally accountable for each and every task happening within your practice. And that's where the team leader's first core responsibility comes into play. Instead of you, the business owner, personally holding every team member accountable for each of their tasks, your business director is holding your team leaders accountable for the tasks of the folks who report to them.

This is one of the most important elements to getting your private practice running on autopilot: knowing that things are happening the way you expect them to happen without your direct oversight. And further, there's incredible freedom in knowing that, when you notice or sense that something is off, you don't have to address it yourself. Instead you can simply pass a quick note to your business director and have them get the problem solved on your behalf through the team leaders who report to them.

It might feel a little more complex than necessary, but I can assure you it's a beautiful dance to watch once everyone is committed to the system. Problems are solved quickly, and you, the business owner, are able to stay focused on production and your core responsibilities.

There's much more to say about overseeing execution, and we'll devote a lot of space to that in the Operations section of the book. There, we'll break down the *how* of execution and, just as important, the art of *overseeing* execution. And if you're getting nervous about raising up quality leaders in your practice, you can put those worries aside. We've dedicated an entire section of this book to the topic of leadership.

Growth Requires Trusting Team Leaders

Jeremy: I never intended for Amelia Aesthetics to grow beyond our one office in Raleigh, North Carolina. Things changed when my friend

YOUR HEDGE OF PROTECTION: THE TEAM LEADERS

Rafi Fredman, one of the best people I know, finished his residency. My father always taught me that, when you come across an A+ person, you should find some way to offer them a job. Rafi is absolutely an A+ person, so I took Dad's advice and offered him a job. He was certainly interested, but he had always planned to return home to St. Louis to build a practice near his family and faith community. So he turned me down. I was disappointed, but his declination turned out to be one of the most important events in my life as a business owner. His no was a spark that incredibly took Amelia Aesthetics to the next level. And it was also the start of one of the most dramatic examples we've seen of how successful a practice can be by following *The Private Practice MBA* system.

Respecting Rafi's decision but still hearing my dad's wisdom in the back of my head, I talked it over with Robbie, and we ultimately offered Rafi the opportunity of licensing the Amelia Aesthetics brand. In this model, he would be the business owner of that St. Louis location, but he would open with the full backing and support of our Amelia Agency team, which would come alongside him and help him run his practice better—putting our experience and know-how together with his initiative and skill as a surgeon.

Leaning on Amelia for the key areas of sales and marketing, Rafi was able to open his business with only two other employees. Just the three of them in that office did nearly two hundred cosmetic operations and $2 million in revenue in their first twelve months alone! With such a lean team, Rafi easily assumed the sole leadership role while still being the business's heart and soul. However, as his production and demand grew, he needed to grow his team to match. And, of course, a bigger team meant entrusting new leaders to take ownership of the different key areas of his business. Like all of us, Rafi was faced with the pressures of growth and the inherent tensions of trusting others with his business.

Today Rafi is just starting to build out his team with excellent people, and as he hires, he's always looking for that little *extra*, that quality that stands out in people who are destined for bigger leadership roles. As his practice continues to thrive, we will work with him to set up the full system we're outlining in this book, including finding a business director and, of course, team leaders for his operations, financials, and clinical teams.

CORE RESPONSIBILITY #2: CREATE JOY AND FULFILLMENT

Robbie: Let's be really honest for a minute. I don't think anyone would disagree that having joyful and fulfilled team members would be a nice thing . . . but does it really belong in the top three responsibilities of team leaders?

As someone who tends to favor the IQ versus the EQ side of things, I get it. When I first began my journey of leading teams, I honestly didn't give the idea of creating a joyful team much consideration. However, my unwillingness to do so bit me in the butt so many times that I eventually realized the extraordinary value that fulfilled team members add to an organization.

When each member of your team is excited to be in their seat, they perform at a higher level, they miss fewer days, they volunteer to work extra hours, they personally identify with the mission of your practice, they hold their peers accountable, they take it upon themselves to grow within their skill set and leadership abilities, and the list goes on and on. And we can't forget perhaps the biggest issue, which is that joyful and fulfilled team members tend to stick around.

Replacing a team member is one of the most expensive staffing issues that ever occurs within a practice. Some studies show that replacing a team member can cost 150 percent of that employee's annual salary.[5] And that's just *one*. What happens if your team is so unhappy that you have to replace several people every year?

If you aren't doing the intentional work of helping your team become joyful and fulfilled at work and in their work, then you're going to be chasing your tail trying to keep good talent over the long haul. The ROI of this core responsibility is immeasurable, and it's one that must be taken seriously if you're going to put your private practice on autopilot.

But if this core responsibility feels a bit . . . *squishy* to you, don't worry. I know they didn't teach employee-morale techniques in medical school. That's why we'll cover all the exercises we use at every Amelia Aesthetics location to create joyful team members and keep our finger on the pulse of team members' sense of fulfillment in their work. That's coming up later in the Operations and Leadership sections of this book.

Wouldn't You Rather Work with Happy People?

Jeremy: Robbie and I work well together because we are so different. What he finds fun, I do begrudgingly at best. What produces happiness in my work life is sometimes a bore in his. As different as we are, though, creating a work atmosphere that inspires joy and fulfillment in ourselves and our team is incredibly important to both of us.

For me, joy and fulfillment aren't just preferences; they're necessities. My life is essentially split into thirds. Out of the 168 hours in a week, I spend fifty sleeping, sixty with my family, and most of the rest at work. If I were sleeping poorly, I'd dig into the reasons why and change it. If my family time wasn't inspiring joy, I'd work with my wife to find and fix whatever the problem is. And if all the hours I spend at work weren't fulfilling, I'd work with my business director to take our whole organization back to its bare bones to address the issue. It's that important to me.

As I said in the introduction, I left the first practice I ever joined because it was not fulfilling. I enjoyed taking care of my patients, but the environment was not well-suited to my feeling joy and fulfillment. So even as a physician, I did the exact thing Robbie just warned you about: I left. If even doctors are willing to leave their patient base by moving to a different practice, how quickly do you think your patient coordinators, nurses, techs, and office staff will leave when they don't feel personally connected at work? And I can't blame them at all. Life's too short to spend a third of every week in misery. No amount of money can make that worth it.

This isn't rocket science: If your people are fulfilled, they will stay until an opportunity for advancement arises. If they aren't fulfilled, they will leave, regardless. That's not just my opinion either. *Harvard Business Review* reports, "In general, people leave their jobs because they don't like their boss, don't see opportunities for promotion or growth, or are offered a better gig (and often higher pay); these reasons have held steady for years."[6] I'd summarize that by simply saying that people leave mainly because at least one of three things is missing:

- Leadership
- Opportunity
- Recognition

These three things are critical for me in both my roles as a member of a team and, more importantly, as the leader of the team. The bottom line is that I like the people I work with. I want to take every reasonable opportunity I can to help make their lives better. That's not just about employee retention; it's part of what brings me joy at work. I've found that my joy and fulfillment is linked to working with people who are joyful and fulfilled. And as the business owner, I'm in a position to help them grow in their joy and fulfillment.

So are you.

Robbie admitted that he didn't start his leadership career being overly concerned with these things. Now that he's more experienced, though, I know he'd agree with me: we just spend too many hours working to not be happy, fulfilled, and outright joyful doing it. And if we in the medical industry—who work to literally improve people's lives and health every day—can't find fulfillment in our work, who can?

CORE RESPONSIBILITY #3: ENSURE 360° COMMUNICATION

Robbie: The third core responsibility of team leaders is a leadership principle I first learned from John C. Maxwell called *360° communication*. That is, you want to ensure that team members are

- communicating with their team leader,
- communicating with one another, and
- receiving communication from higher-level leadership.

The goal with this continual flow of communication is to make sure all team members (including you, the business owner) are always in the loop with what's going on in the business.

Practically every business owner I talk to thinks this is easy to do. They're wrong. This is actually one of the most challenging aspects of running a business because, as a general rule, the person who has the information assumes everyone else already has it too. It's not that business owners and key leaders are intentionally keeping their team members in the dark; it's that they are so connected to the inner workings of the business that they forget most of the people they work with don't have access to all the meetings, conversations, phone calls, and emails between leaders in which decisions are made. Communication can also feel like one of those things that's extremely high effort and low reward—even though we all know how frustrating it can be to feel blindsided by some big shift no one told us about.

We'll cover the nuts and bolts for how to make your communication bulletproof in the Operations and Leadership sections of the book. For now, though, we'll quickly touch on the three 360° communication principles I've mentioned.

First, you've got to ensure that team members are *communicating with their team leader*. I'm not talking about tiny bits of conversation that are tossed back and forth when they pass in the hall. I'm talking about in-depth, meaty, meaningful, eyeball-to-eyeball conversations that cover everything from work to personal life. When team members don't feel seen and heard by their team leaders, an endless array of problems will spring up that could have been easily avoided with a simple communication strategy.

Second, team members must be *communicating with one another*. This isn't just communication about shared tasks and work responsibilities; it also includes getting to know the people you spend forty or more hours a week with. A recent Google study found that the number one trait of a high-performance team is psychological safety, and psychological safety is impossible if team members aren't comfortable engaging in open communication with one another and given plenty of opportunities to do so.[7] Does this mean it's OK for your employees to spend two hours a day chatting about their weekend plans in the break room? Definitely not. We all have too much work to do for that. But it does mean that *some* personal conversation is vital in building relationships, and relationships are a key trait of psychological safety in the workplace. You can't expect your team members to enjoy their work if they don't enjoy being around one another.

Third, team members must be *receiving communication from higher-level leadership*, and the best way to do this is through team leaders. In my experience, the temptation from the business owner and even the business director is to bypass team leaders, take issues directly to the team members involved, and handle all the communication themselves. But this leads to one of the most common communication failures: someone is accidentally missed or someone receives the information in the wrong way, and the negative emotions or tactical outcomes end up costing everyone a ton of time and sideways energy. For example, I have a tendency to be extremely direct with people. If someone doesn't know me well, that can come across as "steamrolling." So the times when I've sidestepped a team leader and taken a concern directly to the team member (who doesn't know me as well) for the sake of "efficiency" has cost me both time and relational clout. Every time. It's never worth it. It is much more efficient to pass information through the team leaders, who already have a strong relational base with each of the two to six people on their team.

We'll come back to 360° communication later. By the end of this book, you'll know everything you need to know about how to tighten up the communication on your whole team and between your individual teams. You'll find that this makes it ten times easier to spot problems, identify solutions, encourage your team members, strategize, and take the business further faster—while making sure everyone else is moving ahead right along with you.

Trusting Team Leaders for Quality Communication

Jeremy: One of the hardest parts of leading an organization—while also working *inside* the organization as the main source of revenue—is understanding my limitations and building systems to overcome them. And if I am being honest with myself, one of my biggest limitations (and weaknesses) is engaging in quality communication with our whole team. It's not that I want to keep them in the dark about anything, and it's not even that I assume they already know everything I know. The biggest problem for me, as the business owner and revenue generator, is that every minute of my day is already spoken for before I step one foot in the office. I arrive around 7:30 a.m. every day, and I leave around 6:00 p.m. Every minute in between is jam-packed either with taking care of patients or taking care of our business. Because the whole day is filled with some form of important decision-making, I struggle to find the time and methods to *communicate* all those decisions to the right people.

Driving communication through team leaders has become an effective workaround for us. Here's what it looks like in action: I will step out of an exam or procedure room, and my business director will be standing there ready to walk with me on my way to the next patient. As we walk, he will present some problem brought forward by a team leader and offer his options for a solution. I will help him decide which course of action to take, and then I'll get back to seeing patients. At that point, the business director understands that he is responsible for not only enacting the solution we discussed, but also for communicating that decision to the relevant team leaders or team members. The business director entrusts the management of those tasks to the team leader. This allows me to keep doing the things that only I can do in my dual roles of physician and business owner, and it prevents my limitations from getting in the way of team members knowing what they need to know.

LAY THE FOUNDATION BEFORE YOU BUILD

As we wrap up this section on "Autopilot People" and before we start unpacking the "four tires" that will drive your business forward, I want to be as clear as possible about one thing: your practice will never truly run on autopilot until you make sure you have the right people in the right seats *and* until you trust them to take the wheel for you while you're focused on other things. *The Private Practice MBA* system won't work well (if at all) if you, as the business owner, are constantly bulldozing your way into every conversation and unimportant decision. The business director role has revolutionized our practice, giving me the freedom and peace of mind I thought would never come this side of retirement. And the team leader role has enabled my business director and me to grow our team and business further and faster than we ever could have done alone. These three roles—business owner, business director, and team leader—are the foundation of everything we're going to build throughout the rest of this book. Do not overlook or underestimate what each role can add to your practice.

SECTION 2
ALL THINGS MONEY

CHAPTER 5

PUTTING YOUR CASH ON AUTOPILOT

Robbie: Cash is the lifeblood of an organization. It doesn't matter how amazing your leadership is, how brilliant you are at sales and marketing, or how much your business is running on autopilot—if you run out of cash, you're screwed.

It's so easy to turn a blind eye to your finances when things are going well. Money's coming in, money's going out, and things are good, right? But then, *life* happens and throws a wild, unexpected crisis in your face ... and your business goes from top of the world to completely underwater in the blink of an eye. Take 2020, for example. We talk about the COVID-19 pandemic a lot because as unprecedented as it was, it represents the kind of upheaval that any business has to prepare for. Sure, nobody was expecting *that* emergency, but smart business owners and business directors were already anticipating *some* emergency—because emergencies shouldn't be all that unexpected. Again, life happens. And sometimes, it sucks.

At the start of the pandemic, the federal government and individual states got all up in the day-to-day operations of small businesses. At best, there were heaps of new regulations and precautions that businesses had to implement in order to stay open. At worst, businesses were forced to shut their doors for weeks, months, or even years. I remember talking to a plastic surgeon in the spring of 2020 who—after driving his brand-new Porsche to his office—had to furlough his entire staff because he didn't have enough cash in the bank to make payroll. The doctors *maybe* had enough money in their personal bank accounts to stay afloat for a few months. Their team members almost certainly did not.

That's the thing about cash management: when times are great, small-business leaders like us look so much smarter than we actually are. But when financially difficult times happen—and they *always* happen—small-business leaders who haven't put their cash management on autopilot will face some pretty brutal situations.

Jeremy: I want to be crystal clear here. When Robbie talks about plastic surgeons who got caught flat-footed and had to lay off their entire team because of their lack of cash, he isn't talking about borderline, poorly run businesses or surgeons who got their medical degree out of a cereal box. We're talking about successful, busy plastic surgeons making up to seven-figure incomes—personal income, not just seven-figure gross revenue.

Because everything was shut down so hard and fast in the early days of the pandemic, I had more free time than normal. So I took the opportunity to catch up with many other private practice owners and surgeons in my field. Over and over, I heard super-successful physicians freaking out about the financial impact of the pandemic. As a business owner, I certainly understand the concern, but the all-out panic I heard in their voices? That was unexpected.

The more we talked, the more it became clear that these business owners had no plan at all for the millions of dollars that flowed through their offices every year. Many, in fact, treated their business bank account like a loosely managed, unbudgeted personal checking account. If there was enough money to pay the bills, they didn't worry. When there wasn't, they did. There wasn't much thoughtfulness or intentionality between the two extremes.

In chapter 1, we introduced you to the "four wheels" that drive your business: Money, Sales and Marketing, Operations, and Leadership. In this section, we are going to dig into that first wheel, all things money. Over the following five chapters, Robbie and I will give you a blueprint for *knowing* your cash, *keeping* your cash, and *protecting* your cash. If you're like many (or most) of my physician friends and colleagues, a lot of this information will be brand-new to you. You may even be tempted to delegate all of this to your business director or bookkeeper. Please, *please* do not do that. Not yet, anyway. Sure, as the business owner, you aren't the one who should be keeping the books for your business, but you cannot turn a blind eye to your practice's finances and hope to run a business that's successful over the long haul. You need to understand how this stuff works and why managing your money wisely is such a huge deal for you, your team members, and even your patients.

But don't worry. You don't have to earn an MBA or an accounting degree in order to understand and apply what we're going to talk about. In fact, you'll find that cash management isn't that complex at all. It's one of those areas that people tend to needlessly overcomplicate.

At the end of the day, if you take care of your cash flow, your cash flow will take care of you. So let's put our nerd hats on for a little bit and explore how to take care of your money.

THREE TYPES OF CASH

Robbie: When you look at your bank account balance, you see one figure: the total. That can make it seem like all the money sitting in the

account is . . . well . . . the same. But it's not. There are actually three types of cash sitting inside your account at all times:
- cash you plan to spend soon,
- cash you plan to spend later, and
- cash you never plan to spend at all.

You probably know this on an intuitive level, but it's time to elevate these three types of cash in your mind. We'll start by giving each type a proper name, acknowledging the differences between them, and creating a plan for how each type of cash should be uniquely treated.

First is what we call *operating cash*. This is the money you plan to spend soon, what you need to spend on a regular basis to keep your business running. This is the money that's used to pay things such as your office rent, payroll, credit card bills, subscription services, utilities, laundry service, and so on. All these things make up the day-to-day operational expenses of your business—hence the term *operating cash*. We know we're going to spend this money, we're going to spend it soon, and we're probably going to spend it on the same things next month. If this money isn't right there at the top of the account, the lights may get shut off or employees may be sent home. That's a reputation and a revenue killer, both to your team members and to your patients, so you always prioritize this cash in the account.

Second is what is traditionally called *sinking funds* in the business world. You probably just call it *savings* in your personal account. This is the money that's building up inside the account that you know you're going to spend later. For example, you may be saving up for a new piece of equipment, your quarterly tax estimate, or your team's annual holiday party. Sinking funds ensure that you don't get caught off guard by irregular expenses, or expenses that don't happen on a set schedule.

Even if these expenses don't come monthly, they are still not unexpected. You know they're coming. Taxes are *always* coming. Christmas is on December 25 *every year*. Equipment wears out. There's simply no excuse for letting these completely *predictable* expenses hit you by surprise.

Third is the cash you plan to never spend, but it is still a necessity. This is your *emergency fund*. Some businesses call it your "float," and the proper business term is "retained earnings," but I like *emergency fund*. Using that name is a constant reminder that this money is not for new furniture in the waiting room, and it's not for a surprise employee luncheon on the receptionist's birthday. It is for *emergencies*. Period.

A good goal for your emergency fund is a solid three months of operating cash. That keeps your savings in line with the size of your business and provides a necessary safety net if revenue dries up for a few weeks or if a bad storm floods your office. You need to have this money set aside for emergencies, and then you need to forget about it until you need it—and I mean really need it—for a surprise financial hit.

You must also avoid the temptation to do anything fancy with this money. It's not an investment, so forget about tying up your emergency fund in a complicated, tax-sheltered investment. Think of it more like insurance. Insurance doesn't make you money; it costs you money. So park it in a simple money market account, pay the taxes on it, and leave it alone. You'll need it when the truly unpredictable financial emergencies happen.

Paying Taxes on Your Savings

Jeremy: Setting aside that much money as an emergency fund causes us, as business owners, to face some harsh realities. Our tax code in the United States is designed to guide you into particular behaviors and steer you away from others. Saving money falls in the latter category. Apparently, the government does not want your business to save money. It wants that money to be moving around throughout the economy, so it actively disincentivizes your retained earnings.

Because most small businesses are considered "pass-through entities," the owner is required to pay taxes on any money left in the business. You don't have to pay taxes on that money *every* year, but all those dollars do have to be taxed once. As a result, if you want to keep $400,000 in your emergency fund, you have to save much more than that to cover the taxes you'll have to pay on that $400,000 balance. Say your marginal tax rate is 40 percent. If you want to *keep* $400,000 in an emergency fund within your bank account, you've got to *save* $560,000 ($400,000 for the emergency fund plus $160,000 for the taxes). That sucks.

This means, depending on your revenue, that saving up a full emergency fund may take a few years. If that's your plan, you might consider opening a revolving line of credit when times are good that you can tap into if or when disaster strikes, and you need quick cash before your emergency fund is fully funded. However, and I can't stress this enough, do not allow this line of credit to become your long-term plan. This is a stopgap measure to take *while* you fully fund your emergency fund. You have to discipline yourself to see your line of credit for what it is: a backup for your backup plan.

THREE CRITICAL CASH REPORTS

Robbie: We've used the term *autopilot* a lot throughout this book. That's a phrase that's becoming more a part of our everyday language as self-driving cars are finally on the horizon. In fact, Tesla even named its enhanced driving mode *Autopilot*, which is widely considered to be a precursor to full self-driving capabilities. Since Teslas have become a modern symbol of success, I suppose there's a good chance you've got an Autopilot-equipped Tesla charging in your garage right now. As a lifelong car guy, I've kept a close watch on this emerging technology and find the whole concept fascinating.

But here's the thing about Tesla's Autopilot and self-driving modes: they aren't much help if the car doesn't know where you're going. You have to start your journey by programming the GPS—that is, telling your car where you're going—before you can take your hands off the wheel on the highway. We can't just hop in the car, fall asleep, and end up where we want to go (at least, not yet). There's still some programming we're responsible for.

Putting your money on autopilot works in much the same way. When it comes to your business finances, there are three critical cash reports that will enable you to program your financial GPS and keep your eyes on the road, even if you aren't micromanaging the steering wheel. Those reports are:

- **Monthly Zero-Based Budget:** for plotting the course.
- **Weekly Budget Review:** for watching out for milestones on the journey.
- **Daily Cash-On-Hand Report:** for keeping an eye on road signs, traffic lights, and other cars as you go.

Your cash management can get as complicated as you want, but just these three reports will get you 99 percent of the way there. No need to overcomplicate things.

Speaking of needlessly overcomplicating things, I've got some good news. Nothing we're going to talk about in the following chapters will require getting your accountant involved. Your CPA, of course, is an important part of your overall business team, but they aren't needed for keeping your money running on autopilot.

And here's some even better news: you don't have to be a math nerd who loves poring over spreadsheets, financial projects, KPIs, and OKRs to understand this stuff. Heck, you don't even have to be a nerd to *enjoy* this stuff. What we're going to cover will help you maximize your cash management, which helps you eliminate financial waste, avoid financial crises, and increase your net profits. Why *wouldn't* you enjoy that? That said, the goal here isn't to stick a pocket protector in your shirt pocket and wrap tape around your glasses. The goal is to help you know that your money is in great shape so you can keep your focus and energy on running your business and caring for your patients.

What about the P&L Statement?

After seeing the preceding list, you may be surprised that I haven't mentioned the profit and loss (P&L) statement. This is a report your accountant will typically send at the end of the month that breaks down the gross revenue you brought in, what you spent in expenses, and the net profit you had left over. Many business owners see the P&L as the pulse of the business, but it drives me nuts when accountants and business leaders put way too much emphasis on P&L statements. Why? Because P&L statements are history reports. In our car analogy, the P&L report is the rearview mirror: they only show where we've been and what has already happened. They show only what we have lost the opportunity to affect. In no world does a P&L statement put your cash management on autopilot.

Don't get me wrong: there *is* real value in P&L statements, but we business leaders have got to stop acting like this is the most important, end-all-be-all report that we need to look at. In my experience, business leaders who primarily look at the P&L statement—to the exclusion of the other cash reports we're focused on here—often feel confused and caught off guard by what's actually happening with the money in their business on a daily or weekly basis. And that makes perfect sense because they aren't looking ahead; they're looking behind. Using only the P&L to track your business is like trying to drive by only looking out the rearview mirror instead of the windshield. Sure, you'll see what's behind you, but that won't stop you from driving headfirst into a light post.

In contrast, the monthly zero-based budget, weekly budget review, and daily cash-on-hand report are all forward-looking. They ensure you're keeping your eyes on the road in front of you, prioritizing *where you're going* over *where you've been*. And they help answer key questions such as:

- Where do we want and need to go with our cash?
- How much cash do we need to get there?
- As of today, how are we doing?

When you set up a system that enables you to quickly and easily answer these questions, you'll be able to activate the autopilot mode on your business, sit back, and enjoy the ride.

COVER YOUR WAGONS

Jeremy: Every Gen Xer and most millennials remember the game *The Oregon Trail*. It was *the* educational video game for an entire generation and then some. In the game, as you and your family made the hazardous journey along the Oregon Trail, you had to make decisions every step of the way. At some point, you'd come to a river and decide what you wanted to do. You'd have options such as riding across if the water was low, sealing your wagon and fording the river if it was a bit higher, or hiring a ferry to take you and your supplies across the river if you had enough money.

Whichever method you chose, you'd get a report once you were "safely" across. (I put *safely* in quotation marks because people were always dying in horrific ways throughout the game.) That report detailed which of your supplies made it across the river with you and which ones floated away, never to be seen again. That report is essentially your P&L.

When I began running our business, everyone told me that our practice would live and die by the P&L so I took it very seriously. However, it quickly became evident that the P&L wasn't helpful at all in our day-to-day operations or cash management. It took me a few years before I really understood *why*.

In *The Oregon Trail* terms, the P&L doesn't help you decide how to cross the river. It doesn't tell you how much money you have with you when you arrive at the riverbank or how much of that money you'll need later when you reach the next town and have to buy food and fresh supplies. It doesn't tell you which members of your travel team can't afford to go with you or cross the river in the way that you want. For all those things, you need to know exactly what you have with you the day you arrive at the river and what you'll need to survive the next day, and then the next day, and so on.

That's where the monthly zero-based budget, weekly budget review, and daily cash-on-hand report come in. These reports show you exactly where you're going, what you have, and what you need to get through another day/week/month in business. Without that information, your business could get washed away (or die of dysentery) on the Oregon Trail.

It's an amazing feeling when you, as the business owner, wake up each morning knowing for certain that the lifeblood of your entire organization—your cash—is in a healthy place for you, your team, and the people you created that business to serve. So let's find out how to get to that wonderful place of peace and safety. We'll start in the next chapter by getting our arms around the monthly zero-based budget.

CHAPTER 6

THE ZERO-BASED BUDGET: A MAP FOR YOUR MONEY

Jeremy: I used to hate budgeting.

Well, it's not so much that I *hated* it; it's that I thought budgeting was fairly useless. I always saw budgeting as nothing more than a *guess* of where you were going to spend your money—and I saw "guesses" around something as complex as business finances as a waste of time. In my (admittedly limited) experience, I thought budgets set you up for failure more often than not by either giving you a false sense of security or a false sense of insecurity. Either way, it was never exactly right, so, I figured, what's the point? As a result, I refused to waste my time on making budgets, either for my business or in my personal life.

That's not to say I was fiscally irresponsible—either at home or at work. We weren't winging it. We had a reasonable idea of how much was in the bank, how much we were spending, and how much we needed to spend month to month. But it wasn't super-detailed, and it was never written down. And it changed all the time depending on the ebbs and flows that happen in every business every month. It was those ebbs and flows—the almost daily fluctuations in income and expenses, the discrepancies between financial expectation and reality that we all face as business owners—that made me think budgeting was a waste of time. What's the point in setting up a "perfect" budget at the start of every month when you know a surprise will pop up in the first week that throws the whole thing out of whack? No thanks.

So when Robbie came in and pushed hard for us to start a monthly budget, I admit I was not on board. I didn't fight him *per se*; I just figured he was another business guy coming in and trying to dress our practice up in all the trappings of a traditional company—which, of course, included a useless spreadsheet labeled "The Budget."

I was wrong.

Robbie introduced me to a form of budgeting called the *zero-based budget*. And to my reluctant surprise, this budget was different than what I expected. It was better. It was useful and dare I say ... useable.

As Robbie will explain in detail, the zero-based budget is a hybrid between budgeting in the traditional sense (which requires all spending decisions to be made and set in stone before you even have the money in hand) and the way I had been running my practice (where decisions were made "in the moment" based on need). My biggest hang-up with traditional budgeting was that it seemed so inflexible. One little surprise (which you can always count on) would wreck the whole thing. Zero-based budgeting solves that. With this style of budgeting, we can have a solid, thoughtful, intentional plan in place for our money each month *and* we can change it whenever a new need or opportunity arises. It's the best of both worlds, and it works.

If Robbie and I agree on the zero-based budget for August on August 1, and then I decide we need to spend $11,000 on August 4, I don't have to wait a whole month or the next quarter to do so. And I also don't have to put our long- and short-term financial goals in jeopardy by blindly spending a chunk of money that was supposed to fund another initiative. I just have to go to the budget, see which categories (which we'll explain) contain the money we need, and move the money from where it was to the new thing I now want to do. If there isn't enough money to do that, or if it's clear that the original purpose for the money is more important than the new opportunity I want to act on, I have to decide if the thing I want to do is worth dipping into our emergency savings. That's it. Nobody's telling me no, and I'm not risking throwing our whole financial month off course. As the business owner, I can still choose where to spend to the money; the only difference is that I'm being much more thoughtful about when, where, and how to spend it, and I'm spending it with the complete financial picture of our business in mind. It has been a massive shift for us as a practice and for me as an individual, and it has revolutionized how I approach basic financial management personally and professionally.

If you think of budgeting the way I always did—as though it's a waste of time—then I've got good news. There is a budget that can and will work for you, and it's something that will immediately create new freedom and margin in your practice's finances. It's the zero-based budget, and it's so easy to implement that you'll want to kick yourself for not doing it before.

TELL YOUR MONEY WHERE TO GO

Robbie: Personal finance expert Dave Ramsey, whom I'm honored to call a friend and mentor, defines a budget as simply "telling your money where to go instead of wondering where it went." How many medical practices do you think get to the end of each month doing just that—wondering where all their money went?

The revenue that flows through our offices is significant—both for the dollar amounts and, more importantly, for what that revenue represents. We at Amelia Aesthetics have patients coming through our doors every day who have spent *years* saving up for their procedure. Every dollar we make represents not only their hard work and diligence in saving, but also their hopes and dreams for improving their lives through the services we provide. It is an honor to serve them and managing the money they pay us is a huge responsibility that we take very seriously. Plus, that's the money we use to expand our business, offer more services to more patients, and, last but certainly not least, pay our team members for their excellent level of care. We can't bless and serve our own employees if we're letting all that revenue slip through our fingers.

So what's the solution? A budget. But not just *any* budget. As Jeremy said, I'm not talking about your run-of-the-mill, make-it-then-ignore-it kind of budget that we all hate. I'm talking about a very specific type of budget that gives focus and direction to your revenue while still giving you total freedom to make big shifts and minor course corrections throughout the month. I'm talking about the zero-based budget. Jeremy already alluded to the benefits; now, let me tell you how it works.

But First...

You can implement a zero-based budget however you like, using any budgeting and EHR software you want, but...

As I said in the introduction, reviewing all the different feature-incomplete EHR packages and listening to all the half-hearted "promises" from software vendors was an excruciating chore for us that ultimately led nowhere. In the end, we knew we simply had to build our own system, so we did. And you're welcome to use it. You can learn more about it at www.AutopilotOnline.com.

Business Budgeting Basics

Zero-based budgeting forces us as business leaders to be intentional and strategic with the most important nonhuman resource we have:

cash. Additionally, it helps us ensure that every single dollar gets used to its maximum potential.

A large percentage of business owners, like Jeremy once did, have strong negative feelings about budgeting. I get it. Private practice physician owners have way too much going on to waste *any* time, so if the concept of budgeting feels like an exercise in futility, it would make sense to skip it. In fact, even though you're reading this book (and apparently haven't skipped past this section), you might still be debating whether this whole budget thing is worth it. If so, please hear me out and put this stuff into practice for five or six months. Things will probably be bumpy for the first few months, so don't bail out too early. By the fourth month, things should be going pretty well as you and your team get into a groove. If you don't feel noticeably more confident and peaceful about your practice's financial management after six months, you can reevaluate. For now, I'm just asking you to trust us.

Step 1: Create Your Budget Categories

Here's how it works: Each month, we're going to predict to the best of our ability how much cash is going to hit our account over the next month. Then we're going to decide, or pre-allocate, how we will spend (or save) every single dollar as it's deposited into the bank.

For example, we know we're going to spend some cash on payroll, office supplies, medical supplies and equipment, cleaning, laundry service, subscriptions, utilities, and rent. So we're going to go ahead and earmark money for those expenses. The good news is that many of these things, such as rent, have fixed costs every month, which makes budgeting easier. Budgeting like this will also force you to think ahead because saving for things such as an emergency fund, equipment purchases, or income taxes doesn't typically come naturally for business leaders.

In fact, when you use a zero-based budget, you're even going to have a line item for things such as your credit card payments and your personal profit distributions. That way, you don't accidentally take home a profit distribution that should have been left in the business for paying your credit card balance.

Let's play out an example month to see how zero-based budgeting works in action. It starts with the business director, who owns the responsibility for *drafting* the budget before bringing it to the business owner to review, change, and sign off. The budget needs to be finalized before the month begins so the process should ideally start no later than the last week of the month for the following month's budget.

Say it's the last week of June, so it's time to prepare July's zero-based budget. The first thing you're going to need is budgeting and cash management software that is capable of zero-based budgeting. Unfortunately, platforms such as QuickBooks or Xero don't work well for this; that's one reason we created our own Autopilot software, which makes this task super-simple. Whether you use the Autopilot software, another software package, or even just a legal pad (not recommended!), you'll list all the different categories that represent where your July money will go. Resist any temptation to overcomplicate this step. I recommend starting with no more than twenty high-level categories for your zero-based budget. To help you get started, here are the categories we currently use at the Raleigh location of Amelia Aesthetics for our zero-based budgeting:

- Emergency Fund Savings
- Equipment Savings
- Professional Services
- Cost of Goods Sold
- OR Supplies

- Office
- Marketing
- Rent and Facilities
- Team Compensation and Benefits
- Sales Tax
- Debt Service
- Business Insurance
- Owner's Distribution

Step 2: Allocate the Cash That's Already in Your Bank Account

Once that is all set up, you'll need to account for any money that's already sitting in your account. All those dollars need a job to do too. For example, if you're just starting out and you have $100,000 in your bank account, you'll need to assign each dollar to a category. In this example, you might put $50,000 into savings, $25,000 into payroll, and $25,000 into equipment savings. That's what I mean when I say every dollar needs a *job*. You're going to use that money for *something*; all we're doing here is allocating the money to the category we know we need it in.

Hopefully, whatever software solution and bank you're using are smart enough to connect to each other so you can automatically import your balance and transactions into your business software. If you're using the Autopilot software, this is easy (as long as your bank offers this feature), but I can't speak for other offerings. You should definitely make this part of your requirements if you're shopping around for other options. Having to manually import or record all your transactions will get really old, really fast. It's easy to avoid this trouble, but it gets more complicated the longer you use one budgeting system. I recommend starting the right way to avoid the irritation later. Once your banking info is imported, you'll want to connect your credit cards and any active lines of credit as well. You need every transaction from every account flowing through your budget if this is going to work effectively for you.

Step 3: Plan Where to Allocate Your Expected Income

Once you have your budget categories set up and you've allocated all the existing money in your bank account to the appropriate categories, it's time to allocate all the money you *expect* to deposit into your account the upcoming month. That's all a budget is—a plan for where and how you're going to spend your money.

For the sake of easy math, let's say you anticipate $100,000 hitting your bank account during the upcoming month. Even if your revenue is ten times that per month, hang in here with me; the principles still work. All you need to do is work your way down the list of budget categories that you created in Step 1 and *pre-spend* the $100,000 you are anticipating. By pre-spend, I mean you need to plan where that entire $100,000 will go once you receive it. We'll continue our example using the list of categories I previously shared:

Once you've spent that $100,000 of anticipated income all the way down the list, you're done! If you get to the bottom of the list and still have some cash unaccounted for, be sure to go back and add that money to *some* category, such as extra savings or even the owner's distribution. Every dollar *must* be assigned to a category. Otherwise that money will disappear, and you'll miss the opportunity to put it to work for you and your business.

There you have it: your first zero-based budget!

Budget Categories	Budget Amounts
Emergency Fund Savings	$ 3,000
Equipment Savings	$ 4,000
Professional Services	$ 2,500
Cost of Goods Sold	$ 3,000
OR Supplies	$ 20,000
Office	$ 5,000
Marketing	$ 5,000
Rent and Facilities	$ 6,500
Team Compensation and Benefits	$ 20,000
Sales Tax	$ 1,000
Debt Service	$ 1,500
Business Insurance	$ 3,500
Owner's Distribution	$ 25,000
TOTAL	**$ 100,000**

BUDGETING THROUGHOUT THE MONTH

Now that you have your budget prepared by your business director and approved by the business owner, you're ready for the month to start. At this point, as the income comes into the bank account, the business director (or their designee) will "fill up" the budget categories according to the zero-based budget plan. Each bank deposit gets you closer to hitting your budget. Simultaneously, your business director has the responsibility of categorizing every expense that hits your bank account throughout the month, being sure each transaction is assigned to its appropriate category per the budget. When your rent payment clears the bank, for example, your business director will tie that transaction to the Rent and Facilities category. That ensures that you're only spending the money you've intentionally earmarked for Rent and Facilities on your rent payment (instead of worrying that the rent payment is "stealing" money intended for an upcoming purchase).

If you bring in less revenue than expected as the month goes on, you'll need to review the budget and see which areas to trim down. Maybe instead of putting $3,000 in the Emergency Fund, for example, you'd put $1,500 to offset a $1,500 shortfall. These are simple, on-the-fly budget tweaks that you should expect. Start by reducing the amounts you planned to put in the less important or urgent budget categories. Unless your business is running on a razor's edge, you should have plenty of room to adjust to the normal ebbs and flows of your revenue.

The goal is to stop viewing the money in the bank as one giant pile of cash. Instead, you're going to see it organized into a series of smaller stacks of cash, each one dedicated to a specific "job." Different budgeting methods and software packages might call these stacks of cash *envelopes* or *buckets*, but we'll stick with *categories*. Ideally, you're using a software solution like our Autopilot software that makes it easy to review the transactions and assign them to categories every day or two. Using Autopilot, I can run through our daily transactions (which are automatically imported from our bank), assign each one to its budget category, and keep an up-to-the-minute view of our cash flow in just a few minutes a day.

Closing Out the Month

At the end of the month, the business director will have a little housekeeping to do to close out the month from a budget perspective. Once all the transactions for the month have cleared and have been assigned to their appropriate categories, the business director will step back and see how the month went. Did you hit budget? Were your plans way off or were they right on target? Did you budget the right amount for each need or do you need to tweak the monthly allotment for one or two categories on next month's budget? What did you learn? What surprised you? Your zero-based budget serves as your battle plan throughout the month, but then it becomes your after-action report when the month is over. You should review it and look for any insights that will help you better plan and manage your money in the future.

The business director will also check to see if you overspent in any category. If so, you'll need to move money from another category to cover the overage. Do not carry any negative or "in-the-red" categories over into the next month. You need to zero them out by moving money from another category, such as savings. I know I keep harping on giving the Autopilot software a shot, but that's because we specifically built it to make running a private practice easier for us and our teams. The software makes budgeting easy. If you're using a different financial software package that doesn't make it clear that you've overspent in one area, you should seriously consider finding a new tool.

Similarly, you and the business director will need to make some decisions about any money that's unexpectedly left in a budget category. Say you planned to spend $5,000 on marketing but you only spent $4,000. That means you've still got $1,000 sitting in the Marketing category so you have two choices. You can either leave that cash in the Marketing category to spend on future marketing or you can move it to a different category. You can put more in savings, speed up an equipment purchase you're saving for, give the team an unexpected bonus, or take the extra profit home with you. Do whatever you want—just do it on purpose and do it in the budget first.

Jeremy: If you run a medical practice, it is likely that you have a team of people helping you. It is also likely that your team is a diverse collection of skill players. Nurses do nursing duties. Front desk/front-of-house team members have their own tasks. Back-office team members do what they do. Imagine now if you had to rehire an entire team. Would you simply hire a random group of humans and *hope* they cover all your needs, or would you hire specific people for specific jobs to ensure all the work gets done?

Zero-based budgeting does that for your money. Instead of pulling money out of a disorganized pile, zero-based budgeting distributes your money into specifically assigned stacks, mirroring the workflow already in place in your business.

A FEW EXTRA ZERO-BASED BUDGETING TIPS

Robbie: Before we wrap up this intro lesson to zero-based budgeting, let's hit a few specific budgeting tips we've found to be especially helpful in our practice.

Tip #1: Get it Done on Time

Set an expectation with your business director that you need to review the upcoming month's budget no later than the twenty-fifth of each month. That way, as the business owner, you'll have time to make adjustments and/or ask questions. You want the budget "locked" by the first of the month so leave yourself enough time to weigh in and come to an agreement with your business director before then.

Tip #2: Cut Yourself Some Slack

Don't beat yourself (or your business director) up when your budget doesn't seem to "work" the first few months. This is a new skill, and it will take some time to master. Much of budgeting is forecasting how much money you'll be bringing in and sending out, and those forecasts may feel more like guesses at first. That's OK. Once you get a few months under your belt, and after you pay more attention to your expectations versus reality (maybe for the first time in your practice), your monthly budgets will get more and more dialed in. Even then, you should not expect perfection on any month's budget. Instead, the goal should be to create a well-informed strategic plan, follow it as closely as possible, and be flexible as different surprises pop up throughout the month.

Tip #3: Watch Out for Credit Cards

Be extra careful with any credit cards and expense accounts. Every charge to your card must be accounted for in a budget category! One feature I love in the Autopilot software is that anytime you categorize a credit card transaction, the software will automatically set aside that cash to cover your credit card bill. That way, you don't risk going into debt by accident, which is much more common than you might think.

Tip #4: Leave Yourself a Buffer

It's important that you keep at least some of your emergency fund inside your operating account at all times. You don't have to keep the whole emergency fund in the same account, but we recommend "hiding" part of it in a separate Buffer or Extra Emergency Fund category. This helps keep your bank account flush with cash just in case you accidentally overspend. Think of it as your own built-in overdraft protection. If you make a budget mistake and accidentally overspend dramatically in one area, cover the overage with the Emergency Fund and then prioritize refilling the Emergency Fund category as quickly as possible.

Tip #5: Your Accountant Doesn't Budget This Way

Let's talk about how zero-based budgeting differs from what your accountants do. When your accountants create categories for all your expenses, they are going to use a far more comprehensive list of categories called a *chart of accounts*. I do not recommend trying to make the categories in your zero-based budget line up perfectly with your chart of accounts. Instead, keep the categories in your zero-based budget as simple as possible.

For example, in our zero-based budget example, we had a category called Team Compensation and Benefits. This is where you'd put expenses such as salaried payroll, hourly payroll, all your contractor payments, 401(k) expenses, health insurance expenses, and so on. That's enough for you to get your job done, but your accountants will want to break that up much more granularly. In your chart of accounts, then, your accountants might prefer to have seven or eight different categories for all the different types of team compensation and benefits. It just isn't necessary for you to go into such great detail for your zero-based budget, especially since we aren't going to be reconciling it to any other accounting system. As long as you have enough categories to ensure you and your business director know where all your money is going, that's all you need. Let the accountants get as nerdy as they want to on their end. That is, after all, what you're paying them for.

Tip #6: Don't Let Your Accountant Boss You Around

Fair warning: Many accountants dislike this style of budgeting. Some outright hate it. In fact, some especially bold accountants may insist that you budget the way *they* want you to. Here's my response to that: screw 'em.

Because accountants necessarily get such an intimate view of your business through their detailed work on your financials, some can start to feel an undue sense of ownership and influence over your operations. But your accountant does not run your business. You do. To effectively do that, you need to know exactly where your cash is and how it's being used on any given day. Some accountants are surprisingly not on board with this and would rather keep things on a theoretical level. While that is extremely helpful in some situations, cash management isn't about theory; it's about the practical, day-to-day, nuts and bolts of how, when, and where you're spending your money.

So stand your ground if your accountant ever tries to dissuade you from running your own zero-based budget for your practice. There's absolutely nothing wrong with running two systems of accounting in parallel if it gives you the information you need as a business owner. Besides, your accountant works for you. If they aren't doing the job you need them to do or if they refuse to work with you because of how you've chosen to manage your cash, no worries. There are plenty of excellent accountants out there who would love your business.

Disruption Is Coming for Accounting

Jeremy: I'll always remember the last time I called a taxi company. It was 2013 and I needed a ride home from a car repair shop on a busy intersection in Raleigh. The dispatcher answered the call and, in a slightly annoyed tone, blurted out, "What's the address?"

I replied, "I don't know. It's a giant gas station on the corner of 6th and Lassiter."

The guy on the line huffed and said, "Well, if you can't give us a numbered address, we can't send you a cab. Call back when you have it." *Click!*

He hung up on me.

I downloaded the Uber app on the spot, set up a new account in less than a minute, and was climbing into the back seat of a nice, clean, newish Infinity less than five minutes later. I've taken hundreds of Uber rides since then—and exactly zero cab rides.

The taxi company prioritized making things easy for themselves even though it made things more difficult for me as a customer. Uber built a business around doing the exact opposite. That's why taxi companies are going out of business across the country while Uber and other rideshare services have exploded in popularity. Now, just ten years after my last experience with a taxi company, it would be practically unheard of for someone in their twenties, thirties, or forties to even utter the phrase, "Call a cab." It's as anachronistic today as phone booths and travel agents, a throwback to a bygone era. And it happened faster than anyone thought possible.

The industries most ripe for disruption tend to favor what *they* want over what the *client* wants, and that distance between the two things continues to grow. Every time someone says, "That's not how we've always done it," the space grows bigger. Eventually the gap between what the industry wants and what the customer wants is big enough to fit a new idea. That's when disruption happens.

I believe the field of accounting is on the verge of disruption. Don't get me wrong: a good accountant is tremendously valuable and an essential member of your business team. The problem is that it's nearly impossible to find one who is both good at accounting *and* good at understanding and empathizing with the challenges of a small business. As a result, there's a good chance that a typical, old-school accountant will not be good at prioritizing your financial well-being ahead of the more mechanical, technical details of their work. At least in my experience, accounting as an industry never cared about how *I felt* about my financial position, so they didn't plan for it. It's not how they've always done it.

Zero-based budgeting is a tool that fits in the space between what the accounting company wants and what the small business operator needs. An accountant will tend to put it in their frame of reference, which, unless you prefer to run your business with a time machine, is unlikely to be very helpful in the now. They have a very important role to play in your practice, but that role is *not* the same as that of a business owner, business director, Chief Operating Officer, or even Chief Financial Officer. Find a good accountant, tell them how *you* want to work, and make them tailor their services to fit your needs. If they can't or won't do that, then move on. Your business is too important to let a disinterested third party dictate how you should run it.

FROM RESISTANCE TO PEACE

What Robbie unpacked in this chapter represents one of his biggest wins as a business director. That's not because he *invented* zero-based budgeting but because he had to overcome one big obstacle standing in the way: me. As I said at the start of this chapter, I was never a big fan of budgeting. In fact, I was never a big fan of planning in general for one reason: In my experience, nothing *ever* goes according to plan. So why bother?

When Robbie first suggested implementing the zero-based budget in our business, I scoffed. I "knew" it would fail. But Robbie's nothing if not hardheaded. He would not stop pushing for it, and since I was supposed to be trusting him to run the business, I relented. Besides, the budget would be *his* thing. I wouldn't have to "waste my time" on it so I let him run with it.

What happened over the next few months blew my mind. My dismissive resistance to the concept of budgeting gave way to something else—what the brilliant Dave Ramsey calls *financial peace*. As a successful plastic surgeon, I should have felt this peace years earlier. Our business certainly made enough money all those years to produce a sense of peace in our finances, but I never felt it. More significantly, my wife never felt it either. She's a much more concrete thinker than I am. I'm comfortable with some ambiguity, but she likes facts. The uncertainty around the business's finances bothered her a lot more than I knew at the time. I constantly reassured her that the business was doing great, but she asked for proof—proof I didn't have and couldn't provide. Those were *not* fun conversations.

To be crystal clear, my wife was right and I was wrong. I'm not just saying that to make sure she knows how much I appreciate her; I'm saying that because I was being careless both as a spouse and as a business owner. I discounted the role that intentional financial management played in my practice and in my family life. Robbie showed me a better way to approach both—with a simple zero-based budget. Now when my wife asks what's going on with the practice's finances, I can show her exactly what's coming in, what's going out, and what we have saved for emergencies and purchases. It's made my life so much simpler on many levels—and isn't that the whole reason we implemented *The Private Practice MBA* system to begin with?

I'll never love the act of budgeting, but now I cannot live without the benefits that budgeting gives me. It adds clarity and simplicity to the complex life of a business owner. It allows me to answer, at any time, three critical questions:

- How much money do we *have* as a business?

- How much money do we *need* as a business?
- How much money do we expect to be available for me to live my life outside of the business?

The best part by far, though, is that the act of zero-based budgeting did what I thought was impossible: it turned my frustration, uncertainty, and resistance into peace. And I had no idea how much I (and my wife) needed that.

CHAPTER 7
STAYING CONNECTED TO YOUR CASH

Jeremy: In the previous chapter, Robbie and I both talked about how you can—and *should*—expect to change the budget here and there as the month goes on. When I'm talking with business leaders about this aspect of budgeting, I often see their confidence in the entire process eroding right before my eyes. This is especially true if the person, like me, is coming from a long-held negative view of budgeting as a waste of time or as something that never goes according to plan. Doesn't changing the budget *after* it was supposedly "locked" by the business owner and business director's mutual agreement seem like ... cheating? Isn't this proof that our suspicions were correct—that budgeting doesn't really work? After all, if you can simply change your budgeted amounts on any given day, if you go into the month knowing full well that what you've agreed to can and probably will change at any time, what's the point of a budget?

If that's the kind of skepticism you have about budgeting, I hear you. It's a common reaction, something I and many, many other business owners have when someone like Robbie comes in and starts talking about doing a budget. You aren't alone in your skepticism. But you're not *correct* in it either.

Being able to change where the money goes—and actively *planning* to change the budget at least once a week with a scheduled meeting or email (which we'll discuss in this chapter)—is not proof that the budget doesn't work. Just the opposite, in fact. Keeping the budget active and nimble is exactly what makes this approach useful. You almost certainly won't see this at first. In fact, things may not start making sense to you until around the third month. You probably won't be good at doing this until month six or seven. But then, about one year into the process, I suspect you will get where I am now: not merely a participant in the budget process, but a strong advocate for it. As I've said, there's no way I could ever go back to the uncertainty that used to feel so comfortable to me. Once the blinders come off about where and how you're spending your practice's precious cash flow, you'll never want to put them back on.

So in this chapter, let's embrace the notion that your budget will be both *fixed* and *fluid*. It's the financial plan you'll live by, but you'll also leave plenty of room to shift gears and move your money around between categories as needed throughout the month. You can't do this haphazardly, though. To keep moving forward toward the financial goals you've set for your business, you'll need to go into these regular revisions with a clear head and with full visibility into what impact each tweak will have on your overall plan. That's what the weekly budget review and daily cash-on-hand report are for.

THE WEEKLY BUDGET REVIEW

Robbie: Let's be clear right off the bat: Yes, you can tweak your budget throughout the month. And yes, you should expect there to be some changes at least weekly. But—and this is a *huge* but—that absolutely does not give you permission to flat-out ignore your budget. There is no reason to go to all the trouble of making a plan with your zero-based budget if you aren't going to do your very best to stick to it. Just because it *can* change doesn't mean it *should* change every time you get a new idea. The budget is still the financial roadmap for your organization and changing it too much will prevent you from getting where you ultimately want to go.

To make sure the organization is operating with an eye on the budget, we recommend committing to a weekly budget review. This doesn't have to take long, and it doesn't even have to be an in-person meeting. Rather, our weekly budget reviews at Amelia Aesthetics are simple emails that I send Jeremy every Friday afternoon. Likewise, the business directors of our other Amelia Aesthetics locations have the option of emailing me their weekly budget reviews every Friday so Jeremy and I can keep an eye on how those practices are doing.

The key to a good weekly budget review is keeping your bank transaction categorized correctly in your Autopilot software or whatever other software solution you may be using. We discussed that in detail in the previous chapter. Someone—probably the business director—will simply import the transactions from your bank into your software and assign each one to the appropriate budget category. For example, you might have a transaction from Amazon that needs to be categorized as an Office expense, or maybe you have a transaction from a piece of equipment you have financed that needs to be categorized as a Debt Service expense. The business director can review and categorize the transactions as often as they like during the week (I do it every two days), as long as they do it *at least once* by the end of the week.

Why have everything categorized by Friday? It's because the business director will prepare a weekly budget review email for the business owner, which will give a financial overview of the week that's ending. There isn't a concrete format for this email, but you'll want to be sure it includes:

- Important observations and things to be aware of;
- Suggested mid-month budget adjustments; and
- Screenshot of the current, categorized budget from the Autopilot software.

Along with these details, the business director should include a brief overview of what's going on with the business's cash and how well you're operating on budget.

Give your business director a Friday afternoon deadline for this report, and every Friday evening before you head home, carve out five minutes of your time to review it. For a business owner, it feels great going into the weekend knowing exactly where all our cash is. Plus, if there's a problem on the horizon as you're going into the weekend, your subconscious has time to chew on it before you have to make a decision about what to do. You'll also want to make sure your business director is available for any questions you may email back to them. It's common to have a few questions about what you see, especially if this is the only time you're looking at the budget each week. Any questions you ask or changes you request will help inform them of what you personally value, and it will help them make better decisions for you when they create future budgets.

DAILY CASH-ON-HAND REPORT

As the business director, I *have* to have a good idea of what's going on with the cash in our business every day. If I can't answer the question, "How's the money today?" early in the morning, the question follows me around all day, creating an undercurrent of anxiety. The opposite is also true. If I know the cash is in good shape each morning, then I'm able to check that mental box and completely focus on whatever that day demands of me. Our business, and especially our patients, deserve Jeremy's and my full attention. If we're distracted, everyone else pays the price. And remember, your cash is the lifeblood of your business. If you run out of cash, everyone has to go home. A six-month waiting list for new patients and a year's worth of scheduled surgeries won't help you if you can't pay your bills and your team *today*. So how do we keep our sense of financial well-being—not to mention our sanity—intact?

Enter the daily cash-on-hand report.

Now, you might say, "But Robbie, I check my bank balances every day. I already know we're going to have enough cash. Do I really need a report for this?" You're not alone. A lot of business leaders make a habit of checking the bank balances each day—but this honestly isn't very helpful at all. We want to have an *active* involvement in the cash, not passive. How you spend money, where you spend money, when you spend money, when transactions clear the bank, what's coming up next, what expenses are due today or tomorrow ... all of that works together to tell a story—the story of your cash flow. And merely checking a bank balance doesn't tell you the story you need to know. It's barely even the CliffsNotes version!

All that changes with the daily cash-on-hand report. This simple email report tells you three things at a glance:
- How much *liquid* (readily available) cash you have today
- What, if any, significant changes have happened since yesterday
- What changes you can anticipate happening over the next several days

Just like the monthly zero-based budget and the weekly budget review, I highly recommend you delegate the responsibility of the daily cash-on-hand report to your business director. Not only will it free you up to focus on more critical tasks, but it will also put an important second set of eyes on your most important nonhuman resource, your money.

Just like with the weekly budget review, there isn't a set form or format your business director has to use for the daily cash-on-hand report. And as with everything cash-related we're discussing, resist the urge to overcomplicate this report. You and your business director have already agreed to the monthly budget so there's no need to rehash all those decisions every morning via the daily cash-on-hand report. The goal with this report is to ease your mind, not to open a new can of worms. So I suggest you keep things to a short, simple morning email with two main parts.

The first half of the email report should include a list of each of your bank accounts and credit cards. For each account, you want to see three pieces of information:

- Today's balance
- Yesterday's balance
- A brief explanation for any significant difference between the two

That's it, two numbers and a sentence or two for each account. Anything more than that and you jeopardize the usefulness of this "glanceable" report.

In the second half of the email, the business director should inform you of any major upcoming expenses or deposits that are expected over the next thirty days. Again, there's no need to go into great detail here because all these things should already be accounted for on the monthly budget. This is just a quick, scannable reminder of those items. This is also an opportunity for your business director to share any new opportunities or expenses that might require a budget tweak or that could come up in next month's budget discussion. This keeps you, as the business owner, from getting surprised by something that hits your business director's radar before it hits yours.

Goof-Proof Your Cash Decisions

Jeremy: The daily cash-on-hand report plays a significant role in my life: it prevents me from making regrettable cash decisions. For example, let's say my wife and I have a conversation on a Sunday night and decide we would like to take a distribution to be able to make a lump-sum payment to pay down our mortgage. In years past, before we implemented *The Private Practice MBA* principles in this book, I might have simply checked the business bank account, seen that there was enough in the account to cover the distribution we wanted, and that would have given me my answer: yes, let's do it.

Being extra-cautious, I might have called my accountant the next morning and asked, "Can I take a distribution?" (Calling my accountant actually *isn't* something that would have occurred to me back then, but it would have been a good idea.) If I had made that call, he would have checked things on his end and seen that we had enough in the account and that, based on previous years, we don't traditionally have big expenses that month. So he would have given me the green light too. With that, my wife and I would have pulled the money out of the business and sent it off to pay down the mortgage. All good, right?

Here's the problem: First, the accountant only knows what the balance is today (which I already know) and what's happened in previous years. That's what accounting is—it's *accounting* for what has happened in the past. It looks at where the money went, not where it's going. As good as my accountant is, he has no idea what's *about to happen* in my business.

Second, what if I didn't know that our bookkeeper had just put a dozen checks in the mail that past Friday to pay our monthly bills, that our American Express payment was scheduled to auto-draft that Tuesday, that our rent check would go out on Wednesday, and that payroll would hit on Thursday? Those are crucial details—details I would have missed. It's entirely possible in this scenario that my distribution withdrawal would have come at the worst possible time. That kind of mistake would create a strain on our business account that would, in past years, have cost me a few nights' sleep.

Contrast that to what might happen today. My wife and I have that Sunday night conversation and one of us mentions taking a distribution to pay down the mortgage. I grab my phone, open my email, and check the most recent daily cash-on-hand report that Robbie sent that Friday. It takes about three seconds to see all the significant expenses set to hit the account over the next week, so my wife and I decide to wait two weeks for the cash in the account to build back up and see how things look at that time.

Given the choice to live in a universe where I make an ill-timed cash decision that hurts my business or one in which I have all the information I need to make the best decision in just a matter of seconds, I'll choose the latter. Frankly, I've already lived in that first universe for far too long, and there's no way I'm ever going back there.

I should also mention that, interestingly, the daily cash-on-hand report has become less urgent as we have grown as a business. It's still important and it isn't going anywhere, but it's not as urgent. That is, it's less likely these days that one ill-timed financial decision will blow a hole in our bank account. That's because we've spent years doing the *other* things we've been talking about—especially building up our emergency fund. Today, if I go off and do something totally reckless, as unlikely as that is, the emergency fund will pick up the slack. It'll prevent the rent payment from bouncing or payroll from coming up short. I don't recommend viewing your emergency fund as your own personal safety net for stupid decisions, but it's there, nonetheless.

More importantly, I think, I've grown in my role as a business owner as our business has grown. Because we've put these simple systems in place, I have a much better intuitive awareness of the rhythm of our cash flow. Spending a minute or two looking over that same report every morning for several years has given me a whole new sense of peace and confidence in not only my ability to make good decisions for my business, but also my business's ability to withstand almost any financial pitfall I might fall into.

FREQUENTLY ASKED QUESTIONS

When I talk to other physicians and practice owners about their cash flow management, I hear a lot of hesitancy and get a few questions. Over time, I've found that many of these business owners ask the same kinds of questions, meaning there's a good chance you are already thinking of the same questions yourself. So let's round out this chapter with a basic FAQ section on how you should be managing your practice's money.

Disclaimer: Remember that I am not an accountant or financial planner. I'm a physician and a business owner so consider all of this advice in that context. This is what I'd tell you doctor to doctor if we were chatting over a cup of coffee.

Q: Should I keep my entire emergency fund in my business checking account?

A: This is a matter of personal choice, but I do have an opinion, and I can tell you how we do it in our practice.

Most accountants, in my experience, advise against storing more money in a business account than is necessary. As such, I prefer to pull the extra out and keep *most* of my business emergency fund in a separate, low-risk, and completely liquid account. If something unexpected happens and the primary business account needs a quick infusion of funds, we can easily transfer the money in seconds online.

This requires personal discipline to never spend that money unless absolutely necessary and only for emergencies, as well as to keep it totally liquid and not in even moderate-risk entities. The emergency fund is there to protect you and your business. That's it's only job, and it can only do that if it's available the minute you need it. This is not an investment (although you'll likely get a small return in a money market account), and it's not a slush fund for purchases. Emergencies only!

Q: Will keeping an emergency fund in my bank account cause me to pay more in taxes?

A: Yep. A bunch.

As we've already discussed, any money sitting in the bank will be taxed. That sucks, but it's the unavoidable price we pay for keeping readily available cash on hand. So if you're at a 40 percent tax rate and want to keep a $200,000 emergency fund, you'll need to *save* about $335,000 in order to *keep* $200,000. The good news is that it's only taxed once, meaning you don't have to keep paying taxes every year on the same $200,000 that's sitting in the bank.

Q: What's the best way to estimate my quarterly taxes?
A: Step 1 is to talk to your accountant. Step 2 is to do what they say. I'm not an accountant!

Q: Should I really let my business director see *all* the numbers in the business?
A: Yes, but...

I think this is a generational thing. My dad's generation tended to be very secretive with money. Gen Z seems to be enthusiastically willing to both encourage and indulge voyeuristic looks into all personal details. Most of us, though, are somewhere in between.

I have made a personal, conscious decision to share numbers with anyone I think can make our business better by knowing those numbers. There are certainly risks in doing so, but I value growing our business over "keeping my secrets." Besides, I'm not at all ashamed of what I personally make as a surgeon, nor am I ashamed of the success of our practice. If someone can genuinely improve my life and our practice, and if the only cost is to let them potentially see my salary, then that's a no-brainer for me.

That said, I always share this information carefully and selectively. I have spent the last fifteen years of my life getting to where I am today as a surgeon and a business owner. You likely know exactly where I'm coming from. I don't expect anyone who hasn't made those same sacrifices or who doesn't know what it takes to run a business to fully understand that.

Giving someone the full financial picture without the context for properly understanding it is a heavy responsibility. I'm not going to put that burden on the twenty-four-year-old, entry-level member who has no context for understanding the big picture of our business or the minute details of my personal income. But if it is someone I have worked with for years and/or someone I trust to handle the burden of knowing such privileged information, and if I believe that entrusting that information to this person will move our business forward, then I will absolutely share it. Your business director should certainly check all those boxes.

Q: What is the best way to prevent theft of my cash?
A: Let's break this down into two categories: external theft and internal theft.

External theft comes from people outside your business. These days, it's most likely to be a cybersecurity issue such as hacking, theft of your patient information, illegal access to your bank accounts, or ransomware (which blocks you from your own data until you pay a "ransom" to the thief). I don't have an answer for this one other than to talk to a cybersecurity expert. There are protections for this, and you need them.

Internal theft comes from people inside your business. This is someone stealing from the cash box, your bookkeeper embezzling money, or a team member breaking into your medicine closet looking for pain meds. Someone I trust once told me, "There are two kinds of small businesses. There are those that discover they've been robbed and have to deal with it, and there are those that have been robbed but never find out about it.

Either way, someone's going to steal from you." Sadly, that's just part of owning a small business.

There's no way to make your business fully immune to internal theft, but there are some safety measures you can and should implement if you haven't already. The big three are:

- Make sure at least two people in your business, preferably two people in different segments of your business, are aware of every transaction. In our business, the person who collects a payment and the person who places that transaction in our ledger are two different people. Additionally, the person putting the transaction in the ledger must compare any transaction against an expected amount by way of a quote created by a third person.
- Let your accountants know you expect them to help with this. For example, a common scam is that an employee will create a nonexistent company that is named something very, very similar to an account you currently pay. For example, say your business occasionally sends a check to a company called "AirSoft." An ill-intentioned employee with access to invoicing can create a fake vendor in your system named "Air Soft NC" and start invoicing you for "services." That "service," of course, is that they're ripping you off. If you aren't vigilant, you'll see "Air Soft NC" among your transactions and not even notice the slightly different spelling of the business's name. Whoever is reconciling charges needs to be aware that you expect a high level of vigilance.
- Read your daily cash-on-hand report every day and get a feel for what expenses happen, when they hit each month, and what each day of the week typically "feels" like. This

will make you nimbler with unexpected results. For example, I've learned that Wednesday and Thursday are our busy cash deposit days. Last year, I noticed we were light on cash deposits for two weeks in a row. No one was stealing (that we know of), but there *was* an error made by our bank that accidentally changed the account where cash was being deposited. It created a nuisance in our accounting, but we caught it quickly because of a hunch. That *hunch* wasn't an accident; it was a skill I developed by learning the rhythm of our money through the daily cash-on-hand report.

BUT JEREMY...

I want to close this chapter with one more FAQ, and this is something you just might be thinking right now:

Q: All this sounds cool... but it also sounds like a lot of work. What if I don't want to do it?

A: You're right. It *is* a lot of work putting all these systems in place and staying on top of your money throughout the month. And it's also all optional. You can do *everything* we're talking about, *some* of what we're talking about, or *none* of what we're talking about. It's 100 percent up to you how far you want to go with this stuff.

But...

Every decision has consequences, and the consequence of not keeping a close eye on your cash flow is... well... ultimately having less cash to keep an eye on. It's all about opportunity cost. Robbie and I don't just want to show you a better way of doing things; we also want to encourage you to consider the opportunity cost of *not* doing the things we're teaching in this book.

If you'd rather not bother with too much of this stuff, that's fine. We won't be mad at you. But at least make that decision knowing it'll cost you something in the long run. If you think the trade-off is worth it, go for it. However, if you'd rather make an investment of time and effort into your business now to create the kind of profitable, low-stress, autopilot business we've built over the past several years, then stick with us. We still have a lot of ground to cover.

CHAPTER 8

THE METRICS THAT DRIVE YOUR INTERNAL AND EXTERNAL ACCOUNTING

Jeremy: I love greatness. Specifically, I love *watching* greatness. It could be in medicine, like watching a master surgeon perform a difficult operation, or sports, like watching a star running back weave through a half-dozen defenders on his way to the end zone. Whatever field it is, if someone is doing it better than anyone else in the world, I am *in*. I could watch any artist, any designer, any builder, any house painter—heck, even any accountant—do their thing if they were a true virtuoso.

For that reason, when I went to a Duke basketball game during Coach Mike Krzyzewski's final year, I was much more interested in watching Coach K than I was in watching the players. I'm sure the players were great, but Coach K is the only basketball coach in recent history who figured out a way to change, evolve, and remain relevant throughout a coaching career that spanned nearly fifty years.

What I got to see that day was remarkable—but not for the reasons I expected. Every time he spoke to a player, assistant coach, or referee, their interactions were surprisingly short. He didn't personally lead the strategy discussions during timeouts. He didn't draw up the plays. During every break, he walked over to speak to a referee. He had an assistant coach on each side, and he constantly leaned over to say a quick word to one or the other. Then that coach would run to talk to a player, no doubt delivering Coach K's message or, more likely, giving that player some word of coaching or encouragement he knew was needed in that moment. Occasionally he'd lean over and speak to a coach for no more than two seconds, and on the next buzzer, that assistant coach would pull a player off the court. Everything Coach K did was intentional, but none of it seemed complex.

Given his unparalleled success, it occurred to me that his in-game coaching probably isn't the thing that makes him special, even though that's what I've always envisioned when I think of a coach. What I expected was very different from what I saw.

My experience running a business has been the same: what I *thought* would make me successful and what actually *has* made me successful as a business owner are very different things. One area in which this is especially true is in our business finances. I once thought that the deeper I dug into the tiny details of the P&L the better I would be at running my business. The reality of running the business, though, has shown me the opposite is true. Again, I can look to Coach K for the reason why.

In 1994, with two national titles to his name, Coach K almost retired due to a back injury. Fortunately, the Duke athletic director convinced him to take a leave of absence instead, which would give him time to heal and more thoughtfully consider his options. When he returned months later, he was a different person—and certainly a different coach. Coach K credits that leave of absence with reinvigorating his career. It led him to get out of the minutiae and forced him to delegate more responsibilities to the capable assistant coaches on his staff. He was able to refocus where and how he spent his time while trusting other professionals to do everything else.[8]

That's something (maybe the *only* thing) I have in common with Coach K: he and I both learned that same lesson in our forties. For me, though, it was more about getting out of the tiny little details of the P&L and trusting other professionals with the financial minutiae of my practice. I realized how much time and effort I was wasting chasing small changes in our P&L instead of focusing on the big changes I could make using my personal strengths and skills. Today I can add the most value to the business by focusing on growing as a surgeon and investing in the three core areas of a business owner that we discussed in chapter 2. That means I have to consciously avoid immersing myself in daily line-by-line reviews of the P&L and balance sheet. I've learned that if I focus on what only I can do, I can push the business to a place where those numbers are always too old to matter anyway. So even though I sometimes *want* to get sucked in, I won't. Forward progress matters too much to me to spend all my time in the financial past, which is where accounting lives.

Of course, that doesn't mean I leave all the accounting to chance, and I'm absolutely not saying that accounting doesn't matter. It is incredibly important to your business! I'm just saying that you, as the business owner and certainly as a physician, aren't the best person to own all those responsibilities. Therefore, let's dig into the nerdy aspects of accounting and figure out how to fully put our finances, from debt to taxes to pricing, on autopilot.

STOP ACTING LIKE AN ACCOUNTANT

Robbie: Small-business leaders waste more time on numbers than on anything else. I've seen this throughout my entire career. You want to see a magic trick? Hand a business owner a spreadsheet of financials and watch an hour disappear. We business leaders can't help ourselves.

I'm not saying numbers and dashboards are unimportant. We just finished an entire section on budgeting, after all. What I *am* saying is that most numbers—especially most accounting—are useless. To be blunt, most accounting doesn't count and is a complete waste of a small-business leader's time. We must resolve to stay out of it as much as possible, and that is only possible if we put systems in place to put the finances on autopilot.

I realize I just gave every accountant and spreadsheet nerd across the planet a seizure but let me illustrate my point. One year my daughter got a telescope for Christmas. While we were assembling it, I realized it came with several different types of lenses. One lens was supposed to be best for viewing expansive star clusters, another for looking at the surface of the moon, and a third for looking at all the intricate craters on the lunar surface. There was one big problem, though: through my eyes, all three lenses appeared to give identical results. Maybe an astronomer would have had a radically different viewing experience through each lens, but to me and my daughter, the different lenses made absolutely no difference. In fact, the variety made our experience worse because we thought we were missing something or that we had assembled it incorrectly. Although they were supposed to enhance our experience, the extra lenses distracted us from simply having a good time looking up at the night sky.

In the same way, your accountant and a stack of business school textbooks will suggest a dozen different metrics, forms, spreadsheets, and reports to give you the clearest possible view of your business. But like those extra telescope lenses, most of them will just be distractions. They're great for the professionals who have been trained to see the intricacies of each, but they're not that helpful to you and me.

Could you follow the rabbit hole of accounting all the way to Wonderland? Yes, of course. But why would you do that? Instead, let's push all the distractions aside, make the decisions we need to make, and get back to growing our business.

What Should Your Accountant Be Doing?

The first thing to know here is that you do, in fact, need an excellent accountant both for your personal finances and for your business. How you partner with that accountant, however, may look a bit different than what you're currently doing. Traditionally, private practice physicians work with their accountants in a very passive way. They wait to hear from the accountant, and then they hope the CPA creates some sort of agenda for the conversation that's more than simply reviewing the P&L statement together. I can't tell you how many meetings I've sat through where an accountant just read a P&L to the room—as if we couldn't do that ourselves. This is unacceptable.

Putting your accountants on autopilot requires having an active relationship with them—one in which *you* are in charge. Specifically, we recommend requiring:

- **A standing monthly meeting. This gives you the opportunity to continually "inspect what you expect." Again,** you aren't personally doing the accounting, but you do need a monthly window into what the accountant has been doing on your behalf. This is also your opportunity to task them with new projects to work on throughout the next month. For example, maybe you need them to research a new tax benefit you've recently heard about. Use this time with your accountants to task them with work so you don't have to do it yourself. Last, as we'll discuss a bit more in a following section, you need to have them tell you how much you need to set aside to pay the previous month's taxes.

- **Thirteen-month rolling P&Ls and balance sheets. Have the accountant prepare and bring these reports to your monthly meeting. Even if you don't review them together (which is not always necessary),** you still need to keep up-to-date copies of these two reports on hand so they'll be easy to grab whenever you need them throughout the month. I promise, there will be some point when you find yourself wondering, *how much do we spend on K-cups in the break room every month*? You aren't going to want to wait a week for your CPA's office to get you that answer. There are also a few specific things on the P&L you'll want your accountant to call out separately. Jeremy will discuss those below.
- **That they close your books by the seventh of every month. Not only will this ensure your accountants never fall behind,** but it will also allow you to pay bonuses and profit sharing as soon as the month ends. It is far less motivating for your team members to receive a bonus for something that happened two or three months ago; closing the books by the seventh should give you time to prepare those bonus checks well before the end of the current month, so your team is always getting paid for the great job they *just* did. (We'll talk more about compensation in the following chapter.)

Putting your accountants on autopilot means actively ensuring they are ready and waiting for you. You need them more than once a quarter so invest in the relationship and make sure they know your specific expectations for them.

Be a Little Annoying

Jeremy: When you interact with an accountant, especially at the beginning of your relationship, they will almost certainly make a few assumptions about you and your business. First, they will put you in your "industry bucket." For example, Amelia Aesthetics is a healthcare practice first and foremost. As a result, every accountant I meet starts by saying, "I've helped many healthcare practices before you." I can't help but roll my eyes at this. Yeah, they've worked with other medical offices, but they've never worked with *my* practice—and we don't fit the industry mold they want to put us in.

Second, they will probably put you in the "passive owner bucket," meaning they'll assume you're just like every other physician owner they've worked with and that you'll expect no more than anyone else. If you are reading this book, though, that's probably not you.

From the start of your relationship with an accounting firm, you must push back against these two assumptions, and that means becoming a pain in their butts whenever necessary to make sure they are doing the job you need them to do. I struggled with this early on. I saw them as the experts so I deferred to them more often than I should have. While that's the right call much of the time, it should not be your default response. No one in the world will care as much about your business as you do. No one. Unless you set the expectation that you are going to ask hard questions and expect quality answers, you are going to be put into whatever generic, lazy box you fit most neatly. *Do not let this happen.*

When I engage an outside firm or individual to work with my practice on an ongoing basis, I make one thing clear up front: Every once in a while, and it doesn't have to be often, I expect an email or phone call from them that says, "Hey, Jeremy, I was thinking about your business today, and I wanted to run something by you." If you never get an email like that from your accountant, there's a good chance that the first time they've seen your P&L is when they sit across the table from you to review together. That is a total waste of a meeting. They aren't going to tell you anything useful because they haven't spent any time thinking about it beforehand. If they can't be bothered to think about my business when I'm not in the room with them, then frankly, they don't deserve my business.

This is not how accountants are used to working with doctors, so you'll have to "train" them. You do that by asking questions—a *lot* of questions. You might even set a reminder to email your accountant an open-ended question twice a month. It will take months of that before the good accountants start thinking about your business on their own. The bad ones never will so this is also a great way to sift out the firms you shouldn't be working with.

GETTING WHAT YOU NEED OUT OF YOUR P&L

Most people outside the medical field would assume that surgery is incredibly difficult, and they're right: surgery *would* be incredibly difficult... for people who aren't surgeons. I remember a time when it seemed more mystical than surgical to me as well. Then I spent ten years learning the ins and outs, working alongside master surgeons, and practicing my craft every single day. Then I spent another ten-plus years *doing* the work, being singularly responsible for the procedures and outcomes and earning the trust of the patients under my care. With all that education and experience behind me, surgery isn't that hard. Without it... good luck.

THE METRICS THAT DRIVE YOUR INTERNAL AND EXTERNAL ACCOUNTING

Have you, as a physician, ever tried to explain a complicated medical procedure or illness to someone with no background in medicine? It's difficult, isn't it? We doctors have a base knowledge of the human body and the practice of medicine that the average person doesn't have, and we often forget that it can sound to others like we're speaking a different language. Well, chances are, your accountant faces the same challenge. This is a professional who spent years learning, practicing, and perfecting their craft. They know accounting just as intimately as we know medicine. So when they try to explain something to those of us who know next to nothing about accounting, it can sound like gibberish. And just like a doctor trying to explain something to a patient, they probably don't realize how useless most of that information is to us.

As Robbie said earlier, we like to have monthly meetings with our accountant, and it took some trial and error to figure out how to make the most of that time. I can't tell you how useless most of those meetings were until we

- found the *right* accountant for our business, and
- outlined exactly what we needed them to tell us.

Once we did that, my eyes were opened to how useful the right information can be to me as a business owner.

Most accountants, in my experience, will hand you a profit and loss statement (P&L) and assume that's all you need. When they look at it they see all the relevant information with zero effort. Their eyes go straight to the most relevant cells of the spreadsheet just like my eyes go straight to the most relevant anatomy on the operating table. They're seeing the P&L through the lens of *their* experience and education, not yours. To prevent this and to save time and misunderstanding when meeting with my accountants, I've learned to tell them exactly what I want to see. Robbie previously set the three main expectations for meeting with our accountants, which include preparing a thirteen-month P&L. Now let's dig deeper into the three bits of information I want them to *pull out* of the P&L for me:

1. **A running thirteen-month picture of all categorized revenue and expenses.**

    This helps us spot outliers and identify trends in our business. For example, if revenue is stable but cost of goods sold is steadily trending up, you may be keeping too much inventory. That's important to know and can identify important tweaks that need to be made. This is the part of the report where it might make sense to spend several minutes of your meeting looking at things carefully while your accountant waits for you to ask questions. No one will care about your business as much as you do, so you are likely to spot something in this review that others would miss. I'd estimate this is where I spend 85 percent of my P&L time, just sitting there looking for trends and outliers.

2. **A separate look at the running thirteen-month top-line revenue and bottom-line profit.**

    By *separate*, I mean I want the accountant to put these two numbers on an entirely separate document from the P&L so it is explicitly clear. Every time, except one, I've asked an accountant for this, they looked back at me like I was asking them to teach me how to read. They may say, "But … it's *right here and here* on the P&L." They forget that their eyes are trained to go straight to that spot. Mine aren't. I don't want to dig through an entire chapter to find the one bit of information I need; I'd rather the author just highlight it for me. Just as with the general P&L, I review this information mostly to spot trends and outliers.

3. **A running thirteen-month profitability calculation.**
This is simply one number. That's it. I just want to know how profitable the business has been over the past thirteen months. I don't care how profitable we were in any *one* month; I'm focused on the overall trends. The timing of a deposit or date a product order comes through—June 30 versus July 1, for example—can make a single month look much better or worse than it actually was.

That's really all I need from our accountant. If they come to the meeting prepared to call out these three things, I can get all the information I need from the P&L in fifteen minutes or less. Of course, I *could* spend hours looking at it, but I'd rather spend that time coaching my kid's soccer team. That's only possible if we can put the accounting—not to mention my interactions with the accountants—on autopilot by getting in, getting what I need, and getting out as quickly as possible.

FIVE CRITICAL FINANCIAL METRICS

Robbie: I've already said I hate it when small-business leaders waste their time pouring over financial reports, charts, and metrics. That's because, if you aren't going to make key business decisions based on the metrics you're reviewing, you're spending a ton of precious time and energy on something that isn't taking you anywhere. That's not to say that *all* financial metrics are a waste, however; there is extraordinary value in regularly reviewing the *right kinds* of data. The trick is knowing which metrics are helpful and which ones aren't.

In the world of private medicine, there are five key metrics that every business owner should use to make critical decisions and keep their finances running on autopilot:

- Total Revenue
- Revenue versus Expenses
- Revenue per Provider
- Total Debt Load
- Budget to Actual

These five areas should always be top of mind, and you should be able to call up these numbers at any time. To make this easier, we suggest having your business director create and provide you with an always-up-to-date financial dashboard of your practice that puts these five metrics front and center. If your software does not generate this automatically, a weekly or monthly email works just fine.

Metric #1: Total Revenue

First is *total revenue*, which I prefer to view as a ninety-day rolling line graph. If you're doing cash-basis accounting, this is the total amount of deposits that hit your bank account. Be sure you are charting both this year *and* last year on the same graph (this is also called a year-over-year comparison). This is especially helpful in identifying any seasonality in your practice, meaning that any dips in revenue might have more to do with the time of year you're in than a problem in your business. Of course, those dips could also be indicating a problem in your business. Either way, you'll know.

Metric #2: Revenue versus Expenses

The second metric you should chart is *revenue versus expenses*. In this ninety-day rolling line chart, I like to see *total revenue* charted together with *total expenses*. This chart reveals how much margin (if any) exists in your business. If these two lines cross, it's costing you more to run your practice than it's making for you.

I also really like this chart because it:
- Shows there is profit,
- Reveals how that profit is moving over time, and
- Informs decisions about adding ongoing expenses.

For example, hiring a new employee requires you to ask, "What will this decision do to our profit margins?" Since this chart allows you to see the delta between revenue and expenses, you'll know if it's wise to make this hire right now.

One expense that should *not* be reported on this chart is owner compensation. Having distributions appear on the revenue versus expenses report will incorrectly deflate your apparent margin.

Metric #3: Revenue per Provider

The third metric to track in your dashboard is *revenue per provider*. I like to view this as a ninety-day bar chart with a year-over-year comparison. The important thing here isn't to represent all your income, but rather, to keep a pulse on your primary revenue drivers to ensure they are staying healthy.

Metric #4: Total Debt Load

The fourth metric is *total debt load*. This one is extremely important because debt is often the biggest long-term risk to a practice. You've got to watch your debt load like a hawk; otherwise, your balances will creep up on you and your practice could end up underwater. A twelve-month line graph is our favorite way to represent debt load because it makes it instantly apparent whether and by how much your liability is increasing or decreasing.

Metric #5: Budget to Actual

Fifth, you will want to track your *budget to actual*, which refers to your budgeted monthly income compared to your actual monthly income. This is as easy as looking at two numbers: the amount of income the business director budgeted for the month and the amount that has actually been received so far.

Again, the bottom line with these and all metrics is that looking at the numbers is a waste of time and attention unless it drives decisions. Business leaders who are successfully running their reporting on autopilot avoid being distracted by bogus vanity metrics, and they don't make a habit of pouring over numbers that don't inform their critical decisions. They look at the numbers that really matter, and then they put that insight to work. Anything more will only serve to puff up your ego or feed your anxiety, and none of us has time for either one.

RECEIPTS: YOUR BEST DEFENSE AGAINST THE IRS

One of the hardest financial things to put on autopilot is receipts. Few things are more annoying than keeping up with and properly archiving every receipt for every purchase your business makes. But as annoying as those little slips of paper can be, forcing yourself to put them on autopilot can save you from a much bigger headache down the road—a headache spelled I-R-S.

THE METRICS THAT DRIVE YOUR INTERNAL AND EXTERNAL ACCOUNTING

As a small-business owner, you have to decide whether you're going to be scared of the IRS. Personally, I'm terrified. The IRS can seize everything you own. They can forcibly withdraw every dime from your bank account. If they audit you and find something wrong, they won't only penalize you, they'll also charge you interest. Although the IRS says that only about 2.5 percent of small-business owners will ever face an audit,[9] I've personally seen two audits happen—one that went really well and one that went terribly. The biggest difference between the two? Receipts.

A lot of business owners have a combative attitude whenever the IRS comes around. I understand that, but I also advise you to put a lid on it. Don't get cocky, and don't be stupid. No small business will win in hand-to-hand combat with the IRS. That's because the IRS doesn't fight hand to hand; they bring tanks. So if the IRS ever walks through your door, you need to be ready. Your attitude should be, "Ah! Welcome! I've been expecting you!" Instead of trying to *beat* the IRS (you won't), you should instead strive to *impress* the IRS. To do that, you're going to show them that you care deeply about the things they expect you to care about, namely:

- You're going to have your tax returns prepared by a certified public accountant every year, and you're going to have those returns neatly organized in a binder by year.
- Along with your filed tax returns, that binder will also include your Articles of Organization, Operating Agreement, Meeting Minutes, and all formal business documents.
- You will have electronic copies of every receipt for every business purchase reflected on your tax returns.

I can't say that these three things will audit-proof your business but having all this information prepared will definitely make the process much smoother and protect you from the most common issues that get small businesses into hot water during an audit.

Now, for the love of God, do not keep *paper* receipts. Paper fills up boxes, filing cabinets, and storage closets. Paper gets lost. Paper fades. Faded paper pisses off the IRS, and we don't want that. We want to impress them, remember? So have your business director or a designee scan or take pictures of every paper receipt and take a screen shot or save a PDF of every digital receipt (including email receipts) and attach it to the appropriate transaction in your accounting software such as QuickBooks or Xero. Without that receipt, the IRS can wave their wand of destruction and decide that you shouldn't have written that expense off your taxes. That's bad news.

Saving receipts may not be a purely *autopilot* function, because someone is going to have to manually scan them and attach them to transactions. But you can at least make it an *automatic* function, meaning everyone in the business knows a purchase must include a receipt, that receipt must be submitted to the appropriate person on your team, and that person is responsible for properly archiving it. Every purchase, every time. Beat this drum with your team until it is a habit, and you'll go a long way toward protecting yourself from the IRS. Besides, putting this expectation on your whole team will also help reduce overspending and potential theft within your business because everyone will know the business director is examining each and every purchase.

This Includes You, the Business Owner

Jeremy: Confession time: I suck at saving receipts. As meticulous as I am in the operating room, I'm fairly absent-minded when it comes to mundane tasks like saving receipts the way I'm supposed to—the way we expect everyone else in the business to do it. In fact, it's probably the one thing my team has to harass me about more than anything else. I'm not proud of that, but I *am* proud Robbie feels comfortable enough with me to bug the hell out of me about it.

I've seen this kind of situation go two ways in most businesses. Sometimes the owner takes a posture of insecurity, obstinately banging his fist on the table whenever the business director asks him to do something important that he doesn't want to do. Other times the owner sheepishly acknowledges his own shortcomings, welcomes the accountability, and looks for systems to help him remember these important things.

Be the latter.

Don't be the type of owner who walks around reminding everyone that they're the boss. That's annoying, childish, and ultimately counterproductive. Instead, be *interruptible*. Our teams must know they can come to us and that we will listen to them when they do. Sure, some of their ideas will be bad, and others won't work in the larger context of the business. You don't need to implement every idea, though; you just need to make everyone on the team know that you will listen ... and that you're not scary.

Don't Get Screwed by Taxes

Robbie: While we're talking about the IRS, let's take just a minute to address another area where we small-business leaders screw ourselves on a regular basis: tax planning.

As a private practice owner, your business is probably designated as a *pass-through entity*, meaning you will pay taxes on every dollar of profit your business earns, regardless of what you do with those dollars. You're going to pay taxes on dollars you take home as W-2 wages, on dollars you take home as distributions, and even on dollars you choose to save inside your business (for things such as emergency funds and sinking funds). Every year, there are private practice owners who bring home more money than they ever have... and then receive a tax bill they can't afford. Why? Because they've *spent* every dollar they've earned, and they haven't been setting any money aside to cover the tax bill.

To avoid this terrible and totally preventable situation, set the expectation with your accountants that they need to tell you each month how much money to budget and set aside to pay the previous month's taxes. This should happen in the monthly accountant's meeting, and they should be able to guide you on whether you should save the money within the business, a personal account, or an interest-bearing option. If you aren't diligently saving an intentionally calculated amount each month for taxes, you could find yourself scrambling to find the cash to pay the IRS. You work too hard to feel that broke—especially when it's so easy to avoid.

DEALING WITH DEBT

Jeremy: Obviously, we can't talk about "all things money" without talking about debt. This is an interesting topic for Robbie and me. You see, Robbie and I agree on a lot of things... eventually. Over several years, we've developed a system of problem-solving that goes like this: I take an extreme position on one side of the issue and Robbie takes an extreme position on the opposite side of the issue; then, we work our way toward the middle. We rarely do this on purpose; it's just where we naturally fall on different issues. By the end of the conversation, neither of us thinks our own original extreme positions was correct, and we agree that the middle ground is the best option for the business. Debt, however, represents one of the rare issues we haven't quite resolved yet.

Robbie strongly believes that debt should *never* be used. I think debt should *always* be considered. As with most of these debates, the answer is probably somewhere in the middle (for your business and ours), but we haven't gotten there on this one issue.

To be fair, I get where Robbie is coming from. There should be an appropriate amount of fear and hesitancy around debt. There will always be a huge portion of the population that is troubled by debt, that abuses debt, and that takes on unreasonable financial risk. Those stories almost never end well, and it's true that debt has shuttered a lot of businesses.

But...

I can't tell you that you should *never* take on debt in your business because I personally took on more than $1 million in debt to buy our business. It would be inauthentic of me to tell you to never use debt when I've carried a huge debt for a long time that I consider to be quite useful. On one hand, signing my name to a seven-figure business debt was an enormous risk. I was personally responsible for it so this debt could have ruined me personally and professionally if something had gone terribly wrong. If I had screwed up or if the plastic surgery market had faced an unexpected crisis, things could have gone very badly very quickly, leaving me holding the bag. Everyone else in the practice would have *only* lost their jobs. I would have lost ... everything.

On the other hand, Amelia Aesthetics as we know it wouldn't be here today if I hadn't taken that risk. I would be performing surgery on some scale, but it wouldn't be what we've built over the past several years. I probably could have still bought the practice eventually even without debt, but it would have taken me years and years to save up enough after-tax dollars to purchase it. And even then, it wouldn't be the same as what we're working with today. By using debt, I was able to start much sooner, and I've been able to invest all the money I would have been saving back into the business immediately, building our brand, launching our Amelia Agency business, creating *The Private Practice MBA* program, and developing the Autopilot software. Instead, I would have spent the past several years simply plugging along, stashing every penny I made into the bank and dreaming of the day I'd be able to own my own practice.

Because of my personal experience, I believe debt is an option. It's one that should be respected—even feared—but one that should always be considered and strategically deployed.

Robbie: Counterpoint!

Jeremy and I obviously have some deep-seated disagreements about debt. I believe debt is by far the most overutilized and underfeared tool available to small-business leaders. From my perspective, if you as a small-business leader don't hate debt, then you have an unhealthy perspective on it. If you look at debt and think of it as a protection or an advantage instead of a liability or a handicap, then I am begging you to consider reframing your perspective.

I'm not saying there isn't a place for debt in your small business. However, in my opinion, debt should always be seen as a "break glass in case of emergency" option. I do not believe that debt is your friend. It is risk, and it steals your cash every single month in the form of principal and interest payments. And as we've said many times, cash is the lifeblood of your entire business. If you ever run out of cash, you have to pack everything up and send everyone home. In my experience, the wisest small-business leaders do not view debt as a set of afterburners on the aircraft of their business; they view debt as a last resort.

My strong feelings about debt come from seeing the aftermath of small-business leaders who use debt regularly to grow their business. The story is always the same: times are good, and making the payments is easy. But then, something happens: the economy stalls, their product or service experiences a problem, a key revenue-producing team member leaves or gets sick, or one of an endless number of "unexpected" other issues arises. My view is that none of these things are ever fully unexpected, because we all know business owners who have faced these exact issues. This stuff is *going* to happen, and if any one or two of them can bring your business crashing down, you're frankly building a house of cards rather than a strong, stable business.

Over the course of your business, you are going to have several seasons when cash flow is significantly reduced. And while it's easy to adjust the cost of your typical overhead expenses during difficult times, it's nearly impossible to make adjustments to the cost of your debt. Additionally, from my experience, using debt almost always leads to a less creative strategy. Debt is an easy, lazy, go-to-first option far too often. Turning to debt *first* prevents you from developing alternative, innovative solutions to the problem or opportunity you're facing. Even if you keep debt as an option but make it your last resort instead of your first choice, I promise you will unlock deeper thinking and better options—quality options—that can get you what you want *and* keep you out of debt. Isn't that at least worth exploring?

Besides, avoiding debt almost always means paying *less* to do whatever it is you want to do. Have you ever watched the television series *House Hunters*? In practically every episode, a home buyer starts the show with a $500,000 budget but then, by the end of the show, buys a $1.7 million luxury condo. Why? Because it's not real money; it's debt. In the consumer world, debt creates a false sense of margin and financial comfort. In the business world, debt creates a false sense of success. It gives you the financial benefit of success you haven't actually had yet. As a result, you feel freer to spend more because you already *feel* the success of the new opportunity. You're flush with cash, and you forget that it isn't really yours. That newfound sense of freedom can and often does turn into a prison sentence the next month when the first bill arrives.

Like Jeremy said, I'm sure the answer to the debt issue is somewhere between our extreme positions. We just haven't found it yet. Nonetheless, there is value to you as a business owner to weigh each extreme carefully. And if you're lucky, your business director will naturally take the opposite position so your business can work toward the middle just like we are.

THE VALUE OF SIMPLE PRICING

Before joining Jeremy at Amelia Aesthetics, I worked for an organization in Nashville, Tennessee, that actively served customers across the entire United States on a daily basis. One November, we had a bad snowstorm—and that was on top of the inch of ice that had already covered the roads. It took forever to get to the office . . . if you made it at all. I saw dozens of cars on the side of the road as I made the slow crawl to work that day. When I got there, it seemed like everyone who had made it was talking about the weather and their drive, and no one was working. You could just feel the general lack of focus throughout the building.

Around 11:00 a.m., our CEO called a company-wide meeting and gave a speech that I'll never forget. The whole speech could be summed up in this one line I can still hear ringing in my ears: "None of our customers gives a shit that it's snowing in Nashville. They need us to get focused on serving them." It was a blunt, yet effective reminder that great businesses do not allow their internal problems to make life more difficult for their customers. We take this idea seriously at Amelia Aesthetics. In fact, our entire mission is to "make it easy to be a patient." If something is making it difficult to be a patient, we fix it—even if that means making it a little harder to run our practice. We think the extra effort is worth the extra ease it brings others.

Unfortunately, that's a novel concept to most private practices. Most physicians have a natural bent toward making decisions that make it easier for them to run their business, not easier for someone else to be a patient. How backward is that? My former CEO used to remind us that "we exist for the people *outside* these walls." If we don't exist to serve the people outside our organization, why do we even exist at all?

And at least in my experience, the biggest area in which private practices make things easier for themselves and more difficult for the patient is pricing. Just like no one cares if it's snowing in Nashville, no one cares how complicated it is to calculate a price for your services. You already know exactly what patients want: they want to be able to go to your website and see clear and simple pricing for the services you offer. They don't want to wait three months for a consultation before finding out if a procedure is even financially possible for them. They want what we all want when we're considering a big purchase: the price. Now. Without having to talk to a salesperson. Honestly, if every major car manufacturer can figure out how to do this, there's no reason you can't.

If you're a surgeon, for example, please stop talking to your patients about anesthesia fees, facility fees, surgeon fees, post-op care fees, bandage and medical garment fees, and on and on and on. Why make it so hard for a patient to figure out how much this procedure will actually cost them? Instead, price all your services as a flat rate and publish them online. It's rude and mean to expect people to call you or wait for a consultation to get an idea of what you charge.

Unless your prices are way out of line with similar practices in your area, you shouldn't be ashamed of what you charge. Own it. Be proud of the level of care you provide and the value you offer your patients. Besides, reducing friction in this one area will likely make your practice ten times more attractive than your competitors. People want to do business with companies that make it easy for them.

STAY AHEAD OF THE CURVE

Jeremy: Times are changing. That's always been true, of course, but it seems like times are changing faster and more dramatically than ever before. The Internet and especially social media have kicked everything up a notch—including our expectations. And I mean our expectations for *everything*, from what we expect from our patients and customers to our vendors and consultants.

There was a time when I think business owners felt they *reported to* their accountants and lawyers. Those people are the experts so we have to do what they say, right?

Wrong.

It's taken some time, but now I'm fully comfortable looking a CPA in the face and saying, "We're not doing it that way." I'm never a jerk about it, but I'm not afraid to make it clear to the people who work alongside my practice that it's ... well ... *my* practice. If I'm paying you to advise us in a key area like our finances, I will absolutely listen to what you have to say, but that doesn't mean I have to do things your way.

That's true in all areas of my business, but it's especially worth calling out here, as we wrap up this chapter on putting your accounting on autopilot. Why? Because most accounting professionals would hate 90 percent of what Robbie and I have said in this chapter. It's different. It's not how they're used to doing things. It's a little outside their comfort zones because it requires them to learn how to translate a complicated spreadsheet into plain English. Just like I want to make it easy for patients to do business with me, I want my accountant to make it easy for me to do business with them. They can do that by following the expectations we've set in this chapter.

Of course, we, as business owners, also need to make it easy for our employees to work with us, and that happens largely through compensation. So before we bring this section on "all things money" to a close, we need to talk about how to care for the all-important human resources in our practice. We'll do that next.

CHAPTER 9

THE INS AND OUTS OF TEAM COMPENSATION

Jeremy: You and I, as business owners, will always see the business differently than anyone else on the team. As owners, we're always thinking about the overarching mission and purpose of the business. If revenue dried up for a few months, would you stop coming to work? No way! You'd double down and work twice as hard to get the business back on its feet. Your team members, however, are coming at this from a different perspective. They may love their jobs. They may love having you as their boss. You may offer the coolest work atmosphere and sense of community imaginable. But the hard reality is, your team members didn't come to work for you just for those things. Most adults go to work because they need the income. If that income went away, they'd go home. If someone else swooped in and offered them a higher income for the same work, they'd at least consider it. It doesn't make them bad, greedy, or disloyal; it just makes them human. While you're focused on growing your business, they're focused on taking care of their families. If another opportunity comes along that gives them the chance to take *better* care of their family, they have a responsibility—a duty—to check it out.

So if we want to hire the best people we can and, maybe more importantly, *keep* those awesome team members, we better be paying them well. That means we've got to talk about compensation.

MENTIONING THE UNMENTIONABLE

Robbie: In all my years in business leadership and ownership roles, I've noticed that there are some topics that business owners love talking about to their teams and some topics business owners hate talking about to their teams. Compensation almost always falls in the latter bucket. Most leaders get uncomfortable getting into the details of how they're paying their team members. They avoid compensation discussions like the plague. We have to get over this avoidance mentality when it comes to compensation, though. Regardless of our comfort level, compensation represents the livelihood of the individuals and families we care so much about, so we have to stop making it feel "unmentionable."

When you intentionally put the area of team compensation on autopilot, not only are your team members going to feel honored by your efforts, but they are going to feel much more connected to the tensions and the realities you personally face as a business leader. Anytime that happens, your entire business improves.

The brilliant Austrian neurologist and Holocaust survivor Viktor Frankl, author of *Man's Search for Meaning*, created a therapeutic approach called *Logotherapy* that helps people find personal meaning in life. According to Frankl, all people have a motivation to find meaning in their lives—something he called a "will to meaning." Additionally, he taught that each of us are made up of body (external), mind (internal), and spirit (philosophical). So, as leaders, if we can help our team find meaning across their external, internal, and philosophical makeup, we can help them find the meaning they are searching for.[10]

This is important in the context of employee compensation because we, as business leaders, expect our team members to be philosophically motivated by our mission and vision from day one. We may altogether miss the fact that team members who aren't motivated externally can almost never be fully motivated internally or philosophically for any meaningful length of time.

What's an employee's initial external motivation for coming to work? Money. If you fail to "hook" them with a compelling compensation package, you'll never get their full internal or philosophical buy-in. That's not because they're greedy; it's because life isn't free. Rabbi Daniel Lapin, author of *Thou Shall Prosper: Ten Commandments for Making Money*, describes money as "certificates of appreciation."[11] When people feel underpaid, then they naturally feel underappreciated. And it's extremely unlikely that someone who feels underappreciated will be excited about working their tail off for the mission of the organization.

At Amelia Aesthetics, we've worked hard to create an atmosphere in which compensation discussions are not awkward but rather welcome conversations. In this chapter, we'll unpack what that looks like and how you could create this same healthy atmosphere in your practice.

TWO LESSONS FROM THE OLD, YELLOW CONFERENCE ROOM

Jeremy: Several years ago, Robbie and I launched a second business alongside our medical practice. We were just starting to get our arms around what would one day become *The Private Practice MBA* and the

Autopilot software, and we decided to develop those initiatives under a new business we called the Amelia Agency. This is also the team that serves our other Amelia Aesthetics locations across the country, offering tools and support to those growing practices so their respective business owners can focus on the other aspects of their practices.

As the agency team grew, we ran out of office space. Even though Amelia Aesthetics could easily afford to lease more space for Amelia Agency, Robbie and I intentionally approached the Agency like a bootstrapped startup. In fact, it wasn't uncommon for new hires to spend their first day building their own flatpack desk and chair. We just kept squeezing them together until the pediatric cardiologist next door moved out. We asked the landlord if we could "squat" in their old office space until he leased it to someone else, and he reluctantly agreed. The agency team picked up their desks, dragged them across the hall, and that catacomb of tiny exam rooms became Amelia Agency's first official office.

The only room big enough to fit more than three people became the de facto conference room. It had yellow walls that were badly faded from the nonstop glare of the afternoon sun, which beamed through the curtainless windows. The roof leaked every time it rained, slowly growing a water stain that threatened to overtake the entire ceiling. It was a mess. However, a lot of crucial decisions were made in that old, yellow conference room. Two of them were focused on employee compensation.

Let's (Not) Make a Deal

First, we decided we were never going to try to "get a deal" on any candidate we wanted to hire. We committed to always balancing as much as we could pay with what the best candidate needed to make, and that was always in the context of what that position and level of experience was worth on the open market. Occasionally, we felt the need to underpay the market rate. Most of the time, though, we did the opposite.

There were times as we grew Amelia Aesthetics and Amelia Agency when we couldn't quite get the offer to where the candidate needed us to go. In those situations, many companies would start with an obvious lowball offer and use that as a way to negotiate the candidate down from the salary they said they needed. We chose to approach that situation differently. We never wanted to disrespect another professional's compensation needs, so we treated them like adults and said:

> You seem like a great fit, and we would love to bring you onto our team. We know you need *this* amount, and we'd love to be able to offer you that. I'm sure you're worth it. However, we just don't have that much to spend on this position. So, *here's* what we can do. It's literally as high as we can possibly go here. We're not trying to lowball you; we just want to be honest about what we're working with.

You'd be surprised how often the perfect candidate will come down from what they said they needed in order to work for a company who treats them with that level of respect and honesty right from the start.

There have been other times when an outstanding candidate popped up, and we went out of our way to bring them on board. It isn't unusual for us to pay someone *more* than they asked if we felt the role and the individual deserved it. I know for a fact that we have paid some team members more than we needed to. In the early days of a business startup, when money is tight, that might seem like a terrible idea. And yet, I've never regretted it. Not once.

Keep Me Out of It

The second big compensation decision that we made in the yellow room was that I, as the CEO and business owner, was not going to have salary and bonus discussions with employees individually. I would have group discussions with the whole team or sub-teams, but I would never have a one-on-one compensation discussion with a team member.

This was an easy decision for Robbie and me for a few reasons. First, he's simply better at it than I am. When you're talking to an employee about their compensation—their very livelihood—every word matters. Those talks can go south in the blink of an eye with just one poorly worded statement, and the emotional fallout from a financial miscommunication can be devastating. Robbie is great at these conversations, which is a huge blessing to me. One of his key strengths as a leader is open, honest, and almost excessive candor. Once he mastered how to use those strengths in the area of compensation discussions, there was no reason for me to even try. So I let him do it.

Second, and this is just my personal preference, I don't want the people in our office to associate me with their salary. I know they do to a large degree anyway because I'm the owner and primary revenue driver, but I don't want to compound that by chiming in on their paychecks. I'm never going to have the full context of what they do, how well they're doing it, what their role is worth on the open market, what they made at a previous company, and so on. Most of our team members are at least two leaders removed from me. I trust Robbie and our leadership team to run the compensation discussions, leaving me to focus on the mission, vision, and culture of our organization when interacting with our team.

WHEN AND WHY TO GIVE RAISES

Robbie: One of the biggest surprises I've had over my years in leadership is how easy it is to screw up something that *should* be a source of joy and celebration: giving an employee a raise. You'd think this is always a positive thing, but somehow, that's not the case. Unfortunately, this is an area that too many leaders take for granted and, therefore, mess up. So, let's examine a couple of land mines that are easy to avoid.

First, you must ensure that you can *afford* to give someone a raise. Just because you want to doesn't mean you ought to. Start by checking your financial dashboard to see how your revenue versus expenses margin is trending. As long as you are proactively budgeting for emergencies, large purchases, and owner's distributions, this singular graph will show whether or not you can afford the increase in fixed costs.

As an aside, this is why I love to regularly talk to our team about how much revenue we're bringing in and how expensive things are. It's easy for employees to get emotionally wrapped up in seeing top-line revenue if they aren't living and breathing the expenses, as well. We as leaders know that revenue only makes sense in the full context of the expenses. Without that complete financial picture, a team member can see a fivefold increase in gross revenue and start to wonder why their paychecks haven't also gone up proportionately. That sounds crazy to us, but it happens every day. Do not be afraid to let your team in on the numbers; they will both appreciate it and understand it far more than you may naturally think they will.

Second, you must identify the right time to give a raise. If you say, "That's easy. Do it every year on their work anniversary," congratulations! You're wrong!

This is one of the biggest mistakes business leaders make when giving raises. While this feels like a natural time and place, it creates an unhealthy expectation with team members that it's going to happen every single year. We all know the problem with expectations: no one is ever grateful for something they expect. Worse, if their expectation goes unmet and they don't get a raise, they get upset.

Giving a raise on a yearly anniversary creates a lose-lose scenario for both the leader and the team member. I know it's easy. I know it's what every other company does. But please... don't do it. Instead give the *person* a raise when the *bar* is raised—or, as Dave Ramsey says, "Your *raise* is effective when *you* are." That is, if you're going to give someone a raise, do it as soon as they do something that increases their long-term value. Maybe they learn a new skill set, or they demonstrate growth in leadership ability, or they start demonstrating new ways to help other team members succeed. The trick is to catch them doing something right, and then reward them. As soon as you notice a sustained level of performance and value increase, that's the perfect time to give a raise.

As for how much of a raise to give someone, you'll want your business director to always check market value for that position in your specific area. This is quick and easy to do on sites like salary.com. You'll want to do this regularly, too, and not just when giving an employee a raise. Doing an overall compensation analysis for the different positions on your team every year will prevent you from falling behind market rates and, thereby, risk losing your best and brightest team members. There's no faster way to lose quality people than to accidentally pay 10 percent more or less than the industry standard for that role.

THE GOOD AND BAD OF BENEFITS

We can't talk about compensation without talking about benefits—health insurance, dental, vision, 401(k), team treatments, etc.—and this is where the whole compensation discussion gets tricky. Your team's benefit package can add as much as 40 percent to the cost of their hourly or salaried compensation. In a growing practice in which you're hiring a few team members a year, these costs can get out of hand over time. When the team is smaller, these extra expenses can fly under the radar, so you might be more inclined to be extra-generous in piling on the benefits. Then you add a few people the next year and a few more the next. Too often, when the practice is smaller, we don't stop to think about what these benefits will cost us at scale. Then, years down the road, if you realize you simply can't afford to maintain the same benefits you started with, you'll find yourself with a huge problem: either endanger your business by sticking with benefits you can't afford, or risk losing team members by pulling back benefits they've gotten used to. Either way, you lose.

The most painful part of benefits to me, though, is that they are generally not appreciated. As amazing as your team members are, they simply will not appreciate most benefits at the level you'd hope they would. That is, a $1,000 benefit will almost never be met with as much enthusiasm as a $500 cash bonus. To a business owner, that sucks. Whether it's cash or in the form of a benefit, that's still money out of your pocket. It hurts to excitedly roll out a new benefit only to have it go largely unnoticed and unappreciated. But then, if you try to take that same undervalued benefit away later, you'll be met with tremendous pushback, grumbling, and complaints. The benefit they never seemed to care about is suddenly a make-or-break issue for them.

Is that fair? No.

Is it true? Absolutely.

With all that said, we encourage you to be selective in what you decide to offer your team within their benefits package. Whenever possible, I'd recommend you keep it super-simple with only health insurance and a 401(k). Those two things seem to make up the most valued pieces of all benefits packages. Everything else, such as vision, dental, life insurance, gym memberships, etc. are certainly nice, but they aren't needed—especially if you're also paying your people well enough to easily buy these things on their own. There are plenty of areas in which you can be over-the-top generous with your team—but benefits shouldn't be one of them. It's just too much risk with too little reward.

The only exception, because we *are* talking about medical practices, would be team treatments. We run a plastic surgery center and medspa, so we include some level of team treatments as an added perk for our employees. If you run a dental practice, you could include free or discounted dental treatments. The biggest danger here is that most people won't appreciate how much these services should have cost them. Even if they know a regular patient would pay around $3,000 for a root canal and crown, they probably won't make the emotional connection that, by doing it for free, you've effectively given them a $3,000 bonus.

We enjoy offering our services to our employees, but we also want them to see and appreciate the financial impact of the benefit. So, we provide them with a total compensation report each year that breaks down how much we're *really* paying them when you total up their salary or hourly wage, insurance, 401(k) matching, treatments, and so on. Giving them this greater context has made a significant difference in helping each team member understand how valuable they are to us *and* how well we strive to take care of them above and beyond their paycheck.

SHOW PEOPLE WHAT THEY MAKE

Jeremy: I believe the world of benefits is more art than science. I see it as more speculative, more of a balancing act between salary, benefits, and work environment. Mainly, though, I believe people don't care about benefits as much as they think they do.

I can't back that up with research. In fact, research technically proves me wrong. According to *Harvard Business Review*, it's probably wiser to add benefits rather than salary when increasing compensation.[12] Other studies suggest that things like culture, leadership, and "perks" are more important, at least to high-income individuals.[13] So, maybe the most valuable thing when hiring and keeping employees happy is benefits. Maybe it's job satisfaction. Maybe it's culture. Maybe it's leadership. It's almost certainly, to some degree, all of the above.

Over and above all that, though, I think people simply want to know what they make. That sounds obvious, but think about it: Do each of your team members know how much they *really* make when you add up everything you're paying and giving them?

When an employee gets frustrated or unhappy at work, it is perfectly reasonable and should be expected that they'll spend some time thinking about their options, possibly looking at job openings at other companies or, at the very least, comparing their current salary to what others in the industry are making. But their paycheck only tells part of the story.

For example, say you have a nurse making $34 per hour, or about $70,000 per year. If someone asks her what she makes, she'd say $34 per hour, and she'd be right. But she'd also be wrong. If she also gets medical benefits, a 401(k) match, and some form of profit sharing, her $70,000 income is actually closer to $90,000 in actual value. Throw in paid time off and free in-house treatments at your practice, and it gets closer to $100,000. That puts her hourly rate at around $50, not $34.

Now let's imagine she's having a rough week, starts to check local job openings on a whim, and sees an open nursing position at another practice that's offering $39 per hour. That's going to look attractive to her, right? After all, $39 is more than $34, so she'll be making more money.

Except she might not be. She's exploring her options using bad numbers. This valued team member needs to know that she's worth more than $70,000 per year to you. She needs to understand that you're paying her six figures! Even if it's not cash *in* her pocket, it's still cash *out* of yours. She and everyone else on your team needs to understand that.

Like Robbie said, the best way to show your team members their full financial value to your organization is through a total compensation report, so let's take a minute to review what that looks like.

Total Compensation Report

Robbie: Knowing that most team members—especially the younger, less experienced ones—equate "what they make" only with what hits their bank account, we've gone to great lengths to help our employees understand that their paychecks only tell part of the compensation story. We want them to see the full context of their income, which includes their paychecks *plus* their benefits and any other expenses we pay on their behalf. Sure, we want them to see all this so they can better appreciate what we're doing for them, but more than that, we want each person to see how much we value them and their role on our team, and that value goes far beyond their take-home pay.

We've created a report that brings all these numbers together and breaks down every dollar Amelia Aesthetics spends to keep each team member on staff. We call it the Total Compensation Report, and it shows:

- **Total Cash Compensation:** This includes base pay, overtime, bonuses, profit sharing, paid time off, and paid holidays.
- **Total Benefits:** This represents the value of their health insurance, HSA contributions, 401(k) matching, educational allowances, and in-house team treatments.
- **Total Government Benefits:** This shows what the business paid toward their government benefits, such as Social Security and Medicare.

We provide this customized report to each team member annually to ensure they're getting the full story of their compensation and not just the CliffsNotes version their paycheck provides.

This report also helps them view their compensation appropriately during those times, which Jeremy alluded to, when they may start checking out opportunities at other practices. How many times have you seen someone change jobs for a $2,500/year raise only to discover they'll be paying $3,000 more in health insurance? That's a bad trade, but it's the kind of mistake employees make all the time because they aren't looking at all the facts.

PAYING INCENTIVES

Jeremy and I both strongly believe in ongoing financial incentives for our team members because of a simple, yet powerful leadership principle: If you show your heart, you'll clone your heart. That is, incentives on top of their regular salary show our team the behaviors we most desire to see repeated. Given that cash flow is the lifeblood of the organization, it makes sense that we would invest in ways to get our team members to help generate more profit. And as important as things like benefits and workplace culture are, nothing is as effective as a cash incentive for rewarding and encouraging great performance.

Too often, business leaders assume their team members know what they should or should not be doing to help drive profit, but our employees can't read our minds. Moreover, they don't see the big picture of the business the way we do; they're usually laser focused on their own small piece of the puzzle. So how are they supposed to know what behaviors we most value if we aren't calling our employees out and rewarding them when we catch them doing something right?

Not only do incentive programs help show your heart to your team members, but they also allow you to show your team what *they* should have a heart for. This is why we love paying our team members a monthly profit-sharing bonus. We set aside a percentage of our profits to invest into the team as a "thank you" for having a heart for the things we have a heart for.

Incentive programs also help you keep your team healthy by sniffing out what we call "More Monsters." You know who I'm talking about, right? More Monsters are those team members you hired who you've later realized will never be satisfied with any amount of money, praise, or benefits.

The tough truth about More Monsters is that ungrateful team members always believe they are somehow being shortchanged and, therefore, feel justified in occasionally taking "fairness" into their own hands to balance the scales. What they may call *fairness* though, the rest of us would call *theft*. This could come in the form of stealing time (leaving early, coming in late, and/or taking long lunches), surfing the Internet instead of working, not submitting PTO for missed days, taking supplies home, or even stealing cash. You are unlikely to have these problems with team members who are grateful for what you do for them, and incentive programs make it blatantly obvious who is grateful and who isn't.

Keep Incentive Programs Simple

Jeremy: Before we lay out some practical tips for implementing an incentive program in your business, I want to suggest one important ground rule: keep your incentive programs simple. This is a lesson I learned the hard way.

I had a meeting with a business consultant a few years ago who specializes in the medical industry. One of the questions I asked her was, "How should we compensate our team's medical and medspa providers who directly serve our patients?"

"There's no standard way," she replied. "Let's figure out what works best for you."

I spent the next hour or so digging into all the numbers and noting the different ways each provider contributes to the revenue of our company. The consultant and I worked up a customized, unique modifier for each of our seven providers' overall compensation that recognized their specific contribution to the business. Clearly, this was a home run.

I was excited to lay all this out for Robbie, who hadn't been able to join me in the consultation. I wanted him to review it just in case I had missed something before we rolled it out.

Robbie studied the document for a minute and then, with a look of confusion (and maybe disappointment), said, "Hey, Jeremy . . . who do you think is going to figure out what number to fill in for each paycheck for each of these people?"

"Uh... you?"

Wrong answer.

Half incredulous and half amused, he replied, "Do you have any idea how complicated that is? I'm going to have to track every service we provide, categorize them separately, weight them individually, and then calculate the total—*for each provider*. For seven people, that's easily ten hours every pay period."

I immediately understood his argument. Our pay periods are every two weeks. That means Robbie would have had to spend ten hours out of every eighty-hour pay period—a full 12.5 percent of his time—calculating the incentive bonus for seven of our forty employees. That would have been a horrible decision for two reasons. First, if Robbie's spending 12.5 percent of his time doing math, it means he's not spending that time doing what he's *supposed* to be doing: leading the business of our practice. Second, speaking strictly financially, considering what Robbie's time is worth to our business, we would have been better off overpaying our providers using a much simpler, less customized incentive program.

If your incentive program is so complicated that you'd spend more in payroll *preparing* it than you would actually *paying* it, you need to go back to the drawing board.

When and How to Pay Incentives

Robbie: There are a few behaviors we often get wrong when it comes to handing out incentives, which in turn cause our team members to undervalue the incentives we're excited to give them. The good news, though, is that these are simple miscalculations that are easy to correct.

THE INS AND OUTS OF TEAM COMPENSATION

First, let's talk about *when* you should give an incentive. A standard model is to pay annual bonuses around Christmastime. From our perspective as leaders, this makes sense. It seems like an obvious way to cap off a great year and celebrate together the success we've had as a company. Because it's around the holidays, we know our team members and their families will get the money at a time when many families need a little "extra." Besides, getting that extra cash out of our business accounts before the end of the year can help us from a tax perspective. Everyone wins!

Here's the problem, though: studies have shown (and most of us have seen from experience) that team members will not connect an annual or quarterly bonus to their work performance. Instead, they're more likely to see these incentive dollars as a "goodwill offering" from the business owner. If that's your goal, then an annual or quarterly bonus is fine. Just understand that your employees probably won't see it as an incentive to work harder. They'll take it as your way of saying, "Hey, I think you're cool. Here's $1,000."

Maybe you've heard the leadership mantra, "What gets rewarded gets repeated." Well... that doesn't work when the reward comes once a year and is more tied to holidays than performance. Instead, when it comes to incentives, the key is, "What gets rewarded *often* gets repeated *often*." For this reason, we encourage you to pay your incentives as soon as possible after the behaviors you want repeated have happened. So practically, if you're going to pay production bonuses or profit sharing, don't wait to pay these incentives at the end of the quarter; pay the incentive for the *last* month in the first paycheck of the *following* month.

Second, you must always surround your incentives with clarity about *why* the employee is getting an extra kick. To reinforce behavior, we must be clear about what they did right and why we'd like them to keep doing more of it. That reinforcement might be providing easy-to-understand calculation sheets to everyone getting paid a production bonus. That way, they can *visually* connect how their behaviors created their incentives.

Or if you're paying your team profit sharing, you can surround that profit-sharing check with the context of what that month looked like for the business overall. You could send a monthly email or have a monthly meeting in which you walk through why profits were up or down, who overperformed, what big expenses arose, what big expenses were avoided, how one team or individual saved the company a lot of money, and so on. This demonstrates in a very real way how their effect on the company's bottom line directly affects the size of their profit-sharing bonus. This is also an excellent opportunity to remind your team members what profit represents: lives changed, long-term stability, the ability to continue reaching more people, or whatever would most inspire your team.

PERSPECTIVE CAN FEEL LIKE A RAISE

Jeremy: I like cars. They help me understand people a little better. For example, when I'm interviewing a potential employee, I'll usually ask them what they drive. It's not because I'm looking for a status symbol; I actually don't *care* what kind of car they drive. What I care about is the story behind that car. Why did they choose it? How long have they had it? Maybe it's a twenty-year-old Honda they've had since high school. Or maybe it's a brand-new Tesla they just leased. Those answers give me some perspective on the person I'm talking to.

During my first two years as an attending surgeon, I drove a BMW 3 Series. When people asked me what I drove, that's what I told them. As soon as "BMW" left my mouth, though, I could see that they had immediately made some decisions about me. It's not uncommon for a surgeon to drive a European luxury car, of course. But at that point in my career, everyone I worked with knew my situation: I was broke! I had only recently kicked off my surgical training wheels, and I was still riddled with student-loan debt. In that context, I felt weird having people assume I was driving around in a new luxury sedan right off the showroom floor. So I told them the story of the car. I overshared, saying, "I drive an old BMW 3 Series with 200,000 miles on it that I bought from my parents for $4. It gets me where I need to ... even though I use safety pins to keep the roof lining from falling on me while I'm driving."

Those factual details immediately changed what people thought about me as a person. Their perspective of my car shifted from *luxury status symbol* to *broke guy's transportation*. It mattered to me that people knew that. I wanted them to have more information when evaluating me than just the make and model of my ride. I wanted them to know *why* I drove that old BMW and that I wasn't the stereotypical, show-off, hotshot surgeon but was instead a smart, scrappy young surgeon who was paying his dues.

I also know this isn't true for everyone. Some people care about the why, and some people don't. That's not something I can control.

In the same way, you can't decide how an employee is going to view their compensation—but you *can* influence it by giving them all the facts. Some won't care. Others will care a great deal. When an employee making $65,000 a year understands they were also given $2,500 in retirement funding, $8,000 in health insurance coverage, $3,400 in profit sharing, and that you spent a gazillion more dollars in taxes and government expenses, you give them a piece of information that has the potential to change their perspective: that $65,000 team member's total compensation is more like $82,000. That's something they won't realize unless you show them because nobody is doing this kind of math on their own.

This new perspective could be eye-opening for the team member. It changes the story they tell themselves about their work and the commitment you've made to them by hiring them and keeping them. And emotionally, it could hit them almost as much as a raise because they're seeing, maybe for the first time, that you value them much more than they thought.

SECTION 3

ALL THINGS SALES AND MARKETING

CHAPTER 10

UNDERSTANDING THE PATIENT JOURNEY

Jeremy: We've worked hard over the past few years to make the Amelia Aesthetics brand stand out to potential patients who are researching plastic surgery options. Several of my surgical patients travel from out of town every week just to have their procedure done in our office by me or one of our other providers. Is it because there are no qualified surgeons in their own city? Absolutely not. In fact, I'm sure many of these patients are leaving cities with far more skilled and experienced plastic surgeons just to have me do their surgery. Part of me thinks that's nuts. As I've said before, I know I'm a *good* plastic surgeon, but I'm certainly not the best in the world. Why would people choose our practice over other providers, and why would some travel hundreds of miles to do it?

The answer—which we're going to explore fully in this section of the book—is our approach to sales and marketing. It doesn't matter how skilled you are as a physician; if you fall short on your sales and marketing, your practice will never come close to its full potential.

About once a quarter, a surgeon I've never met will reach out to ask about our marketing and see if I'd be willing to have a phone call to discuss it. I've done enough of these calls to know exactly how they're going to go. The other doctor will always start enthusiastically, hoping to find *the* answer to their marketing problems. By the end of the call, though, both of us will feel discouraged and deflated. As we hang up, I can usually say with 99 percent certainty that the other person isn't going to do any of the things we discussed. Why? Because I didn't have an easy answer. Almost every person who has reached out to discuss our marketing has been looking for a quick and easy solution they can simply turn on like a light switch. They want a silver bullet. But there isn't one.

Oftentimes professionals outside the business world have an unrealistic view of sales and marketing. They see another business's recent social media post "go viral" and think, *Hey, we should do that too!* Or they think it's about creating the perfect ad, launching a fresh marketing campaign, mastering SEO (search engine optimization), or throwing a thousand before-and-after photos onto Instagram and waiting for the phone to ring. That's not how marketing works at all—not *good* marketing, anyway.

Marketing is about relationships and trust, and relationships built on a foundation of trust do not come quickly or easily. Sure, a stellar add or an investment in social media can get a lot of attention, but that attention rarely turns into a sale on its own. Instead, that new relationship has to be nurtured and allowed to mature. You have to see that exposure for what it is: a little bit of trust that the potential customer has placed in you. That trust earns you the right to pursue a relationship with the customer but, handled poorly, you can squash that trust long before it ever turns into a sale.

For example, you might post a particularly compelling before-and-after photo on Instagram with a link directing visitors to "Book a Consult." If they click, congratulations! They've placed a little trust in you as a provider for a service they're interested in. But if they click the "Book a Consult" link only to find it's merely a contact form that doesn't give them the ability to *actually* book a consult, their trust will start to erode. If they still have enough trust to fill out the form but then several days go by before anyone contacts them to follow up, that trust erodes further. Say they *still* have enough trust to have a conversation with your team about a consult but need to know up front how much your offering costs. If you say, "You have to come in to get your individual plan before we can set a price," whatever is left of that trust will evaporate entirely.

Speaking as consumers ourselves, we know this is a justifiable response. They stated plainly what they needed to make a decision (a ballpark price), and you basically told them you'd only answer that question if they made an appointment, waited weeks or months for a consult, and then stood naked in your office discussing a procedure they can't afford. I wouldn't want to be treated that way. Neither would you. So why do so many physicians treat everyone else like this?

Every part of the patient's experience is an opportunity either to *build* trust or *lose* trust. That's marketing. And if you are a good steward of that trust and have given the customer everything they need to make the best, most well-informed decision, only *then* will a sale occur.

Of all the things we discuss in this book, sales and marketing is the one area I believe medical practices get wrong more than anything else. But that's good news. It also means this is the area that's ripe for the most dramatic improvement—*if* we're willing to take the slow road and learn how to develop relationships with our customers that are built on trust over time and how to put that whole process on autopilot.

THE WHY AND HOW OF THE PATIENT'S JOURNEY

Robbie: As we get started with this section of the book, you may be wondering why we couple sales and marketing together instead of addressing them separately. Simple: Sales and marketing are synergistic. They go hand in hand. Sales and marketing, taken together, is simply the act of showing a patient why they should take one step after another toward your offering. You can think of marketing as the *why*—showing a patient *why* they should take another step forward—and you can think of sales as the *how*—showing a patient *how* to take their next step forward. These two disciplines, while unique in their own regard, cannot be successful without the other.

Think of it like a track-and-field event. Some people view sales and marketing like one company competing in two separate races, with a marketing team and a sales team each competing against other companies in their respective areas. Here's the problem: if they were running separate races, marketing could lose and sales could still win. But that's not how it works. In business, sales and marketing win or lose *together*. They aren't separate events; rather, sales and marketing are running a relay race—and the customer is the baton they pass back and forth. If that handoff isn't done carefully and intentionally, the customer could be dropped in the process.

The process I'm referring to should be inherently familiar to you. Every person who has ever bought any product or service has done so as part of a process. It can go fast or slow. It can be a joy or a chore. It can be an agonizing decision-making process over several sleepless nights, or it could happen so easily that you don't even know the process happened at all. It can also be unpredictable, like spending a month picking out a new hairstyle versus five minutes picking out a tattoo. The item, the features, the options, the providers, the location—all of it swims around our minds as we race (or crawl) toward a decision. And even then, we're left with the aftereffects of the decision. Was it "the best money I've ever spent" or are we suffering from buyer's remorse?

Whatever the product, service, or provider, there is a psychological journey every consumer takes when they're considering a major purchase—anything from a new car to a vacation to plastic surgery. You'll often hear this referred to as a *marketing funnel*. Others may call it *experience mapping* or *user journey*. As a medical provider, we prefer the term *patient journey*, and this journey represents the path a patient takes from their initial thought about a procedure all the way to your offering.

We've identified five key phases in the patient's journey, and each one represents an opportunity either to take the relationship further... or to drop the baton. We'll spend the rest of this section of the book breaking down each phase, including

- what they are thinking, feeling, and doing during each phase;
- how a patient moves toward or away from each phase; and
- what you can do to help patients make the wisest decision.

These three areas will put a spotlight on the main reasons patients usually bail on the journey they started with you. By becoming aware of them and how you can build your sales and marketing around these concerns, you can put the patient journey on autopilot in your practice.

THE PATIENT JOURNEY IN A NUTSHELL

Once you learn the patient journey, you will begin to see this kind of consumer process everywhere—even in your own life. There's a misconception that "no one likes to be sold to." That's not true at all. The real truth is that no one likes to be sold to *poorly*. When done correctly, it is an absolute pleasure to go through a well-thought-out sales and marketing process. If you're having a great experience that's fun and exciting for you as the customer, you can be sure the provider is serving your needs *for the phase you're in*. Anytime you get frustrated during a sales and marketing process, though, it's because the organization you're interacting with has violated something about that phase. It goes back to the trust issue Jeremy mentioned at the start of this chapter. A bad experience usually means the provider did something to erode the trust you have in them.

Identifying where your customer is on the journey is critical to serving them well. There is simply no better way to attract more patients than to serve them exactly where they are in the patient journey, and there's no better way to lose patients than to violate something about the phase they are in. Making the perfect sales pitch at the wrong time in the process will guarantee you'll lose the customer. Making a mediocre sales pitch at the perfect time in the process will probably get you the sale. It's all about timing and paying attention to the customer's progress through the process.

We will do a deep dive into the five phases of the patient journey over the following three chapters. For now, though, I want to quickly run through each phase to give you an overview of where we're going. And because I'm a car guy, I'll use a current car-based example to follow a typical customer's journey through the five phases.

Phase 1: Awareness

First, there's the *Awareness* phase. This is where the vast majority of our culture is when it comes to plastic surgery. They are aware that

Patient Journey Funnel

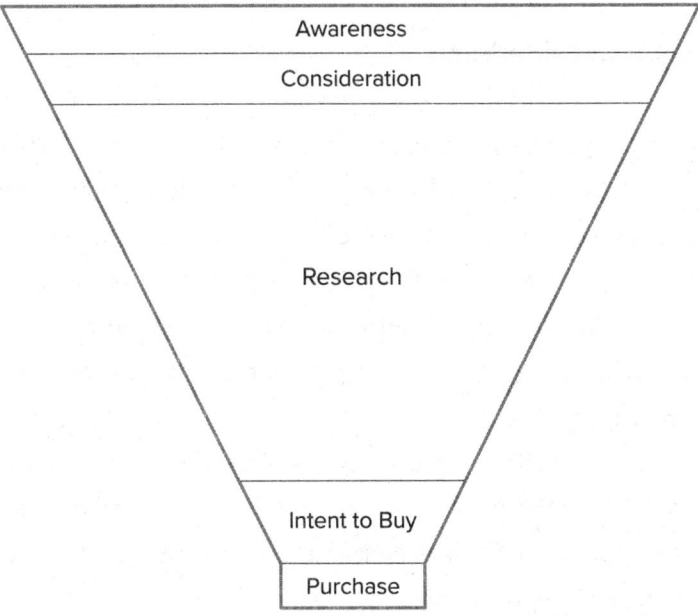

plastic surgery exists, but they aren't putting any regular emotional energy toward it. Maybe they would consider having a cosmetic procedure someday, and maybe they wouldn't. Either way, when it comes to the patient journey, most people are aware that plastic surgery is an option, but they are not actively pursuing it. That puts them in the Awareness phase.

To give you an example from outside the space of plastic surgery, most of us live in the Awareness phase when it comes to Tesla. That is, we've heard of the brand, we've seen it become more common on the road, and/or we've seen the brand's owner, Elon Musk, in the news. We may think Teslas are cool or we may think they are gimmicky. Regardless, we are aware they exist, but most of us are not actively walking down a path that is leading us to purchase one. That means we are in the Awareness phase when it comes to Tesla.

Phase 2: Consideration

Let's say a patient who is in the Awareness phase begins taking steps toward having surgery; the second phase they will enter is called the *Consideration* phase. The Consideration phase is an uncomfortable place for us all to be in because it is full of cognitive dissonance. That is, most of the energy we put toward the Consideration phase happens inside our minds. We aren't *doing* anything yet—no online research, no asking friends, no reaching out to possible providers, no *anything*. We're just... thinking.

The Consideration phase is where a person starts to untangle the mental ball of yarn that was created during the Awareness phase. A potential plastic surgery patient in this phase will find themselves driving down the road asking:

- Am I the type of person who could get plastic surgery?
- What will my mom think if I get plastic surgery?
- What if I don't like my results?
- How much would this even cost?
- What if I end up on an episode of *Botched*?

In the Tesla example, we might think:

- Is it really an all-electric car?
- What happens if I'm on the road and run out of charge?
- How long does it take to recharge?
- Will the money I save on gas make up for the higher sticker price of the car?
- What if Tesla goes bankrupt?

Again, we aren't doing anything but noticing these questions filling up our conscious mind. We know those answers are available; we just haven't started looking for them yet.

Phase 3: Research

The next step after Consideration is called the *Research* phase. This is when the energy moves out of our minds, and we begin to take some form of action. These days, this almost always starts with a barrage of Google searches. While paid Google ads usually fill the top of the list, research-driven consumers are primarily interested in unbiased expertise they feel they can trust. This is why many people find the user reviews on Amazon much more helpful than the actual product description. When we're neck-deep in research, we want to know what others who have real-world, hands-on experience with the product or service think about it.

This is an extremely important moment in the patient journey so I want to risk repeating myself to make sure you hear me clearly: at this point in the process, the patient/consumer is not seeking out the help of a *provider* for whatever they're researching. To be blunt—they do not want to talk to you yet. They want to hear from unbiased sources because they know the providers are trying to sell them something. And they are not ready to be sold to yet. This is probably the phase when you're most likely to lose someone because your sales pitch will not only be unwelcome but may also seem threatening at this point. They'll stiff-arm you just like how we *all* go on the defensive against overly enthusiastic salespeople, effectively saying, "No thanks, I'm just looking."

In the Research phase for our Tesla example, we would spend this time:

- reading tons of articles and reviews about the cars,
- learning which models are available and what the features of each are,
- watching YouTube videos of Tesla owners and professional car reviewers,
- lurking in online Tesla communities and Reddit groups, and/or
- asking questions of Tesla owners we personally know.

While we don't want to talk to a salesperson or fill out a contact form yet, we might even go to Tesla's website and start configuring different car models with the available options.

A key question for most consumers during the Research phase (unless the person is fabulously wealthy) is, "How much is this going to cost?" As we've said a few times already, medical practices are notorious for hiding their pricing. Do not make someone in the Research phase call you or make an appointment to find out the basic cost for your services! At the very least, give them a ballpark just so they can learn—on their own, away from any perceived sales pitch—if a procedure is even possible for them.

Phase 4: Intent to Buy

Once a patient is satisfied with the research they have done, they move on to the *Intent to Buy* phase. During this phase, the patient or consumer has made up their mind that they will likely make a purchase... eventually.

There are still some open questions, of course. Remember, they've only researched on their own, so they don't have all the details figured out yet. Someone considering breast augmentation, for example, may not have the time frame nailed down, and they may not know what size implant to choose, but they are almost certain they will make a purchase. Now, therefore, it's time for them to come out of hiding and start contacting actual providers to find a practice they're comfortable with, meet the surgeon, check scheduling and availability, and get firm pricing information. In the world of plastic surgery, this is where a patient will feel ready to book a consultation.

In the Tesla example, this is when we'd visit a dealership, take a test drive, and maybe apply for financing. Even if we aren't 100 percent sure which model we're going to buy or what color we're going to select, we feel pretty confident that we will purchase a new Tesla soon.

Phase 5: Purchase

The last phase of the patient journey is called the *Purchase* phase. As the name implies, this is when the patient makes the purchase. They've thought about it, researched it, found the best provider for their needs, and received satisfactory answers for all their questions. All that's left is to hand over the money and get the deal done.

In the world of plastic surgery, this is when the patient schedules their procedure and pays either in full or at least a deposit, depending on the practice. The train is moving at full speed now, and very little will stand in the way of them completing the journey.

In the Tesla example, this is, of course, where we'd pay for and take delivery of the car. The journey that began with a general awareness of this strange, new car company has ended with their latest offering parked in our garage.

A Patient/Customer for Life

If you guide a patient through their journey with respect, giving them what they need at each phase—even when what they need is space *away* from you—you'll turn a patient into a fan of your business. Ideally, when the journey is done well, you'll have a patient for life. Plus, by providing excellent service and stewardship throughout their journey, they are now able to proudly tell their friends and family about you and leave a glowing review online. We saw in the Research phase how important these first-person, unbiased testimonies are to future patients.

Now, before we jump into each of the five phases in much greater detail, Jeremy and I need to explain the lenses through which we will examine each phase in the following chapters.

THOUGHTS, EMOTIONS, AND ACTIONS

I am going to ask you to do something right now that you may not be comfortable with. I need you to take off your physician hat. Now I need you to take off the business owner hat you wear *underneath* the physician hat. If you want to get to the heart of your patients' thoughts, emotions, and actions—and specifically to understand them in the context of which of the five phases of the patient journey they're in—you have to totally get out of the doctor/practice-owner mindset. Instead, you need to learn to see things the way *they* are seeing things. This shouldn't be too difficult since we can all relate to the patient/customer journey as consumers. But it won't be comfortable...because it's going to force you to change how you've likely been making decisions for your practice.

It shouldn't surprise you to learn that patients are going to be thinking, feeling, and doing a unique (yet predictable) set of things during each phase of the patient journey. If we can find a way to tailor our approach based on exactly what they're thinking, feeling, and doing *and* on which phase of the journey they're in, we can immediately become much more effective in serving them—and more effective in closing sales.

I realize this creates a certain amount of anxiety. I've worked with enough private practice business owners to know we all have a natural bent toward making *business-first* decisions. That is, we tend to make decisions that make it easier for us to operate as a practice. The problem is, this involves a trade-off we seldom consider. Almost every business-first decision we make will make life more difficult for the people we exist to serve: our patients. Even if it's just a small change here and a tiny tweak there, every time we put the business's needs above the patient's needs, we put more and more distance between us. Ultimately, all those decisions could leave us with an incredibly efficient practice ... with no patients. No patients mean no revenue, and no revenue means no business. If this sounds dramatic, that's because it is. But it's also true. Business-first decisions rarely create the outcome the business wants.

Let me illustrate my point. You've probably heard of CarMax®, the chain of large, sprawling car dealerships, which focuses on a wide selection of quality vehicles and up-front, no-hassle pricing. When the company first opened in the early nineties, it prioritized matching a salesperson to each customer immediately. This made a lot of sense for CarMax as a business; having a salesperson make contact as soon as someone walked in gave employees a chance to collect the customer's information, make a personal connection, and provide a path for personalized follow-up.

However, this created a horrible experience for every customer who walked in. In those early days, a potential car buyer would walk through the front door and immediately hit a wall of salespeople lined up to "attack" (from the customer's point of view). As you can imagine, shoppers hated this. It's not that they didn't want the help of a salesperson at *some* point in their journey; they just didn't want to feel bombarded the moment they arrived and creepily followed around the lot while they were "just looking."

Unsurprisingly, CarMax struggled throughout the early and mid-nineties. Their goal of harvesting customer information immediately left them with too few people sticking around long enough to buy a car. Why? Because they had approached the car-buying process from their own perspective and made business-first decisions. Once they finally got the message and considered what their customers were thinking, feeling, and doing, everything changed. They got rid of the long line of salespeople visibly waiting to pounce and instead had a single salesperson on the showroom floor as a new customer arrived. This friendly salesperson would greet the customer, hand them a card, and say, "Please let me know if there is anything I can do for you while you are browsing our cars. If you want to test drive, talk about financing, or check the stock at a different location, just give me a quick call. No rush. I'll be inside waiting to hear from you."

Once the customer began browsing the lot, a new salesperson would rotate in from the back room to greet the next customer, and the cycle continued, giving every salesperson an opportunity to make "first contact" and giving every customer a less stressful first impression. When CarMax's financial results came in for 2000, they had generated their very first profit. This is what happens when we put the needs of our patients/customers first. Therefore, in the following chapters, we are going to spend a lot of time digging into what a patient is predictably thinking, feeling, and doing during each phase of their patient journey.

Stop Saying "No" First

Jeremy: Robbie frustrated the hell out of me all the time when we first started working together—specifically around making decisions that affected both the business and our patients. To be clear, my frustration was due to the fact that Robbie is so good at looking at things through the patient or customer's eyes. But I'm ... not. Or at least I wasn't.

Early on, I would go to him with a problem and a solution I wanted him to implement. Invariably, he would push back, telling me everything he's shared in this chapter. Mainly, he'd argue that my proposed solution wasn't easy enough for the patient. I would push back, usually with the same response: "Robbie, you just don't understand yet. The medical field is different from what you're used to." I wielded that line like a trump card, and I played it all the time.

We fell into a routine that played out over and over again. I would raise an issue and suggest a mild change to accommodate. Robbie would counter my suggestion by proposing something preposterous. I would resist. Robbie would disappear into his office for a while before returning with an entirely workable plan for his formerly preposterous suggestion—one that would be much more beneficial for the patient. Then I would relent, and we'd put his plan into motion. Every time, this resulted in not only a better experience for the patient but also a better outcome for our business. Every. Single. Time.

After several years, I can now see what was happening back then, and I can recognize that my first instinct when I hear a problem is much different today than it was fifteen years ago.

Like most physicians, I learned how to do my job by watching those who were further ahead of me. And those ahead of me, when asked to implement a change, almost always said no. This was true of doctors, nurses, MAs, techs ... literally everyone I worked with in the hospital system. I learned early and often that, in healthcare, we say no, we say no immediately, and we say no every time. It's our gut reaction to every change.

After years of Robbie pushing back on me so unrelentingly, I've changed. Today, my first answer is almost never no. Going straight to no cuts off creativity. It ends the discussion. Changing that no to even a *maybe* creates a little pause, and that pause is critical. It gives you a moment to dream, to consider, *What if we really could do that?*

What I've found time and time again is that the thing that benefits the patient almost always benefits me and our practice. Our interests are not mutually exclusive; we can both win. In fact, the practice can *only* win when our patients have a good experience. Ultimately, happy patients in need of and buying our services create a happy staff and happy surgeons. That's the real trump card—winning together by focusing on the patient's needs first.

LANE CHANGES AND OFF-RAMPS

Robbie: So we've seen there are five phases of the patient journey, and patients are thinking, feeling, and doing something different at each point. There's still one more thing we need to consider before we can do our deep dive into the journey, and that's how patients move from one phase to another.

Unless a patient gets stuck in their current phase—which we'll talk more about below—there are two options a patient has to continue down their patient journey. The first option is the most obvious: the patient moves from one phase to the next. We call this a *lane change*. Examples are when a patient moves from Consideration to Research or from Research to Intent to Buy. The idea is that the patient will ultimately work their way across all five "lanes" of the patient journey until they take the exit at their destination. In our world, that destination is successfully going through with a plastic surgery procedure.

The second option a patient has is to abandon their patient journey altogether. We call that an *off-ramp*. Regardless of what phase of the journey the patient is in, there is always the possibility that they will decide to take the off-ramp before reaching the destination.

It's worth mentioning that off-ramps, though they may feel like a lost sale, are actually a good thing for your practice. For example, say a woman considering a breast augmentation is in the Research phase. She's only willing to spend $2,000 and, because most practices hide their pricing, she assumes that's enough to move forward. As part of her research, she learns about Amelia Aesthetics and finds our simple pricing on our website. At that point, she realizes she can't afford the procedure at this time. So, she takes the off-ramp. She might come back later after she's saved some more, and she might not. Regardless, it would have been a waste of everyone's time if we had brought her in for a consultation at that point. We don't want a patient changing lanes from Research to Intent to Buy if they aren't ready, so this off-ramp was a good thing for our practice and the patient. Strategically designing obvious off-ramps into each phase of the patient journey is one of the best ways to increase your conversion rate and profitability.

I also want to call out the fact that, on the patient journey, there is no cruise control. That is, with the exception of the Awareness phase, patients do not enjoy being stuck in any one phase for too long. If they don't see an obvious lane change ahead, they'll start looking for the off-ramp. It takes little-to-no energy for people to stay in the Awareness phase; it's where we live our lives on most things. Moving into the Consideration phase requires more mind space and emotional energy. The further we go in the journey, the more mental space the idea takes up and the more emotional energy is required to manage it. If this effort isn't leading us anywhere, we'll exit. We've all done this ourselves a thousand times on purchase decisions.

The patient journey is an uncomfortable place to be. Our brains simply do not enjoy considering big decisions for an extended period. That's why it's so important that we serve a patient where they are in the process, giving them exactly *what* they need *when* they need it so they can make the wisest choice between making a lane change to advance the possibility or taking an off-ramp to put this idea to rest.

QUALIFIED, NOT QUANTITY

Jeremy: Surgeons like me are taught very little about marketing. We aren't taught about sales, finance, or business management either. Our education is entirely focused on the practice of medicine. That's not necessarily a bad thing; we obviously need doctors who know how to give the best medical care to their patients. These doctors graduate, finish their residency, and often start their own practices. That's where new problems arise—problems no one ever warned us about. We know everything we need to know about being a doctor…and nothing about being a business owner.

This leads to a lot of bad assumptions, backward thinking, and wasted energy. The biggest offender in my view is our often-misguided view of marketing. Most new doctors hang up their shingle and assume the best thing to do is invest in advertising to get as many people as possible through the door. That may work in general practice or some other insurance-driven specialty, but it's a total failure when it comes to private, cosmetic, and elective practices. If the patient is personally paying out of pocket for your services, the last thing you want is a flood of people filling your office from an advertising blitz.

The most valuable thing we have is our time—and the wrong person coming through the door wastes far too much of that precious time. Who is "the wrong person"? It's the *unqualified* patient. That's a sales and marketing term that essentially means *someone who can't afford or doesn't really want your product or service*. Scheduling unqualified patients for consultations is a net loss for your business. It costs you some of your time, and you get nothing in return. This happens all the time to practices who hide their pricing and force patients to come in for a "free consultation" before telling them how much their service would cost. This is so strange to me because we all know as consumers that the number one thing the patient wants to know before they ever talk to us is how much a procedure costs. But most practices hide it and then convince the person to come into the office for a consultation. If the patient goes through that only to hear a price that is far outside the realm of possibility for them, everyone loses. Not only did we drag the patient around by the nose, but we also wasted our office staff's time, our nurses' time, and our own time. Plus we wasted a spot on the schedule that could have gone to a better-qualified patient who's ready, willing, and able to follow through with the procedure.

When you guide a patient through their patient journey and when you help them navigate their lane changes and provide clear and easy off-ramps, you're left with happy, well-served patients who not only *can* pay for your services but who are *excited* to pay for your services. It's a win-win for everyone.

With that in mind, let's spend the next few chapters breaking down each step of the patient journey in greater detail, examining their thoughts, emotions, and actions and identifying clear lane changes and off-ramps that ensure we're narrowing our scope to only the best, most-qualified patients.

CHAPTER 11

THE PATIENT JOURNEY PHASES 1 AND 2: AWARENESS AND CONSIDERATION

Robbie: In the previous chapter, we ran though the five phases of the patient journey and talked about the lenses we'll use to examine each one. With that done, let's jump right into the first two phases of the process, Awareness and Consideration, to examine the thoughts, emotions, and actions the patient is experiencing in each one and discuss specific ways we've found at Amelia Aesthetics to help guide a patient through a lane change to the next phase or toward an off-ramp.

PHASE 1: AWARENESS
THOUGHTS, EMOTIONS, AND ACTIONS

Nobody *decides* to enter the Awareness phase. There is no lane change that gets you here. Instead, we're here already. Whatever your medical specialty is, my guess is there are very few people in this country who've *never* heard of it. They certainly don't understand it fully, but they are at least aware of it. That's all it takes to be in the Awareness phase for any given topic. Similarly, it takes no emotional or mental energy to stay in the Awareness phase. In fact, most adults stay in the Awareness phase for any given topic for their entire lives. Take the Tesla example we used in the previous chapter. As of the end of 2021, Tesla had sold around 2,000,000 vehicles. The total adult population of the US is around 335,000,000. That means 99.5 percent of the US adult population might be *aware* of Tesla but have not (yet) become Tesla customers. They may buy one someday, and they may not. Either way, it takes no effort for them to keep Tesla's existence in a tiny corner of their minds, just sitting there until it becomes more relevant to their lives.

Someone in the Awareness phase may technically be on the patient journey as we've defined it, but they are not *actively* on the journey yet. So what are they thinking, feeling, and doing here? Nothing. The Awareness phase is a zero-thought, zero-emotion, and zero-action space on the patient journey. Even though they see it, they aren't pursuing it.

That doesn't mean a person doesn't have an opinion on your specialty, however. When the topic of plastic surgery comes up in conversation, for example, most people have *some* perspective on the matter, and that perspective is usually based on what they've passively heard from others or seen in the media. If a friend or loved one had a life-changing experience through plastic surgery, they may hold it in high regard. More likely, their opinion is driven by the negative stereotypes that are commonly portrayed on social media and reality television. Those extremes are common in practically every field of medicine.

The main lesson for us here is that it does not matter if you agree with what the person thinks or feels about your specialty, especially in the Awareness phase. Their opinion is not a conscious decision they've made; instead, it's largely based on assumption, hearsay, misperception, and stereotypes. But that doesn't mean it's not true. It *is* true . . . for them. Perception is reality. That means, as we try to guide them toward a lane change into the Consideration phase, we have to accept the challenge to overcome whatever negative impression they have about us and our work. Don't be offended by it, but don't ignore it either. Whatever they assume about you is their starting point on the journey, and it's up to you to change their minds by serving them right where they are.

Overcoming Shame and Public Misperception

Jeremy: For years, whenever I met someone outside of work—in a social setting, at a school function with my kids, a new neighbor—the conversation went like this:

"So Jeremy, what do you do?"

"I'm a physician."

"Really? What kind?"

"I'm a surgeon."

"That's so cool! What kind of surgeon?"

Hesitation. My eyes wander. I look to the ground.

"I'm...well...a *plastic* surgeon."

It was as if I didn't want to tell them. Even though I'm immensely proud of what I get to do every day, the term *plastic surgeon* got stuck in my throat. I used to think I was the only one in my field to struggle with this. Turns out, it is a lot more common than I thought.

As I've talked with other plastic surgeons about this, I've realized the reason we often struggle to own our role in aesthetic medicine comes down to one word: *shame*. But it's not my shame. I know what plastic surgery is and how much value it adds to the world. When other people—people outside the industry—hear the words "plastic surgery," though, they get uncomfortable. It's not their fault.

They're simply reacting to the impression Hollywood and Instagram have given them about my field of medicine. They don't picture the thirty-four-year-old mom who's had three kids in five years and has become insecure about her body. They don't see the incredible forty-seven-year-old man who's lost a hundred pounds in the past year and needs help to remove the extra skin his weight loss has left him with. No, most people hear "plastic surgery" and think of all the irritating stereotypes you'd imagine.

It's not their fault. The problem is that we've lost control of the conversation. We've allowed Hollywood to own the conversation, and they present hardworking physicians like me as greedy morons. Heart surgeons get TV series about their brilliance and heroism. Neurosurgeons get documentaries. Transplant surgeons get national news coverage. And plastic surgeons get... *Botched*, *Dr. 90210*'s sleeveless scrubs, and the ex-husbands of the *Real Housewives*. And frankly, many doctors in my field are contributing to this gross misunderstanding of aesthetic medicine. Every day, I see more and more ads on social media promoting some self-aggrandizing, plastic surgeon goofball who's all aglow in Instagram filters and iPhone cinematic mode.

Fellow physicians... we have to stop.

We have to stop contributing to the misperception the general public has about what we do. We have to stop implying that plastic surgery is about making other people jealous. We have to stop the trend on Facebook where grown, intelligent women refer to themselves as *dolls*. Yes, these things are specific to plastic surgery, but I've been around enough doctors to know the same thing likely exists in whatever field you practice.

Why bring this up now when we're supposed to be talking about the patient journey? It's because all the garbage out there about what we do has fed into what the public believes about us and our work. The first two phases of the journey, Awareness and Consideration, aren't based on facts, evidence, and research; they're based on assumption, on a general awareness about the services we provide. Whatever irritating stereotypes bother you the most about your profession, *that's* what most people think about you and your work. The general public lives in the Awareness phase most of the time for most topics, and that awareness is driven by whoever controls the conversation around that topic. That's why it's so difficult to get people to make a lane change from Awareness to Consideration when it comes to plastic surgery: you don't want to be seen as one of *those people* portrayed in the media. You may be ashamed, just like I used to be when I met someone because they don't want to bump up against someone else's misperceptions.

Imagine how many more people we could help if they weren't afraid that their parents, siblings, and friends would think less of them. Imagine how many more people plastic surgeons like me could serve if we could convince them that aesthetic medicine isn't about vanity but about being comfortable and confident in their own skin? Whatever your specialty is, what could you gain and how many more people could you serve if you could simply help them see your industry for what it really is and not what others portray it to be?

Thankfully, there are ways to regain control of the narrative. So let's talk about that.

PHASE 1: AWARENESS
OFF-RAMPS AND LANE CHANGES

Robbie: Amnesia and dementia notwithstanding, there is no off-ramp for the Awareness phase. Once you're aware of something, there's no going back. You either stay in the Awareness phase forever or you change lanes into the Consideration phase. So that's where we'll start, using plastic surgery as our example.

People in the Awareness phase have a passively formed opinion about plastic surgery, but they are not actively considering having a procedure done. What can we do with that information? Given that we currently have our sales and marketing hats on, the entire goal of your sales and marketing efforts within the Awareness phase is to simply get people thinking. The only reason someone will make a lane change out of the Awareness phase and into Consideration is if someone gives them a compelling enough reason to reconsider their existing beliefs. Those beliefs aren't necessarily negative either. Someone could have a positive view of plastic surgery in general but simply not believe it's for them, at least not right now. To get them to consider it at all, you have to challenge that paradigm in a compelling way.

Here's an example from outside the medical industry: The first "Got Milk?" TV commercial aired in 1993. Titled "Who Shot Alexander Hamilton?" the one-minute spot features a guy sitting in his home, listening to classical music, and making a peanut butter sandwich. The camera pans around his surroundings. There are multiple portraits and busts of Alexander Hamilton. There's an entire bookcase labeled "Hamilton's Memoirs." There's a depiction of Hamilton's famous fatal duel with Aaron Burr. There are two eighteenth-century pistols facing each other on display, and there's an old, round bullet in a glass case labeled "The Bullet." Clearly, this man is a huge history buff and Alexander Hamilton fanatic.

As he stuffs his entire peanut butter sandwich into his mouth, the radio host announces the $10,000 question of the day: "Who shot Alexander Hamilton?"

"Let's go to the phones," the announcer says.

THE PATIENT JOURNEY PHASES 1 AND 2: AWARENESS AND CONSIDERATION

The phone rings. Mouth full of peanut butter, the historian's eyes open wide with excitement as he answers. "Hehwoh?"

"Hello! For $10,000 ... who shot Alexander Hamilton?"

Proudly, but fighting through the wad of sandwich in his mouth, he proclaims, "Awon Buh!"

"Excuse me?" The radio host can't understand him.

"Awon Buh! Awon Buh!" It is no use. He can't swallow the sandwich and he can't get his tongue unstuck. He frantically grabs the milk carton, but there are only a few drops left. Time is running out!

"I'm sorry," the voice says. "Maybe next time." *Click!*

The screen fades to black as the man whimpers, "Awon Buh" one last, sad time. And the soon-to-be iconic phrase "Got Milk?" appears onscreen.

The hapless historian lost. But the milk industry won—big time.

Over the next twelve months, a twenty-year decline in milk sales miraculously came to an end and the California milk industry saved more than $250 million—all because a brilliant marketing agency found a way to remind consumers how terrible it can be to run out of milk.

In short, they got people thinking about something familiar in a new, more urgent way. As a result, as people went about their regular grocery shopping, that question rang in their minds: *got milk?* Most people have no idea how much milk they have in the fridge, so why not pick up a carton just in case?

Now, back to plastic surgery. At Amelia Aesthetics, we've found two strategies that have helped us get people thinking, which then causes them to reconsider their existing paradigm about plastic surgery. These two strategies have specifically helped us create lane-change moments, moving people out of Awareness and into Consideration, thereby activating their patient journey.

First, we have learned that *meeting* someone *moves* someone. When any of us meets someone else who is like us yet has a much different belief system than we have, it surprises us. As a result, we naturally begin to challenge our own belief system. For example, picture someone who has a stereotypical negative view of plastic surgery. If we can compel that person to watch a touching patient video about a young mother who had regained her confidence and overcome her deep insecurities with a procedure, the natural byproduct is a newfound open-mindedness. This is also why word-of-mouth referrals are especially powerful. Meeting someone moves someone.

Second, we've found tremendous success by investing in our local business community. This has become one of our passions. We've developed many deep business relationships among our corporate neighbors throughout the Raleigh area, and I love how surprised other business owners are when we express genuine interest in what they are doing for our community and for the world at large. Not only does this give Jeremy and me opportunities to "talk shop" with other leaders, but this investment of time has also created a positive, powerful reputation for Amelia Aesthetics as a strong, vibrant North Carolina business. And in doing so, it's forced other well-respected and influential professionals in our area to reconsider any preexisting negative beliefs they had about the practice of plastic surgery. Again, it's gotten them to think about us and our field in a whole new way, which is the key to moving someone out of the Awareness phase and into a more active phase of the journey.

Help Them See Themselves

Jeremy: Dale Carnegie, the legendary author behind *How to Win Friends and Influence People*, famously said, "Talk to someone about themselves, and they'll listen for hours." If I had to distill everything I've learned about marketing into one simple statement, that'd be it. If marketing is about reaching people, then that marketing has to be *about* those people—the ones we're trying to reach. That's why real estate agents encourage you to remove family pictures and personalized décor before they list your home for sale. It's why you never see the face of the driver in a car commercial (unless it's a celebrity). Advertisers know that buyers want to immediately be able to see *themselves* living in that home or driving that car. Once you list your house, it isn't *your home* anymore. It's a model home. It's generic. It's a blank slate that the homebuyer can seamlessly step into. It isn't about you; it's about them.

Our marketing for Amelia Aesthetics is no different. Someone is more likely to consider a cosmetic procedure if they can see themselves getting that surgery—not because they see a picture of a beautiful model and not because they're impressed with the doctor's credentials. It's because, when they look at us, we help them see a slightly improved version of themselves. We've learned how to give our potential patients a way to see themselves in our media. As a result, more and more people are trusting us to help them discover that new version of themselves.

Most plastic surgery marketing does the opposite. We make it about how good we, the doctors, are. We talk about how good we are at surgery, where we've practiced, who we've worked with, how well we care for our patients, and so on. It's all about us. Why is that? Well, it's because we've depended on the wrong people for marketing support.

Plastic surgeons are not trained in marketing or advertising. It would be unreasonable to expect us to be experts at everything we need to be medical experts *and*—without any additional education or training—to be good marketers as well. This is a need we outsource to "the professionals." As such, physicians have traditionally leaned on predatory plastic surgery marketing companies. But there's a problem. When we speak to one of these marketing companies, *we* are the customer. They are the professionals, the ones with the formal training in education who know how to sell. And they use all those skills to sell to *us*.

Do you see the problem? They are focusing their marketing efforts on us, not on the patients. They are more focused on selling us their marketing plan than they are on selling our services to potential patients. These professional marketers are effectively selling me ... to me. And I was buying it! I get so mad when I think about all the time and money I wasted on marketing that made me look great but did little to drive our business forward or reach the audience we wanted to reach.

Once I learned about marketing and thought about how backwards ours was, our marketing shifted immediately to focus on the patient. Since we primarily serve women, we changed everything about our practice to make it more comfortable and appealing to women. Our entire patient experience was refocused to better enable a patient to see herself when she interacted with our office. We even changed the name of the business itself. Up to that point, our practice was named Davis and Pyle Plastic Surgery. Why? Because it was *our* names, the names of two male surgeons—me and Dr. Glenn Davis, whom I've mentioned previously. We were marketing who *we* were. We changed our name to Amelia Aesthetics because that's who the *patient* is. Amelia—named for aviator Amelia Earhart—is a stand-in for all the brave, bold, powerful women we want to work with. We didn't even choose the name; our patients did. We asked them to help us choose a new name, and Amelia was the runaway winner.

Marketing gives you the ability to track everything, including how people react to your ads, which piece of media first leads them to your site, how long they stay on each page, which emails are most compelling, and just about everything else. What we've found by sifting through all this information is that people interact with companies that look and feel like them and use language they use and do things they do. That kind of customer-first approach is rare in medicine, so it has made us stand out from the crowd. And it can do the same for you.

Remember, the customer will not leave the easy, stress-free comfort of the Awareness phase unless you give them a reason to do so. That reason *has* to be about them. They won't make a big life change simply because they think you're cool. They'll only do it if they see how it can make their own life better.

PHASE 2: CONSIDERATION
THOUGHTS, EMOTIONS, AND ACTIONS

Robbie: Once the patient is able to see themselves improving their life through your services, questions will begin to creep into their minds. This is the start of the Consideration phase. This is typically the shortest phase of the patient journey, consisting of about 5 percent of the total experience. However, it is a critical time. You can think of Consideration as the short bridge that takes the customer out of the passive Awareness phase and into an active observation of your business. If they don't cross this bridge, they'll never even bother to learn how you might be able to serve them. I'm going to stick with plastic surgery as our example here because it's what I know best, and the principles are applicable across different fields. If you're a psychologist, dentist, or anything else, I'm sure you can see how this will apply to your practice.

Consideration is unique among the five phases of the patient journey in that it is entirely emotional. Facts, statistics, and qualifications are irrelevant here; this is all about how the patient *feels* about the type of services you offer. Here the patient is forced to untangle the ball of emotional yarn they've created in their minds—especially around the topic of plastic surgery. As we've said, people generally have preexisting ideas about what plastic surgery is and the type of person they think would have a cosmetic procedure done. The Consideration phase is so emotionally charged because it forces the patient to test and challenge their existing paradigms. They were comfortable in their assumptions for years in the Awareness phase, but then something crashed into their life that caused them to begin a patient journey. Something made them start thinking—and those thoughts are probably annoying the hell out of them.

Many patients spend a significant amount of time arguing with themselves, having mental conversations like, *I'm not the type of person who would get plastic surgery... am I? What would my mother think? Can I even afford it? Will my friends be embarrassed to go to the beach with me? What if something goes wrong? What if someone sees my scars during an intimate moment? How would I explain this to my kids? How long would I be stuck in bed recovering? How would this affect my exercise routine?*

It's also common for patients to begin vetting these ideas with their closest friends and loved ones. They might start dropping little hints to see how others react to the topic, such as, "Hey, did you hear Cathy had some work done? I saw her the other day and thought she looked great." Or, "You know, I've started getting random plastic surgery ads in my Instagram feed. It kinda makes you think, doesn't it?" These are simple ways to introduce the topic into a conversation—little trial balloons people use to test their own judgments against the reactions of those closest to them.

THE PATIENT JOURNEY PHASES 1 AND 2: AWARENESS AND CONSIDERATION

If this sounds over the top, it's important to remember that what's normal in our lives as medical professionals is far from normal for the average person. We get so comfortable with the idea of plastic surgery, the safety of plastic surgery, and the outcomes of plastic surgery, that it's easy for us to forget how uncomfortable, potentially dangerous, and scary any kind of elective surgery can be to a newcomer.

But even beyond that, let's think strategically for a moment about what this phase teaches us. And at the risk of being offensive, there's a really, *really* important principle we have to discuss. It's a principle that—in our little ego-filled bubbles—the entire field of plastic surgery has seemingly forgotten about. Here it is: Your competition is not the handful of other plastic surgeons in your city. If we as private practice and business owners continue to believe our competition is *one another*, we're missing the bigger picture. Patients don't start comparing surgeons to each other until the late stages of the patient journey. Here at the beginning, they're comparing our industry as a whole to other industries.

As patients move through the Consideration phase, their questions shift from judging themselves—*Am I the kind of person who would do this?*—to judging the industry itself. Those questions might sound like, "If I have this much money to spend, shouldn't I spend it on something else instead? My family could really use a new car. We could take a dream vacation for this amount. Maybe I should use it to finish my degree."

Again, your competition is not the handful of surgeons in your area; your competition is Tesla, Disney World, and state universities—and they are *way* better at sales and marketing than you are. If you believed your website was going to be compared to tesla.com, I bet you would have hired a better design agency. If you believed the quality of your photography was going to be compared to Disney's photos, I bet you'd insist on better quality before-and-afters. If you believed your value proposition would be compared to a business degree, I bet you'd do better than "500 off your breast augmentation."

I know this sounds harsh, but when our team stopped paying attention to what was happening across the street and started paying attention to what was actually happening in our patients' lives, we immediately noticed dozens of things we needed to change and/or improve. And when we did, we experienced dramatic results in both the number of qualified patients we had walking in and in the quality of the experience we were able to provide them. If we would all start paying attention to what our patients are paying attention to, there would be more demand for our services than our entire industry could meet!

Our Own Consideration Phase

Jeremy: Remember back when you were a med student trying to figure out what exactly you were going to spend your career doing? It was a short period when you already knew you were going to be a physician but didn't know for sure what *kind* of physician you were going to be. You probably had these random thoughts filling your head as you drove down the interstate or lay down to go to sleep. *Could I do this? Am I cut out for that? Which do I find more interesting? Which is more challenging? Do I like that kind of challenge, or do I prefer something simpler?* Those thoughts drove me crazy for a little while.

That's the Consideration phase. A big part of that short, emotionally charged season of my life was spent trying to figure out who "my people" were. Then within the first hour of my surgery rotation, I felt at home. Surgeons immediately felt like "my people." Seeing myself in that world, performing surgery every day, was perfectly natural. That was it. The questions that had been keeping me up at night evaporated. I knew I was going to be a surgeon. With that decision, I moved out of the Consideration phase and into Research.

I imagine you know exactly what I'm talking about. Most doctors remember that time in their lives, but they never stop to see how it relates to the path a patient takes from simple awareness to going through with a procedure. Notice it. Draw on your own experience. Remember how emotionally charged that season was for you. Now use it to better understand where your potential patients are and how they're feeling on their journey—and, of course, how you can help them navigate the lane changes and off-ramps ahead.

PHASE 2: CONSIDERATION OFF-RAMPS AND LANE CHANGES

Robbie: When a patient decides to take the off-ramp from within the Consideration phase, it's typically because they weren't able to justify getting surgery, or they weren't ready to clear the hurdles they felt certain would be in their way.

While they're taking the off-ramp, some common things patients tell themselves are:

- Plastic surgery just isn't who I am.
- My life is too complicated to consider this right now.
- The timing isn't right for me.
- My family would never accept my decision.
- I need to use this money for something else.

They stopped trying to untangle that ball of emotional yarn and instead decided to put it back on the shelf for another time. It's not that they didn't decide to do *something*; it's more likely that they chose something *else* besides plastic surgery. That's why not competing with one another, which we talked about earlier, is so critical for the long-term health of our industry. If the patient bails out at this stage, they didn't reject *you*. They rejected plastic surgery—at least for the time being. It could be an indicator that we as an industry aren't doing a good enough job overcoming the negative impression many people have about what we do.

It's also worth saying that taking the off-ramp is very often the right decision. Don't assume that someone exiting the patient journey early means a mistake was made. As we've said, we should be pursuing *qualified* patients. If a patient removes themselves from the process at this point, there's a good chance they never would have gone through with the procedure anyway. It's better for them to leave the journey here before wasting more of their time or any of yours.

But what about those patients who decide to keep going down this road? Those who look to the future and think, *You know what? This might actually be the right choice for me right now.* Remember, the active patient journey is an emotionally uncomfortable place to be, and the Consideration phase is especially uncomfortable. So as soon as a patient gets that ball of emotional yarn untangled, they are ready to make a lane change into the next phase.

To be clear, they have not decided to have surgery at this point. Instead, they have decided that they're comfortable enough with the idea of plastic surgery that they want to know more about it. They know they're on their way to a decision, but that decision will require research. This is the moment when they advance out of Consideration and move into the Research phase.

ACTION REQUIRES CLARITY

Jeremy: Medical school is hard. Actually ... it sucks. Early on, it sucks because the classwork is overwhelming. Halfway through, it sucks because of the crippling anxiety of not knowing for sure if the desired next step in your career is going to work out or if you made the right decision at all. Then, in the third year (at most schools), you have your first clinical year. That's the first time you get to walk the halls with the people in medicine and start to get a feel for who "your people" are—and who they aren't. The clinical experience tends to confirm your decision to focus on a particular field or it proves you made the wrong choice after all.

Either way, there is some newfound clarity, and that clarity enables you to take action, to take the next step in your education and career by diving headfirst into research mode, learning everything you can about your specific field of medicine. Looking back, I see that the moment I decided for certain that I wanted to go into plastic surgery is the moment my focus sharpened. Instead of spending my time wondering what I should do for the next six years, I spent it learning about everything I could do in those six years, how I could position myself to succeed, and what success would even look like. Once I had clarity, everything else fell into place.

That's what it feels like when a patient moves out of the Consideration phase of the patient journey. There's clarity in being able to say, "Yes, this really is something I'm interested in pursuing. I'm ready to take the next step." And that clarity is what enables them to enter the Research phase and ultimately end up in your office for a consultation. Every patient you meet for a consult has already been through an emotional journey just to get that far. Now, finally, you have the chance to personally help direct their next steps, to make sure the path ahead of them is well-lit and filled with the information they need to make the best decision for themselves and their health. Let's talk about how to do that next.

CHAPTER 12
THE PATIENT JOURNEY PHASE 3: RESEARCH

Jeremy: Confession time: Robbie and I both, for different reasons, were extremely hesitant to include a section on sales and marketing in this book and in our online course. We went back-and-forth on it for a while, and while it could very well be the most valuable information in our material, it almost didn't make the cut.

From Robbie's perspective—and he may not like me saying this—our sales and marketing techniques are what separates Amelia Aesthetics from every other plastic surgery practice in the world. It is one of our key unique differentiators as a business. For that reason, this information is immensely valuable. Giving that information away for free (or for the cost of this book), represents a big risk for our practice. What if every plastic surgery practice in the country started doing this? Wouldn't that negatively impact our business?

Well...yes.

However, we know every plastic surgery practice will *not* implement our approach to sales and marketing. Nowhere close. The reason is that most practices aren't willing to wait for this process to work. It's slow. It's not an overnight fix. If you've seen anything from the way we run our practice, it's that we carefully implement slow-moving solutions with an eye on the long game. We aren't running a sprint; we're plodding along in a double Ironman competition. That takes time. It requires a long-term investment with a slow draw. It's not the flashy, sexy solution most practices are looking for.

We went all-in on our revamped sales and marketing approach in March 2020—the month the entire world came to a screeching halt due to COVID-19. It seemed like the perfect time since our business was already facing unprecedented interruptions. If there was ever a time to risk short-term profits by making a long-term play in implementing a system that had never been tried in the world of private practice, this was it. Regardless, we knew it would take at least a year to see any payoff whatsoever. That's because much of our new process was focused on educating the consumer, and education doesn't have an immediate payoff. Plus, when you educate the aesthetic medicine consumer—or at least when you educate them honestly—you make it *less likely* that some people will ever book a consultation. Your overall volume of potential patients dips, and that scares most practices away.

In 2020, we decided it was worth the risk. We had time to be patient, and we were willing to sacrifice several months of profits in exchange for a decade or more of new growth and opportunity.

And…it worked. We went from a two-week waiting list for surgery to a several-month waiting list. Then we had to add another surgeon. Even then, our waiting list grew absurdly long for all of our providers. That was without any big publicity stunts, "sales," spectacles, or me dancing on TikTok. No offense to you TikTokers out there; I'm just not a good enough dancer.

So Robbie's hesitation was that we'd be giving away our key differentiator. My hesitation was different. I was worried that you wouldn't believe us.

That may sound strange, but it's a concern based on experience. We've had many surgeons spend time with us in our Raleigh office, and we are open about everything we do—our processes, resources, tools we've developed, and even our financial information. The feedback I've heard time and again is either,

- they think we're lying to them or at least holding back some key information, or
- they grossly underestimate how difficult it is and how long it takes to do what we've done.

As a result, I come across looking like either a liar or a simpleton. Neither is a good option for me. So I seriously considered holding back this information.

In the end, obviously, Robbie and I agreed that this part of *The Private Practice MBA* is too important to leave out. What good is teaching you how to get your money, operations, and leadership in great shape if we don't also help you get the right people in the door? As we move into this discussion on Research, then, I'm going to ask you to suspend your disbelief. What you're going to read in this chapter will probably cut against everything you think you know about educating a patient—especially if you're a plastic surgeon. But hang with us. If you're willing to do what we've done and risk a short-term lull in exchange for long-term growth, I imagine *this* is the missing piece of the puzzle you likely need the most.

PHASE 3: RESEARCH
THOUGHTS, EMOTIONS, AND ACTIONS

Robbie: The Research phase is almost certainly the most neglected, unappreciated, misunderstood, and undervalued phase in the entire patient journey. To be blunt, this is the area practices screw up the most. Is that mildly offensive? Probably. Does that make it untrue? Not even close. Remember, the business of medicine is sick. The only way to get the business of medicine back on its feet is to honestly diagnose the problems and provide a new treatment plan. Few things we'll talk about in this book are more radical than our approach to sales and marketing—and specifically the Research phase, the phase when the medical consumer gets educated.

Picking up where we left off in the previous chapter, we have a patient who has been through the Awareness phase and has just finished the Consideration phase. At this point, the individual has spent time addressing the nagging questions going through their mind and has decided they need more information before they can either exit the process or take the next step toward treatment. What do you think this person is thinking, feeling, and doing here?

The Research phase is all about the patient's information-gathering. We all know what this is like. Say you were considering a dream vacation for you and your family. You can imagine the overwhelming number of questions you'd need to find answers for: where you should go, when you should go, how far in advance you'd need to book, how much it would cost, who offers the best flights, what the weather is like there, when the best time of year is for that destination, how hotels compare to Airbnbs there, and a million other "unknowns."

The Research phase is no different for those considering plastic surgery. They go into it with a long list of questions, no idea where to start looking for answers, and a general distrust of most providers as a source of fair, unbiased, and non-sales-driven information. With no other options, they do what we all do when we have questions like this: they start with Google.

To be clear:

- **They are thinking,** *How am I going to find answers to all these questions?*
- **They are feeling overwhelmed,** insecure about what they don't know, and unsure of who to trust.
- **They are doing a lot of research,** starting with Googling their high-level questions, such as patient experiences/testimonials, details about the procedure, and cost.

And this, my friend, is where the business of medicine—and plastic surgery in particular—overtly underserves our patients. For whatever reason, we've made it much more difficult than it needs to be for patients to get the answers they need to make a quality, informed decision. We believe this largely comes down to three myths private practice providers have come to believe about this phase of the patient journey, so let's pull back a bit and explore these three myths, how they're affecting your business, and how you can change your view on these common misperceptions.

MYTH #1: THE PHYSICIAN SHOULD BE THE EDUCATOR

The first myth our industry believes is that plastic surgery education should come exclusively from a surgeon. This myth is so harmful because it seemingly forces patients to get their early information from the one group of people they do not trust: us, the providers. They don't trust surgeons, business owners, or anyone on their staff... yet. Of course, we want them to trust us, and hopefully they will in the future, but it's too much to ask the patient to lay down their natural—and *healthy*—suspicions right at the start of their search for answers. Why? Because they know we have something to gain by their decision to move forward. Think about it: how many car salesmen would tell a potential buyer *not* to buy a car? We wouldn't trust a salesperson to help us make the decision that's best for *us* because we know what's best for *them* is to make a sale.

I'm not suggesting that's actually your motivation, and I'm sure you'd never actively talk a patient into any medical procedure that would be dangerous or unnecessary. But they don't know that. The bottom line is that they don't trust you yet. They have their guard up just like any wise consumer would.

When any of us enter the Research phase of a patient or customer journey, we all want the same thing: clear, accessible answers from an unbiased source. So in the first half of this phase, the patient will go out of their way to avoid talking directly to a provider, whether that's a surgeon, a salesperson, a business owner, or any member of your team. Requiring them to talk to a provider before they're ready will likely either scare them off or feed their existing distrust in you and your practice.

Now, please do not misunderstand. I'm not saying that surgeons and salespeople don't have a role in the patient's journey. They absolutely do. I'm simply saying they don't have a place in *this part* of the patient's journey. That's actually good news because when you realize you don't have to be the one to personally do all the education, you're suddenly freed up to do a whole lot more, which we'll talk about in a bit.

My Hardest Job

Jeremy: My hardest job isn't being a surgeon or a business owner. The hardest job I have—the hardest job I've *ever* had—is coaching my kids' soccer teams. Young children are high-energy, low-focus, no-filter little humans with zero regard for order. It can be chaos on the field at any given moment. I've coached my older son's team for seven seasons now, sticking with many of the same boys as they've grown. After seeing these little boys grow into young men, I've noticed something remarkable: they are starting to coach *themselves* and teach *each other*. One kid will see an opportunity to improve his teammate's game, and he'll pull him aside and "coach" him through it. It's a thing of beauty. These guys are learning that the best advice doesn't have to come from the coach; it can come from their peers. As ruthlessly difficult as coaching is 90 percent of the time, these moments make it all worthwhile.

What does that have to do with our practice's sales and marketing? For years, the hardest part of my job as a surgeon came down to two things:

1. Staying mentally engaged in consultations while repeating the same basic information the same way for the twelfth time that week (which usually includes debunking a lot of bad information the patient read online).
2. Encouraging a post-op patient who is struggling mentally because the result is not what they expected.

Over the past few years, though, I've realized I can avoid these situations by helping the patient find the best information early in their research—and by personally backing out of that early education as much as possible.

At Amelia Aesthetics, we've invested a lot of time and money into an educational resource called Bustmob Academy, which we've separated from our plastic surgery business in both branding and marketing. We're not trying to "hide" our connection to this resource, but we are intentional about not injecting the Amelia Aesthetics brand

and surgeons into it unnecessarily. We know the prospective patient doesn't want that at the start of their research, so we make the information available, and then we back off, giving the patient the opportunity to learn everything they need without worrying about a salesperson emailing them five times a day to set up a consultation.

Our resource is video-driven curriculum that breaks down the most common plastic surgery procedures and answers the questions people are most likely to ask. It also includes a huge social component in which patients of *any* plastic surgery practice can interact, encourage one another, answer questions, and offer support to those who are struggling or who are simply interested in learning more. The best part is that I'm not the one doing all the talking and teaching. They bring me in for some Q&A every now and then, but it's clear I'm only there as a resource. The first time someone meets me, then, they've already learned all the basics from other peer-level instructors, they don't see me as someone who's trying to make a sale, and our practice hasn't bugged the hell out of them for the past month, trying to coerce them into something.

The result is that almost all my consultations now are with patients who have a strong knowledge base of the procedure we're discussing, they're qualified—in that they already know what they're in for *and* how much it'll cost—they're excited to be here, and they're grateful for how we've treated them so far. I spend much less time having to convince them that Dr. Google was wrong, and I have fewer post-op patients who are surprised by their results or swelling. Instead, I just get to meet people, hear their stories, make a plan for their care, and then return them to the educational system I know will continue to nurture them.

Robbie: Where does that leave us? If we shouldn't even try to get involved in this part of the patient journey, are we supposed to just sit back, cross our fingers, and hope qualified patients magically appear in our office? Of course not. Instead, we must meet the patient where they are and give them what they want: clear, accessible answers from an unbiased source. That's why we must overcome the *second* myth of sales and marketing...

MYTH #2: INFORMATION ISN'T FREE

The second myth our industry believes is that information isn't free. That is, we believe research should come at a cost.

One of my favorite marketing experts, Donald Miller, has an entire curriculum and book called *StoryBrand* around this idea. As Miller explains, there are two critical roles at play in every consumer journey: the "Character" and the "Guide." The Character is the consumer who has a problem or felt need, and the Guide is the professional who knows how to solve that problem. In this model, then, you are the Guide, and your patient is the Character. Your job is to guide the patient along a journey that will lead them to the outcome they desire.

This is the same dynamic that's at play in your favorite movies. In *Star Wars*, Luke is the Character and Obi-Wan Kenobi is the Guide. Forty years later, in *The Last Jedi*, Rey is the new Character and Luke has grown into the Guide role. In *The Hunger Games*, it's Katniss and Haymitch. In *The Wizard of Oz*, it's Dorothy and Glinda the Good Witch. In *The Karate Kid*, it's Daniel and Mr. Miyagi. In *The Matrix*, it's Neo and Morpheus. Over and over, we see the clear presentation of the Character and the Guide. But there is one more element we cannot overlook—and this is where many businesses screw things up. In each of these movie examples, who would you say is the *hero*? Is it Kenobi, Haymitch, or Glinda who saves the day in the final climactic moments of the film? Of course not. The hero is never the Guide; the hero of every story is the Character.

As Miller explains, the story is always about the main character, not the supporting cast. And the Character wants to be the hero of their own story. We all bristle when a Guide enters into our story and tries to steal the show, don't we? This is the person we go to for advice who then attempts to take over, tell us what to do, and relegate us to a supporting role in our own lives. That never works. We are each living our own lives, and we each want to be the hero of the story our life is telling. So when we as consumers have a problem, we want to find a Guide who doesn't position themselves as the hero. Instead, we want our Guide to come alongside us, offer perfectly timed advice and counsel, point us to the solution, and then get out of the way.

OK, let's take this out of fantasyland and see what the Character–Guide relationship looks like in real life. Here's how you as the physician know you're positioning yourself as the hero in your patient's story: if you don't make it easy for them to learn virtually everything they need to know about the service or procedure they're considering *without talking to you*. You simply aren't much of a Guide if you are actively hiding the answers they need. It's more likely that you are holding that "secret" information back so you can swoop in as the hero and save the day. But they don't want you to save the day. Your patients aren't helpless; they're heroes. They simply need someone to provide directions to the next step in their personal heroic journey.

Plastic surgeons who position themselves as the hero almost always view information and education as something to hold with an iron grip. We know from experience what information they need, but we still wait for them to ask the right questions before we educate them properly. In doing so, we essentially force the patient to pry the information out of our tightly clenched fist ... and then we blame the customer when we "lose the sale." Information about our services and education about the procedures we perform should be free. They are essential pieces of the journey our potential patients are on. And remember, the end goal of this journey is for these people to fully become our patients by coming to us for our services and then becoming champions who help promote our brand to their friends, family, and anyone who will listen. Providing the information they need—when they need it and how they need it—isn't just what's best for the patient; it's what is best for us as well!

Don't Be the Sales Rep We All Hate

Jeremy: How many times a week does a sales rep show up in your office, unannounced and with no appointment, asking for a few minutes of your or your office manager/business director's time? When that happens, especially if it's someone you don't even know, do you ever tell your front-of-house team to send them away? Of course you do. We all do, because in that situation, we know the rep is showing up on their schedule, not ours. They're here for their benefit, not ours. They want to show us what *they* want us to see when *they* want us to see it so *they* can make a sale. How in the world did it become an industry norm for salespeople to show up in a busy physician's office and expect to be seen immediately? If we can't do that for our patients, why should we do it for pushy salespeople?

To be clear, not all salespeople are like this—and that's my point. You probably immediately thought of a half-dozen examples of a bad sales experience as you read the preceding paragraph. But you also probably thought of a handful of excellent sales reps you enjoy working with. What I want you to see is that our potential patients see us the same way we view sales reps. There are the good ones who help us make wise, well-informed decisions that we're comfortable with ... and there are those who think if they can just get a minute of facetime with a potential customer, they'll magically charm and wow their way into a big sale. Don't be that person.

Robbie said, "Information about our services and education about the procedures we perform should be free." This means a patient should never have to pay actual money to receive the vital information they need to make a good decision about a procedure. It also means it should be freely available, not tethered to anything ... such as a consult. I've tried for years to figure out why we doctors are so secretive with our knowledge. I don't believe we actively *want* to withhold information; I think we simply aren't taught how and why to make it free.

When I was a resident, I once sat in a private practice plastic surgeon's office discussing sales and marketing with the business owner. He taught me what I'm sure his mentors taught him twenty years earlier: the goal is to get the patient in the office for a face-to-face encounter. Once they're in the office in front of you, he explained, they are much more likely to become a patient. I'm sure that's what the bad sales reps we all hide from think too. But is that what we, as consumers, want? Do we want to schedule an appointment, travel across town, sit in a waiting room for a consult that's running thirty minutes late, and make small talk with a stranger in order to get the same information we could have gotten on a webpage or five-minute YouTube video? Is that what you want when you're considering a new car, investment, or home purchase? No.

As we've said a few times, there is nothing wrong with face-to-face meetings *at the right time*. What we usually get wrong, though, is when that *right time* is. In Donald Miller's parlance, that's for the main character to decide... and we're not the main character in this story. When a patient is ready to sign up for surgery or interview a few providers, an in-person meeting is totally appropriate—but not until the patient is ready for that step.

I have nothing but respect for the surgeon who gave me that sales and marketing advice when I was a resident, but he was wrong on this issue. The consultation should not be about forcing an early face-to-face meeting, educating the patient on the basics of the procedure, or making a sale. The consultation should be laser-focused on making a plan. So let's talk about how to make the most of that precious time between doctor and patient, by debunking the most harmful myth about the Research phase.

MYTH #3: CONSULTATIONS SHOULD BE EARLY IN THE RESEARCH PHASE

Robbie: The third myth about the Research phase we need to dispose of is that consultations should come early in a patient's research and that they should be seen as the primary way a patient should do their research. Wrong on both counts. Of the three myths we've been talking about, this is undoubtedly the most harmful and costly of them all—for patients, for surgeons, and especially for your business.

The Research phase makes up about 85 percent of the entire patient journey, meaning patients are going to spend the vast majority of their active patient journey doing research. And don't miss this: the patient does not decide to go through with a procedure until they enter the Intent to Buy phase. That means everyone who is still in the Research phase has not even decided if they'll go through with it yet—and yet we still bring them into the office as early as we can.

This is terribly inefficient for one mind-blowing reason: Most private practice surgeons intuitively believe they have a consultation-to-surgery conversion rate of around 70 percent. And yet, when the data is actually measured, only 30 to 33 percent of patients who have a consult go through with the procedure *with that surgeon*.[14] They'll likely have surgery eventually, but statistically speaking, it will be with someone else. And that's not because they actively want to choose a different surgeon; it's likely because they simply were not ready to make a decision after one conversation.

That's the result of bringing unqualified potential patients in for a face-to-face consultation. None of us should be comfortable knowing that one in three patients who have a consultation with us will ever go on to have surgery with us. Further, why would you as the most expensive member of your team be investing so much time and resources into a patient who statistically is so unlikely to have surgery with you? This costs you a fortune in opportunity cost, and you don't even realize it.

Let's say a typical consultation takes an hour of your time. If the patient decides to go through with that procedure, then that's an hour well spent. However, knowing that only three in ten patients who have a consult ultimately have the procedure, it was most likely an hour you wasted. It's reasonable to assume a plastic surgeon can generate around $4,000 of revenue per hour in the operating room, so every hour you spend on an ill-timed patient consultation is *costing* your practice $4,000 in unrealized surgical revenue. Want to feel queasy? Try this: look up the number of consultations you did last year that did not go through with the procedure. Multiply that number by $4,000.

That's how much revenue you missed out on by forcing unqualified patients to come in for a consultation instead of making that basic information freely available to them without a face-to-face meeting. If you have multiple providers, spread that exercise out across them as well to see the opportunity cost your total practice is paying for doing consultations wrong. My guess is you'll want to throw up. And then you'll want to change how you do consults.

If you could make a change to how and when you do consultations, and if that change resulted in a 2x increase in your consultation-to-surgery conversion rate, you could *double* your revenue by doubling the amount of time you're spending in the operating room. This practice is the main reason our practice went from a two-week waiting list for one surgeon to an eight-month waiting list for multiple surgeons!

When SHOULD Consultations Take Place?

If the consultation shouldn't take place early in the Research phase—or maybe not even in the Research phase at all—when should they happen? Our answer will almost certainly surprise you. Based on our experience over the past few years, if most of your patients don't already have a surgery date on the books *before they arrive* for their consultation, you are most likely talking to them too early in their journey.

As of this writing, every Amelia Aesthetics surgeon at all our locations has a consultation-to-surgery conversion rate of over 92 percent, and they are all booked several months in advance. Plus, 85 percent of our patients are already scheduled for surgery by the time of their consultation. I'm not saying all this to brag; I'm just trying to give you context and to show you that it is possible to have a sky-high conversion rate if you move past the three myths we've discussed.

Our team radically changed how we view consultations. We started probably in the same place you are, believing that consults are the best place for a patient to do their research. Over time, we moved to the opposite position: we now think consultations are the *worst* place for someone to do research. Further, we resolved that it's flat-out mean to ask a patient to pay a consult fee, take their clothes off, and show a surgeon the part of their body they are most insecure about—just so they can get the information they are looking for.

A patient who arrives for their consultation with a surgery date already on the books has moved out of the Research phase and into Intent to Buy. If they aren't prepared to lock down a surgery date before the consultation, it means they're still researching and were not able to find all the information they needed on their own. As such, they defaulted to a consult for information-gathering, which prematurely involves us in their process. That's expensive for us and frustrating for them.

You might argue, "But shouldn't the patient get to know the surgeon before they book their surgery?" Absolutely! They should learn everything they need to know about you to trust you to be their surgeon. The vast majority of patients, however, are completely comfortable when none of this happens in person. Most of the patients who come into our office for consultations say something such as, "It's so nice to finally meet you! I feel like I know you already!" That can only happen if you make it easy for them to find information about you, your beliefs, your techniques, and your results during their Research phase. And if you can do all this in video form on your website, the patient likely already feels like they've had a face-to-face first meeting with you.

Having patients show up for consultations with a scheduled surgery date is uncommon enough to warrant an explanation of how it happens. Since we've put so much effort into our free online educational materials, getting past this hurdle isn't difficult. When someone books a consultation online with us, one of our patient care coordinators will follow up with a text message, asking to schedule a fifteen-minute onboarding call before their consultation. During this phone call, the patient care coordinator double checks that this patient is ready and able to have surgery within the next six months. If they are, we educate them on why they should go ahead and schedule their surgery. If they are not ready to have surgery in the next six months, we explain to them that a consultation is a terrible place to do their research. Instead, we point them toward the relevant research materials that we have already created for them. We will talk more about these tools below.

The Art Is in the Planning

Jeremy: My wife is an anesthesiologist. Although she and I don't work together in the operating room, she has seen all the different procedures I perform. For years, she and I have joked with each other about how "easy" the other's job is. More than once, I *may* have suggested that all she does is push meds into an IV and set a timer for however long the surgeon tells her. In return, she *may* have said all I do in a breast augmentation is make a cut, dig a hole, insert a balloon, and close it up. While we are both clearly joking, it does make me realize something about my job that most people don't realize: there is an artistry to the work I do, but most of that art is the result of what happens *before* I step into the operating room.

The real magic of aesthetic medicine, at least for me, is found in the planning. The time I spend talking to a patient, hearing her story, listening closely to her goals for the procedure, and then working with her to create a personalized, customized plan of action is critical. It can and should be a time of connection and excitement—certainly for the patient, but also for me as the surgeon. I may do ten breast augmentations that week, but I've never done *this* augmentation because I've never operated on *this* patient to achieve *this* desired result. That artistry is only possible if I've talked and listened to the patient...a lot.

You'd think that would make my consultations exciting, that they've always been the best part of my week. Not so. The truth is, I used to despise walking into a consultation with a patient. They were *so* boring. That's not because they weren't important; they were. And it's not because the patient didn't deserve my complete attention; she did—every time. No, it's because I had to say the same thing over and over again. As soon as I met a patient in a consult, I'd push the "play" button in my brain, and the whole speech would pour out of me practically verbatim. I'd use the same words, explain the same things, and draw the same diagrams up to twenty times a week. It was mentally exhausting, but it was important. I knew there were things the patient needed to hear, and the only way I could be sure she heard them was to say them myself. After all, it may have been the millionth time I've said all that, but it was the first time *that patient* had ever heard it.

I need an average of ten procedures per week to fully book my surgery calendar. Back then, I had a conversion rate of 50 percent. That meant I had to have twenty consultations to book ten surgeries. I could also see that the consults when I felt especially bored almost never resulted in a surgery. My attitude was clearly affecting my performance. That not only impacted our revenue, but more importantly, it gave the patient a poor experience. That wasn't fair to her. So I was mentally checking out, and my conversion rate was dropping. Something had to change.

THE PATIENT JOURNEY PHASE 3: RESEARCH

I gave Robbie and our Amelia Agency team a goal: figure out how to make every consultation interesting for the patient *and* for me. The answer was to turn my same rinse-and-repeat lecture that I had been giving during consults into a series of short videos the patient could consume at home before coming in for a consultation. That gave her the chance to hear it multiple times if she wanted to, and it gave me the chance *never* to have to hear it again. By having consultations only with patients who've already heard my little speech, all my consults immediately became less of a lecture and more of a conversation. Now I get to spend that consultation time with my patients, learning about them, hearing exactly what they hope to accomplish, and customizing a plan to make it happen. We've effectively off-loaded to the web all the other parts of my old consultations that are boring to me but vital to the patient.

As a result, I'm more energized and engaged in my consults, which has resulted in a drastically higher conversion rate. Today it takes me *eleven* consults to book ten surgeries. That has effectively given me back nine extra hours per week that I once spent doing fruitless consultations. We took full advantage of that time by extending my time in the OR an extra hour per surgery day, adding an hour of dedicated CEO time to the end of my schedule five days a week, and even adding an additional surgery day when needed.

Fundamentally changing our approach to consultations resulted in my spending less time doing something I didn't find interesting, spending more time in my sweet spot (the operating room), mentally showing up for every patient when I walk into a consult, nearly doubling my conversion rate, gaining more time to devote to my business owner duties, and adding 30 percent more revenue to our bottom line. Perhaps best of all, because the last hour of my day is now dedicated office time and not dependent on wrapping up a conversation with a potential patient, I leave work at pretty much the same time every evening. That sends me out the door to my wife and kids in time to have dinner or coach soccer...every night.

That's what I do with the time I reclaimed from bad consultations. What could you do with the time you'd save?

PHASE 3: RESEARCH
OFF-RAMPS AND LANE CHANGES

Robbie: The Research phase we've discussed here is huge, and helping a patient through it by providing all the information they need, when they need it and how they need it, is no small feat. But all that work (theirs and yours) during this phase has a major payoff. If a patient feels like they got all the information they needed, and if they feel confident about booking their consultation and surgery, they will excitedly change lanes from Research to Intent to Buy. Or if they got all the information they needed and that helped them realize a procedure is not right for them, at least for now, they will take the off-ramp and return to the Awareness phase. That's where they'll stay until or unless they change their minds, at which point they'll start the journey over. I want to reiterate that *either* of these options is a good outcome. There is nothing wrong with helping a patient decide not to book a procedure if it's not in their best interest. Sometimes, that's how we as medical providers serve the patient best.

The only time an off-ramp is a problem is if it's because the patient did not get the information they needed during their Research phase. In that case, their decision isn't based on what they learned; it's based on what they *didn't* learn. They exit the journey either out of frustration

THE PATIENT JOURNEY PHASE 3: RESEARCH

by the lack of information or because they're reacting to bad information they received.

Sadly, it's rare for a typical patient in our industry to get through their Research phase feeling like they got all the information they needed. That's how so many unqualified patients end up sitting in consultations that ultimately go nowhere. They're only there to get the information they couldn't find on their own. Too many providers make it so difficult to get the right answers that many patients simply give up. What started as genuine interest in a potentially life-changing procedure devolves into a mess of frustration and confusion, and the patient ultimately runs out of steam. At that point, they choose the off-ramp to end what has become an irritation rather than an adventure.

Here's how we know this is true: The average lead-to-surgery conversion rate (not to be confused with consultation-to-surgery conversion rate) for private practices is 1.7 percent.[15] That means fewer than two out of one hundred potential patients who fill out a form or download a lead magnet on your website will ever go on to have surgery. And again, our own practice was right in line with this industry statistic until we stopped believing the three myths we discussed in this chapter. After implementing the strategies I'm about to share with you, though, our lead-to-surgery conversion rate has increased by 7x to 10x across the board.

I'm not going to pretend there's only one way to do this or that our team at Amelia has figured out the silver bullet. What I can say is that the changes we've made in this area have been some of the wisest decisions we've ever made as a practice. So I'm going to give you a high-level overview of how we've chosen to meet patients wherever they are in their Research journey, which has given them the confidence to book their surgery date before ever coming in for a consultation.

The first way we have done this is by staffing marketing personalities we call *micro-influencers* who are positioned outside of the Amelia brand. While these team members are paid by Amelia, we have built their reputation on their own names, rather than on our Amelia brand. Their entire job is to empathetically meet people and serve them where they are in their patient journey. Each of these marketing team members specializes in something, such as breast surgery, body surgery, or skin care. They each have a dedicated platform—again, built on their own name, not the Amelia brand—to provide patients clear, accessible answers from an unbiased source. That said, I should say that these people are clearly *associated* with Amelia, even though they are not operating *as* Amelia. We are not trying to fool anyone.

The second way we meet patients where they are in the Research phase is by providing them a community platform to get involved in. We call that community Bustmob, and it's a thriving, drama-free group of women that was built specifically for those who are considering an aesthetic procedure. The members of Bustmob heavily lean on each other for information, peer-level education, and support.

A third way we meet patients where they are is through a mobile app called Bustmob Academy. As Jeremy mentioned earlier, this app is not branded as being part of Amelia because most people would prefer not to learn from a plastic surgery practice while they are researching. This app contains hundreds of educational videos to teach patients about plastic surgery, skin care, and medspa services. All the videos are taught by our marketing personalities, not by our surgeons because, again, patients can't relate to someone whom they know will profit off their decision.

THE PATIENT JOURNEY PHASE 3: RESEARCH

RESEARCH TAKES TIME AND MONEY

Jeremy: I know this may seem like a lot ... because it is. It was also expensive, but we've viewed it as what it is: an investment in our business. These are a few of the ways we've tried to help our potential patients make the most of their Research journey, but there are many others. As we said at the beginning of this sales and marketing section of the book, we made a conscious decision to play the long game with this stuff. None of it had an immediate payoff, but it's grown our practice exponentially over the past several years.

If I could leave you with only one takeaway from everything we've discussed in this chapter, it's this: the patient journey does not start in your office; it ends there. You can't afford to spend your time meeting one-on-one with patients who haven't yet been educated in what you do, from pricing to procedures. Your office is not the place for that kind of research. In fact, your office is the *worst* place for a patient to conduct their research when they're still deciding whether to have a procedure. Make whatever changes necessary from what you learned in this chapter to meet only with highly qualified, well-educated patients who are ready to move out of Research and into the Intent to Buy phase, which we'll talk about next.

CHAPTER 13

THE PATIENT JOURNEY PHASES 4 AND 5: INTENT TO BUY AND PURCHASE

Jeremy: In the previous chapter, we shared that your goal should be to have a patient book a surgery date before you as the surgeon ever meet with them for a consultation, meaning they're already in the Intent to Buy phase before you sit down with them. My guess is that you're still debating whether this is possible or even wise. I get it. It took a little while for me to come around to the idea too.

When Robbie and the Amelia Agency first presented that idea to me, I pushed back. I argued that trying to make people commit to a surgery date before the consult feels coercive. If a person meets me and doesn't feel like I'm the best fit for them, I don't want them to feel like they *have* to stay in my care because they've already committed to a date and put some money on the line. You may be thinking the same thing right now, so let me explain how I came around to the idea—*and* how I now believe it's the only way we should do it.

We can never know for sure what someone else is thinking or feeling, but I'd expect someone who's feeling coerced into a decision would appear hesitant or anxious during our consult. And to be fair, I do sense that occasionally when I'm meeting a client in person for the first time. I wouldn't say it's common, but it does happen. That's why

I'm so happy with the changes we've made to the consultation process—because now I have the time to spend digging into a patient's apparent concerns...whether they've voiced them to me or not.

Before these changes, you'll remember that I spent the entire hour of the consult going through my little lecture. I had so much information to share with the patient and so little time to do it. I did my part first and then used whatever time was left to answer the patient's remaining questions. The problem is, I knew how long it took me to give my speech, but I had no idea how many questions the patient had. We've all had patients who bring an exhaustive list of questions into the consultation. Not knowing how much time we'd need at the end for questions prevented me from slowing down, really listening to the patient and paying attention to their body language. More importantly, I was always nervous to ask open-ended questions that were outside my scripted speech. A simple question like, "What worries you the most?" could take some patients a full hour to answer, and we didn't have time for that. There was too much education to cram in to risk talking about their feelings.

Today things are radically different. First of all, I have less pressure going into a consult because I know my surgery schedule is already full. Because we pre-book surgery dates, I'm not distracted by the old 50/50 odds of *this* consultation working. I know the person in front of me *will* have surgery unless I screw up or, more commonly, unless I notice something is...off...with the patient. That brings me to the second big difference: I have time and freedom to slow down and engage with the person who seems hesitant about what they're doing.

Since we've off-loaded so much of the educational component to our online tools, I have plenty of time to sit and talk with a patient during the consult. If I notice someone is unusually anxious about the procedure or process, I can say:

I know all this can feel like a fast-moving train by this point, but it's OK to slow down and reevaluate things. One of my jobs is to help make sure you're choosing the right surgery at the right time. Can you tell me what you're most excited about and what you're most worried about?

That's a question I got from my friend and fellow surgeon Rafi Fredman. It gives the patient an opportunity to be vulnerable, and it gives the surgeon insight into why they may not be ready. You may be surprised by the answers you'll hear when you do this. Believe it or not, many of my patients have expressed concerns about disappointing *me*, their surgeon! Some don't want to "bother" me with their questions. Some are afraid of looking like a coward if they cancel their procedure. Some are worried that *I'll* be disappointed with *their* results. It sounds strange but we all know people can have a million different insecurities wrapped up in how they see their bodies. And we as physicians (and especially plastic surgeons) get exposed to all of them.

I've found, however, that their anxieties are often centered around legitimate concerns. Sometimes it's a timing issue. The patient may have scheduled a tummy tuck three weeks before a big family ski trip. In that situation, she's correct; this is the wrong time. I'd validate her concerns and tell her to reschedule the surgery and enjoy her trip. Oftentimes, the most freeing, encouraging thing a surgeon can say to a patient is, "Don't have surgery." Some of them will look at you as if you're insane because they're so emotionally invested in going through it. Others, though, will let out a huge sigh of relief and say, "Thank you! Thank you! I do think I need to reconsider." If that happens, it's a win. Like I said in the previous chapter, it takes me about eleven consults to do ten surgeries. And I'm just as happy for the one "no" as I am the ten who went through with it—as long as everyone is making the right decision for them.

People in this Intent to Buy phase are riding high with excitement, but it's not a done deal yet. So assuming they've exited the Research phase and entered the Intent to Buy phase by scheduling a procedure and having a consultation, let's examine what's going through their heads. As you read this material, though, keep in mind that sales and marketing isn't a precise science. Just like medicine, it contains a modicum of art. The suggestions you'll read in this chapter represent the proven plan that's worked for us. We can't guarantee your results, but we are confident that there are a few things in this chapter that, if implemented correctly, will make a big impact on your business.

PHASE 4: INTENT TO BUY
THOUGHTS, EMOTIONS, AND ACTIONS

Robbie: The Intent to Buy phase is an exciting thrill ride for most patients. At this point, most of their questions have been answered, and they've mentally accepted the idea that they're almost certainly going to go through with the procedure. They've also put some skin in the game by committing to a surgery date, paying your consult fee, and starting a personal relationship with you as their likely surgeon. They haven't paid for the surgery yet, but things are certainly moving that direction. All the momentum of the previous three phases is now pushing them faster and more forcefully into making their dream of surgery a reality. To be blunt, this is when shit gets real.

During this phase, the patient is thinking things like:

- I really hope this consultation goes well.
- I think I'm really going to like my surgeon.
- I can't believe I'm finally doing this!

THE PATIENT JOURNEY PHASES 4 AND 5: INTENT TO BUY AND PURCHASE

- I have so many details to iron out before my surgery date.

They are feeling excited and nervous, and even though they have left the Research phase, they are still researching, seeking out patient stories and experiences, and absorbing information like a sponge. This is another reason why many of the resources we talked about in the previous chapter are so important. When you create your own ecosystem for the patient, you can help eliminate confusion and anxiety by continuing to give them resources for exactly where they are in the process. This is especially helpful while they are in this purgatory state between their consultation and surgery date, which could be several months, depending on how far out you're booked.

This is also the part of the patient journey where we as the practice have no excuse for screwing this up. When the patient comes in for their consultation, we should already know five things:

1. They are ready to have surgery and are a great fit for surgery with us.
2. We've provided clear education about the procedure they are considering.
3. We've earned their confidence, and they trust our team's track record.
4. They have an expectation for the cost of their procedure and can afford it.
5. They are going to leave their consultation with a crystal clear, step-by-step path to their surgery date.

If you ensure all five of these things are true, your consult-to-surgery conversion rate is going to go through the roof!

This is the power of giving patients everything they need—not just *when* they need it, but *how* they want to receive it. By the time someone books a consultation and enters the Intent to Buy phase, they are ready to commit and are excited to have surgery with you and your team.

PHASE 4: INTENT TO BUY
OFF-RAMPS AND LANE CHANGES

At the Intent to Buy phase, you might fool yourself into thinking the patient is 100 percent going to follow through with a procedure. They're committed, they have a surgery date, they've either had or scheduled their consultation, and they've paid a consultation fee. Perhaps more importantly, they've mentally shifted into a frame of mind that says, "I'm doing this." Frankly, it would be mentally and emotionally difficult for the typical patient to suddenly take the off-ramp at this stage. But they might do it anyway.

As we were going through the difficult process of reevaluating and revamping our patient and sales and marketing processes, we identified two primary reasons why someone would take an off-ramp at this point in their journey. The first reason is obvious, and it's something I'm sure has happened to you many times in your career: the patient has a sudden, unexpected life change, which takes their planned procedure off the table. Examples would be a pregnancy, job change, relocation, or family tragedy. Whatever the reason, life steps in and forces them to change their plans. The patient may come back when things settle down, or this may be the last you ever see of them. Either way, it's nobody's fault. Stuff happens.

The second reason is more likely, and unlike an unexpected life event, this reason *is* someone's fault: ours. I'm talking about something

THE PATIENT JOURNEY PHASES 4 AND 5: INTENT TO BUY AND PURCHASE

going wrong in the consultation. Maybe the patient wasn't prepared well enough beforehand and is surprised by some important bit of information they receive in the consult. As we've said, the consult is a terrible time for them to do research, and any new bit of potentially negative or disappointing information can bring the whole journey to a sudden end.

In this situation, you may have done everything 90 percent perfectly, but that last 10 percent tripped you up. There are other times, though, when the entire consultation is a disaster. Because we do this every day, it can be hard for medical professionals to see things through the eyes of a patient. Imagine a woman coming in for a breast augmentation consult. It might have taken her last bit of courage to walk through the doors, knowing she was going to have to undress and have a doctor she's never met examine her body as they discuss her deepest physical insecurities. What if she is neglected by the front-of-house team member who was supposed to make her feel welcome? What if she's kept waiting for two hours before anyone sees her? What if she hears your office staff making inappropriate comments about another patient? What if everything about her in-person meeting is so disorganized she can't help but think, *If this is how things are when I'm here and awake, there's no way I'm trusting these people to put me to sleep!*

Bad consultations can happen for any number of reasons. In the Operations section of this book, we discuss ways to get honest patient feedback at every stage of their journey. It's worth mentioning now, though, because these critiques are crucial to improving your business and creating a winning patient experience. You as the doctor and/or business owner aren't with the patient at every step. In fact, you may spend the least amount of time with the patient of anyone on your team (at least while the patient is awake), so there's no way you have a complete picture of their experience with your practice *unless you ask them*. Practices that ask for feedback get it—in all its painful glory. Those who don't ask *don't* get it, leaving massive problems and blind spots festering for years before they ever come to light.

Our patients were very gracious—yet honest—in the feedback they provided as we were making changes in our practice several years ago. You know the lecture Jeremy mentioned giving to every patient during their consultation? Yeah . . . that lecture appeared on our feedback surveys. A lot. A large percentage of our patients reported leaving that consultation feeling overwhelmed by all the information that had been thrust upon them in such a short period of time. They appreciated the amount of time their surgeon and patient care coordinator gave them, but it was simply too much information for them to process, especially when coupled with the anxiety of an embarrassing physical exam.

Those of us who do this every day have the curse of knowledge. What feels easy to us doesn't feel easy to someone who's just hearing it for the first time. In fact, one patient reported that she left her consultation, got to the parking lot, sat in her car, and cried for fifteen minutes because she knew she wasn't going to remember everything she had been told. She was panicked that she was going to forget some key detail that would ruin the whole experience.

That was heartbreaking for us to hear, but we needed to hear it. Based on that feedback, we created a game-changing resource for both our patients and our patient care coordinators. It's a simple step-by-step booklet that outlines every part of the patient's journey with us. In each consultation, the patient care coordinator walks the patient through the booklet page by page so they can see exactly where they are in the process, where they're ultimately going, and all the steps in between. Plus, this beautifully designed resource goes home with the patient to help them review what they learned and discuss with their significant other.

How frustrating would it be for a patient to get all the way to this Intent to Buy phase—just one step away from their desired outcome—before deciding not to go through with surgery? That's like spending six months researching the perfect car, placing your order, waiting for the big day, and then bailing out the day you're supposed to pick up the keys because your salesperson made just enough mistakes to scare you off. That would be a huge letdown, but that's what we're doing when we lead a person all the way to the Intent to Buy stage and then drop the ball.

The consultation should be an underhand pitch to you and your team. If you're not knocking almost every one out of the park (as in, booking the surgery), then I can almost guarantee your problem lies in either underserving patients during their Research phase or in unknown issues that patient surveys would quickly uncover.

Appropriate Expectations

Jeremy: Because my wife and I are both busy doctors, we knew as soon as we had children that we'd need full-time help with them. Meghan and I both hoped to find a long-term nanny, someone our kids could grow up with and be comfortable with for the long haul. For that reason, we prioritized one thing above almost everything else (except, of course, the safety of our children): making sure the nanny *liked* us. Because we were so focused on being liked, we were hesitant to set clear, firm expectations for what we wanted her to do for and with our children throughout the day. We were afraid of being seen as "difficult" or "hard-to-please" parents. So we were vague in what we asked for. We figured giving the nanny some freedom and autonomy would help us all get along and make her want to work with us for many years.

That plan failed. Miserably.

Instead of making us the "cool, drama-free" parents and employers, our unwillingness to set specific expectations caused us to have a series of difficult conversations over several months. Rather than being up front about what we *wanted* her to do, we instead kept reacting to the things she was doing that we didn't like. That relationship suffered and ultimately fizzled out. Not surprising.

I asked Meg what she thought we needed to do differently next time, and she replied with a gem of wisdom I'll never forget: "A person will never meet expectations they don't know about."

That is so obvious, but how often do we expect an employee—or a patient—to just *get it* when we have not clearly defined what *it* is?

Flash-forward to when Robbie surveyed all our patients, asking for feedback on their patient journey and specifically, their consultations. It was apparent that we didn't know what our patients were expecting of us because we had never asked them. And because we didn't know what their expectations were, we were failing to meet them in some way nearly every time.

The feedback I received about my perfect little speech that I gave every patient in their consult made me sick. Seriously. You'll remember that I hated giving that lecture; it bored me to death every time, but I thought it was beneficial for the patient. Turns out, they hated it too. It wasn't helpful for them and was actually hurting many of them. After seeing the same comment for the twentieth time, I started to wonder how *any* of them actually went through with their surgery.

Reading the comments sucked, and I eventually took myself off the feedback distribution list (because they kept me up at night), something I could only do because I knew our business director and clinical director were paying close attention. However, we would not have an almost 100 percent consultation-to-surgery conversation rate today if we had never faced the unseen expectations our patients had for us. We can never forget that a patient can take an off-ramp at any point in the process, right up until they're on the table and the anesthesiologist tells them to start counting backward.

Robbie: If you and your team have served the patient well during their Research phase, and you meet their expectations during their Intent to Buy phase (including the consultation), then the patient will gladly keep going on the journey with you and change lanes into the Purchase phase.

PHASE 5: PURCHASE
THOUGHTS, EMOTIONS, AND ACTIONS

In nearly every marketing discussion in any company in any industry in the world, someone will mention Apple as the company to emulate. Whether it's a discussion about creativity, design, market reach, penetration, saturation, customer service, customer experience, supply chain, presentations, stock prices, social influence, or "cool factor," Apple almost always gets a mention. There are reasons for that—a *lot* of reasons.

As someone who's worked in the field of customer or patient experience for most of my career, one thing about Apple's business has always stood out to me. Did you know that fewer than 10 percent of all Apple products are purchased in person at an Apple Store?[16] That means 90+ percent of all Apple products sold are purchased online or through a phone carrier. In almost every sale, the customer does not walk into a retail store, and they don't see any retail packaging until *after* they've made the purchase. Why, then, would Apple invest so much time and money—not to mention complicate their supply chain—creating beautiful, innovative, industry-leading packaging for every one of their products? To be blunt, why would they care so much about the customer's "unboxing experience," especially since it happens after they already have that customer's money?

It's because, psychologically, Apple knows the Purchase phase of the consumer journey is uniquely important. Just as we want to feel like we're making a great decision *before* our purchase, we also need to be reminded that we made a good decision *after* our purchase. Not only does it prevent buyer's remorse, but it's yet one more thing for us to tell someone else about.

Your patients see their journey the same way. So even after they have paid for their surgery—and even had the surgery—they need us to keep creating experiences that remind them they made the right decision. This can and should include the clarity and availability of your post-op care instructions, the demeanor of your clinical staff when your patient calls with a follow-up question or concern, and the excitement you convey to them about their results when they come in for follow-up appointments. Our surgeons call every patient on the night of their surgery to check in, see how they're feeling, offer encouragement, and answer any new questions about their recovery so far. They also send a handwritten note to every patient to say thank you, making sure their handwriting is legible and not the stereotypical doctor scribble. Plus, we offer a free medspa treatment to every patient after surgery.

These touchpoints and experiences we create for our patients after their surgery are every bit as important as the ones that led them to have surgery in the first place.

Our whole team has become so focused on the entire patient journey—up to and including the Purchase phase—that we are constantly talking about how to tweak small things to improve every aspect of the experience. One of our team members recently summed it up this way: "After someone has surgery, I feel like we should be working just as hard to earn their five-star review as we did to earn their decision to have surgery with us." I love that.

Isn't this how we want to be treated when we make a $10,000 or $20,000 purchase? Imagine you just paid $15,000 to a business that you spent a lot of time with over the course of several months. You made personal connections with some of their team members. You talked about your family and heard about theirs. You made several visits to their office and trusted them with something deeply important and personal. What is something you'd expect them to do for you at the end of the journey? What is something you'd *want* them to do for you to make you feel valued and special, rather than just another nameless, faceless customer? What is something they could do that would absolutely blow your mind? Seriously, spend time thinking through these questions. When you come up with a few answers, see how you could implement them into your own business. I promise it will remind them that they made the right decision by choosing you, and this, in turn, will help make them a raving fan of you and your practice.

It's All about Relationships

Jeremy: The key to so much of what we've been discussing is building healthy, enjoyable, mutually beneficial relationships with our patients.

All that intentional relationship building we've done throughout the patient journey has a huge payoff here at the end for at least two big reasons. First, happy patients will almost certainly come back if or when they ever want another procedure or ongoing medspa treatments. This is more important than you may realize because *replacing* an existing patient is far more expensive than anything you may do to better serve—and therefore *keep*—existing patients. Harvard Business Review reports that finding a new customer is five to twenty-five times more expensive than keeping a current customer.[17] So whatever money you spend in thank-you gifts and free post-op treatments more than pays for itself if you create a medical home for that patient.

The second reason it pays to build strong relationships with your patients is much more important to me, and that's quality of life. We all have patients we enjoy seeing on the schedule, patients we've made a strong connection with, joke around with, have interests in common with, and so on. Depending on the type of medicine you practice, you may see a patient a half-dozen times per procedure from consultation to follow-up visits. If you've done the work to build a good relationship with your patients, the payoff is getting to enjoy seeing them again and again. I love seeing patients who seem to lift the mood of the entire office when they're around. If my schedule was full of those people, my life would be better.

On the other hand, every physician also has a few patients they *hate* seeing on their schedule. These are the ones who are never happy, who are always anxious, who question everything you tell them, and who seem to trust Dr. Google and Aunt Ida more than you. If I *only* had these patients on my schedule, I probably would have retired by now. I don't want to dread coming to work every day; I want to be excited to do the work I love with people I love being around. When you view the entire patient journey as your opportunity to build strong, enduring relationships, you get to build that kind of professional life for yourself.

Patient retention, then, is one of the most important ways I invest in myself. It makes my days better. It helps me tip the scales toward people who already trust me and my practice. Being a surgeon and business owner already comes with enough stressors. I don't want to add more by filling my schedule with patients who suck the life out of me. I'm willing to do whatever it takes to fill my practice with happy, trusting, friendly, *grateful* patients—and that certainly includes giving them the best possible patient experience all the way up to and after their surgery and recovery. It's not only what's best for them; it's what's best for me and my team too.

SALES AND MARKETING TOOLS

Robbie: Before we wrap up this Sales and Marketing section, I want to pass along a couple of different resources that have made a significant impact in our sales and marketing process at Amelia Aesthetics. By no means is this an exhaustive list, but I do think of the following three resources as the bare minimum requirements for any healthy practice.

Online Price List

The first sales and marketing tool you should absolutely implement into your practice is an online price list. Yes, we've said this a few times before. And yes, I'm saying it again. I'm sure I'll say it a few more times before the end of this book. It is *that* important. To be blunt, you *must* publish your pricing online. It is *the* way to stand out among the crowd of other providers. More importantly, you have to do this if you ever hope to make the best possible first impression on your potential patients.

You could even use this as an opportunity to capture a *tiny* bit of information about the patient. For example, when someone clicks the "View Our Pricing" link (which is prominently featured on our website), they are taken to a page that asks only for their email address. That allows us to gently market to them. Once they provide that and click the big "Get Our Price List" button, they go straight to our price list, which is broken out per location and per procedure. When someone selects a procedure, they see the price estimate in big, bold letters—because we aren't ashamed of our pricing. They also see a link to our financing options, a bulleted list detailing everything that's included in that price, and a link to our before-and-after photos of other patients who have had that procedure. We provide this additional information because we assume the next two questions after "How much?" are "What are my payment options?" and "What all do I get for that price?" So right at the start, the patient knows we're not just committed to answering their questions but also to anticipating their needs.

The good news is that you don't have to start with a full marketing campaign that is triggered by someone downloading your price list. Sure, that would be great, but it's not the most important thing right out of the gate. The bare minimum here is to answer the price question you know they're thinking. We know the patients have a need, and we also know that most surgeons won't publish pricing. That makes this a no-brainer way to surprise and delight a patient before you ever even meet them.

Sales Pipeline

The second basic sales and marketing tool you need to implement is called a *sales pipeline*. Simply put, a sales pipeline is a visual representation of two things:

THE PATIENT JOURNEY PHASES 4 AND 5: INTENT TO BUY AND PURCHASE

1. Each major step in your sales process
2. Which patients are in each stage

I regularly talk to practices that don't use a sales pipeline, and their patients fall through the cracks all the time. Someone calls to ask for information, and they never become part of the follow-up process. Something is written on a Post-it® note, which soon falls behind the desk. A patient comes in for a consultation, and we get busy and totally forget something specific (and important) about that patient—or we forget about them altogether. Implementing a sales pipeline will keep you and your team from ever having a patient fall through the cracks again.

A basic sales pipeline could be side-by-side columns labeled "Stages," each with its own name. These stages represent the major milestones on a patient's sales journey with your practice. For example, the stages we use at Amelia Aesthetics are:

- Called for More Information
- Consultation Booked
- Onboarding Call Booked
- Awaiting Consultation
- Not Yet Booked
- Awaiting Pre-Op
- Pre-Op Done
- Treatment Done

Your stages may be similar, or they may be completely different. If ours work for you, feel free to use them. If they don't, make up your own. The goal is to identify the major milestones in a patient's journey through your practice.

Inside each of these columns are individual cards—each representing a patient. The cards include key information, such as the patient's name, what procedure they are considering, how much they were quoted, where they are from, and when your team promised to follow up with them. Each time a patient progresses to the next stage, we click that patient's card in the Autopilot software, add any new information, and drag it to the next stage.

The ability to literally "see" where each patient is in their journey is a game changer. We've said several times that your success in the patient's journey depends on meeting them *where they are* on the journey. You can't do that if you aren't tracking their progress through your sales and marketing process.

Online Appointment Booking

The third sales and marketing tool that every practice on the planet must implement is online appointment booking. For whatever reason, our industry has historically been against this idea. I understand it creates some business problems to solve, but I do not understand why most practices have not taken this need seriously yet. Consumers expect to be able to book their next haircut, manicure, dinner reservation, and movie ticket online and/or in an app these days. Many people won't even bother with a company that doesn't offer this basic convenience. If the little mom-and-pop Italian place down the street can figure out how to take reservations online, how foolish and disconnected do we look when we can't do the same?

Even worse, many physicians unintentionally deceive patients on their websites. Take plastic surgeons, for example. It's common for a surgeon's website to have a big, bold, eye-catching button labeled,

THE PATIENT JOURNEY PHASES 4 AND 5: INTENT TO BUY AND PURCHASE

"Book Your Consultation Now!" But what happens when someone clicks that button? Do they go straight to a calendar showing the doctor's earliest available spot and the ability to claim it? You know the answer. Nine times out of ten, rather than the ability to "Book [Their] Consultation Now," they get a long form to fill out, followed by a frustrating wait for someone to call them to set up an appointment over the phone. I'm sorry, but that's deceptive. If you're doing this, you're promising your patients one thing and giving them another. You're starting the relationship by eroding their trust, as we discussed in chapter 10.

Not only is this unintentionally deceptive, but it's also bad business. If someone is clicking a button to book a consultation, they are *activated*. In that moment, they are ready to take a step forward. If we don't allow them to do that, there's a significant chance they will change their mind or go somewhere else, to a place that *will* let them take action right now.

Again, I understand this functionality creates some business problems to solve. For example, how do you make sure that the person who booked a consultation online is actually *ready* for a consultation? That's a business problem. To solve it, maybe you follow up by requesting an onboarding call or directing the patient to an orientation video they must watch before their appointment. In this example, not only are you solving the business problem, but you're creating an immediate positive perception for the patient that they are being super-served.

Since we implemented online booking for our practice, more than 98 percent of our appointments are booked online, and our patients love it! Very few people still want to have to call a practice to get an appointment. That's an old way of thinking and an old way of doing business, which communicates something to the patient: your practice isn't keeping up and is out of touch with the modern patient's needs.

Trust me, that's *not* what you want to communicate to a patient who is actively trying to take the next step with your business.

PROVIDING THE BEST CARE POSSIBLE

Jeremy: As we wrap up this section of the book, I want to go back to the first thing I said in chapter 10 when we opened this discussion on sales and marketing: Every part of the patient's experience is an opportunity either to *build* trust or *lose* trust. That trust is vital to creating a long-lasting, positive relationship with a patient. They need to know they aren't only going to get the best possible *medical* care, but also the best possible *human* care. Each patient should know that you see him or her as an individual—an individual with questions, concerns, anxieties, hopes, dreams, fears, and everything in between. Recognizing the five phases of the patient journey is our way of trying to meet each patient where they are at every point of the process. It's not about increasing profits or improving your consultation-to-surgery conversion rate; it's about taking care of people—and that starts long before and extends long after the time they spend in the operating room with us.

SECTION 4
ALL THINGS OPERATIONS

CHAPTER 14
YOUR OPERATIONAL ETHOS

Jeremy: It bears repeating, as we start this section on the operations side of private practice, that the business of medicine is sick. It's not just sick at the patient experience level (although it is). It's not just sick at the bottom line (although it is). It's also sick for physicians. How do I know? Besides having two decades of personal experience, I know this is true because nearly every email I get from any medical society includes an article about how to solve the issue of physician burnout. But none of these articles ever gets to the root of the problem: we are so freaking busy learning how to take care of our patients that we never learn how to take care of anything else—our personal well-being, the well-being of our colleagues, the well-being of our team members, the well-being of our businesses, and the well-being of the entire health system we're all trying to survive in. It's all so much to handle. It's killing us, and it's killing our industry.

The medical field represents some of the smartest, most educated, and most dedicated people in the world. Together, we are a collection of intelligent, motivated, exceedingly capable people from diverse backgrounds and capabilities, yet we have very few ways to advance in our industry. As a result, we end up angry, tired, unfulfilled, and forevermore burdened by decisions we didn't make.

Take the mountain of new regulations regarding pain medicine, for example. I'm a surgeon. Obviously, my patients need pain medication after their procedure so I'm writing narcotic prescriptions at least ten times a week. Just in the past few years from the time of this writing, a new system has been introduced, which requires us to prescribe, then confirm narcotic prescriptions using an independent and poorly designed system. That wasn't complicated enough for the "decision-makers" so they added an additional step that requires us to visit a different website to enter the name, date of birth, and other personal information of each patient getting a prescription. Then we have to go back to the website after the service has performed a review of the patient and determine whether the patient has too many prescriptions. Of course, no one actually defines what "too many" means. *Then* we have to go into a separate system, look up the patient, and write a note verifying that we checked the website. THEN we have to sign in to yet a different system, which allows the script to actually go out to the pharmacy. For God's sake. It's a weighty and poorly designed system *at best*. But we have no choice but to waste our time trudging through it. For every prescription. For every patient.

Now, because that giant wad of red tape isn't irritating enough, the government decided to drop a whole new problem on those of us who practice plastic surgery. A different set of decision-makers came up with a new fifteen-page consent form for breast implants. And it's not just a form for the patient to sign. As the surgeon, I have to sign a different form that confirms I've read the entire fifteen pages of government-approved consent nonsense to each patient before they're allowed to sign it themselves. Again, for every breast implant patient.

These are just two examples of recent industrywide changes that have made my business operation infinitely more annoying. But the real kicker is that the same organizations in charge of all this ridiculousness keep sending me email after email warning me about the danger of physician burnout. That, to me, is the perfect picture of bureaucratic oversite—"Here's an additional five hours of work you need to add to your already overstressed, overburdened, overworked week. And hey, if you get a second, here's a pamphlet you should read about avoiding burnout. Have a nice day."

Organized medicine cannot solve physician burnout. It can't. It's too sick. That's like asking the patient on the operating table to remove his own appendix. If I know anything, it's that organized medicine's solution to physician burnout would be adding *more* red tape and regulations, not less. That's the last thing we need.

There's only one way to avoid burnout in our industry: take control. And the only way I know to take control is to build operational systems that free us as much as possible from the direct impact of these ridiculous and overwhelming burdens that others have put upon us. The things we're going to discuss in this section, which Robbie will introduce, aren't exciting. They aren't sexy. They aren't what drove us into the medical field. But these things can and will save your sanity if you're up to your neck in operational chaos and bureaucratic bullshit.

AN INTRODUCTION TO OPERATIONS

Robbie: Clearly, Jeremy isn't a big fan of the operational side of business. I get it. His home base is the operating room; that's where he shines, where he makes the biggest impact using his skills, passions, education, and experience. But me? I'm an organizational nerd. I love digging into systems and processes, turning knobs and tweaking things here and there to squeeze as much efficiency as possible out of an already well-oiled machine. That's why this section on All Things Operations represents one of my favorite areas of business. As much as I love it, though, I'm willing to bet you're more on Team Jeremy. You'd probably rather stay in the operating or exam rooms with patients than focus on how the business side of things runs day-to-day. Well, that's what I want for you too. The goal of this section is to free you, the business owner, to focus on your core strengths and responsibilities by putting as much of the bureaucracy as possible on autopilot.

Cleaning up the operational side of things represents some of the best, ripest, lowest-hanging fruit in your business. Because most doctors hate this stuff, and because regulators keep adding more and more hoops to jump through, operations is one of the most overlooked and neglected areas of maturation in most private practices.

Let's change that. Let's turn one of our weakest areas into one of our greatest strengths. How? By automating the crap out of our businesses.

In this section, we won't just cover the *how* of putting your operations on autopilot; we'll also discuss the *how come* behind it. That extra step is crucial because a handful of new systems and processes won't do much to move the needle on your business unless you have a clear ethos on *why* you're doing the things we're going to discuss. In the rest of this chapter, we're going to focus on,

- Who your competition is and why it matters,
- The art and science of creating a memorable patient experience, and
- The most toxic tradition in the space of business and medicine.

Once that's out of the way, we'll spend the following three chapters examining the three critical components that will keep your private practice running as smoothly and efficiently as possible:

1. Checklists: living, breathing documentation of how your day-to-day operations are supposed to run... every single time.

2. Issues: the inevitable tensions and problems that arise on a regular basis and need to be prioritized for attention.
3. Meetings: the regular, routine gatherings that drive communication, motivation, and expectations throughout your team.

Let's be real, I've never met a doctor who was excited to talk about procedures for managing checklists, issues, and meetings. That's fine. All I ask is that you keep an open mind. What we at Amelia Aesthetics have done in the area of operations is likely different than anything you've seen in this industry. You've probably seen operations at their sickest. Now let's see what they can look like healthy, strong, and running on autopilot.

OPERATIONAL ETHOS ISSUE #1: WHO YOUR COMPETITION IS AND WHY IT MATTERS

We'll start with one of the most important questions that every private practice owner should be asking themselves: "Who is my primary competition?" As in, who is your practice primarily competing against?

We discussed this in chapter 11 so you'll remember that your competition is *not* other physicians in your field. Your real competition is *anything else the patient could spend their money on*. That includes anything from a new car to a dream vacation to going back to college for another degree. As we've seen, that means your marketing should focus more on winning the patient over to your service or industry in general than on taking shots at the physician across the street. If we can get someone to seriously consider plastic surgery at all over a new Audi or a trip to Disney, we consider that a win.

What I didn't discuss earlier is how much damage we do to each other and ourselves when we view other medical providers as our competition. Frankly, I believe this is one of the top reasons why so many other industries achieve a much higher level of operational excellence than medicine does. However, if we can shift our teams' paradigms on this topic, it will revolutionize the way our practices make decisions, *and* it will increase the level of excellence each of our team members demands of themselves. That requires us to reframe what we mean by *competition*.

We most often understand *competition* to mean someone who is working against us and/or someone we need to defeat, whether that's in business, sports, or any other arena. I like to think of it differently. The *StrengthsFinder* personality test (one of my favorites) lists competition as a strength metric that can be measured within any individual. In that context, it describes "healthy competition" as a situation in which you pit yourself against someone you know is better than you, someone you want to become more like, someone who is going to push you to become greater than you ever could have been otherwise. Is that how you've traditionally viewed other practices in your city? Probably not.

I've worked in a few different industries, and I've never seen such toxic levels of competition as I've seen in private practice medicine. I've heard so many doctors verbally tear other physicians apart (usually behind their backs, either to other doctors or, worse, to patients). Why? Because they view them as competitors in an unhealthy and insecure way. But other doctors are not our true competition, remember? All of us in private practice medicine are competing against the car industry, vacation industry, education industry, real estate, investing, and any other area with big-ticket price points. And we should view that through the lens of *healthy* competition, looking to Apple, Nike, and Lululemon as leaders in marketing and product desirability, recognizing that they're doing a much better job selling their product than we are, and asking, "How can we become more like them?"

Can you imagine how much more inspired we would all be if, instead of comparing ourselves to people who annoy and distract us, we started comparing ourselves to our "hero" organizations, those companies we wish we were more like? That's what our patients are already doing. We are not in competition with one another; we are in competition with the other things our potential patients could buy with $10,000 or $20,000. And that should inspire us to new growth.

One of our team's favorite exercises is to share each person's favorite "hero organization." We've heard everything from Southwest Airlines to Apple to Yamaha Motorcycles. This gives us a chance to discuss what each of these companies has done to impress and super-serve their customers. Then we work together to see if we can figure out how to create those same kinds of experiences for our patients. Some of our most significant innovations have come from sharing these *wow moments* we've seen in other businesses. Our custom online booking application, onboarding sales process, and pretty much every feature in our Autopilot software all came out of intentional examinations into what other industries—our true competitors—were doing.

We learned from the best of the best, and we used those lessons to dynamically improve our own business. That is such a stronger, more inspirational position than sitting around the office talking trash about the "500 Off" and "Free Consultation" offers the doctor down the street is running.

We Can Win Together

Jeremy: I don't want to belabor the point about competition, but I'd regret not adding one more thing to this discussion. I've said before that we've always held our business practices—from sales and marketing to operations to leadership—with an open hand. Other business owners are in our office all the time watching everything we do. I've also said that many of these visitors are skeptical about what we tell them, as though we're leaving out some secret sauce that brings everything together. I'm sure that's because no one expects one successful practice to share *everything* they do with another ... because we're supposed to be competitors, and competitors don't help each other succeed, right?

I hate that perspective. Here's how I see it: if someone has a wonderful, world-class experience with *any* plastic surgery practice, every *other* plastic surgery practice benefits. That patient is going to be a walking, talking billboard for the benefits of plastic surgery. Everyone around her will see the change in her, whether she actually talks about her procedure or not. Her family, friends, and coworkers will be more open to the idea of plastic surgery. It will be "normalized" just a bit more than it was before. It will be a little less weird, something that may not be only for "other people." That's what people mean when they say a rising tide lifts all boats; when the pool of interested consumers increases, every provider in that industry benefits.

Maybe you're a plastic surgeon like me. Maybe you're not. Whatever field you're in, even if you're next door to me and consulting with the same patients, I want you to know that you are not my competitor, and I am not yours. I'm going to do my best to help you grow your business by doing the only thing I can do—grow my own.

When we each win, we can *all* win.

Together.

OPERATIONAL ETHOS ISSUE #2: DO MORE THAN MEET THE NEED

Robbie: We spent most of the Sales and Marketing section of this book unpacking the patient journey and discussing how we can create unbelievably positive, memorable experiences for each and every patient. There's one crucial piece of the patient experience, however, that I've held back for this section. Why talk about something as customer-facing as the patient experience at the start of a more inward-facing section like Operations? Because everything about our operations—every system, process, and workflow—should be focused on creating the hands-down best possible experience for our patients. Too often, doctors are led astray by parroting what they have previously seen. They sometimes think the patient is there to serve them. No. Everything we do is *for* and *about* the patient. Without patients, there's no practice. This is another lesson we can learn from our true competitors in the other customer-facing industries we've discussed.

For example, one of the best customer experiences of my life happened in the absolute last place I would have expected. It was 9:00 p.m., and I had been driving for twelve hours. I was tired, cranky, and hungry. I had finally made it to my destination, and all I wanted to do was eat something and go to sleep. I had neither the brainpower nor patience to make any decisions, so I pulled into the first place I saw after exiting the interstate: Taco Bell. Not five-star dining, but I didn't care. Besides, I will admit I've been to Taco Bell enough to have a "regular order." I pulled up to the speaker box primed and ready to say, "7-Layer Burrito, please." Because that's what I say at Taco Bell. Every time.

I heard the static of the speaker and braced for the typical, apathetic "What do you want?" type attitude one might come to expect at a Taco Bell speaker box. What I got both surprised and delighted me.

"Hello there! Thank you so much for choosing Taco Bell this evening. If you aren't familiar with our menu, all our specials are located on the left-hand side. Are there any questions I may answer for you? If not, I'm happy to go ahead and take your order."

I honestly don't know what came over me. I unexpectedly heard myself say, "Well, let me see . . ." as I begin scanning the specials. "Can you tell me about the Cheesy Gordita Crunch?" *Cheesy Gordita Crunch? What was I doing?*

The voice came back over the speaker, "I would love to tell you about the Cheesy Gordita Crunch! It's one of my favorites. It's the perfect combination between the crunch of a hard-shell taco and the simple-to-eat nature of a softshell. It also pairs very well with our cheesy potatoes."

"That sounds wonderful," I said. So I got the (more expensive) combo, and as I pulled around the building to pay, the same woman leaned slightly out the pick-up window, smiling and motioning to me (as if I'd never done this before). As I approached the window, she said, "Good evening! Your order will be ready in about sixty seconds. I've made you an ice water for you to enjoy while you wait."

I don't typically seek out Taco Bell tap water, but as the window closed, there I was, happily sipping on my water with a stupid grin on my face. I didn't have a clue what was going on, and frankly, I didn't care. Thirty seconds later, the window opened and the woman handed me my bag of food. "I've put three or four of each of our sauces in the bag for you. My favorite on the Cheesy Gordita Crunch is the medium flavor. Is there anything else I may do to make your visit with us any better?"

For a half second, I thought about offering her a job at our practice on the spot. Instead, I simply thanked her for creating such a memorable experience for me, and I went on my way.

Here's the point of this story: Every time you or I interact with an organization as a consumer—whether it's with an employee, via their website, on the phone, and so forth—we go into the interaction with a felt need and an idea of how the interaction will go. The organization knows this and 99 percent of the time, they have a singular goal: meet the need. As business owners, we think the goal is to meet the need—*period*. However, if we stop there, we've missed the biggest, most obvious opportunity in all of business.

Meet the need should not end with a period. It should end with a comma because there is *always* a next step. Our patient interactions should never end with us simply meeting the need. That's the baseline. Anyone can do that. If that's where we stop, we don't deserve that patient's business any more than any other practice. What makes the difference, where we truly shine, is what we do *after* we meet the need. In other words, the difference is what's on the other side of the comma.

The other side of the comma is what I experienced that night at Taco Bell. Getting something to eat was my need. What that lovely cashier gave me was something more. She met the need—comma—and then went on to *surprise and delight* me. She turned a 10-out-of-100 fast-food stop into a 100-out-of-100 dining experience by going the extra mile, by doing something so unexpected, so caring, and so helpful that I couldn't help but tell everyone about my experience.

Meet the need—*comma*—surprise and delight.

It's a two-step process.

Our strongest memories are created in situations that happen radically differently from what we expected. You drive to work on a Monday morning and get there uneventfully. You drive to work on a typical Tuesday morning and end up skidding across three lanes of rush-hour traffic in the rain, ultimately slamming your car into the concrete median. Which one are you going to remember?

Now, consider this: Every patient who interacts with you, your staff, or your website has essentially the same baseline expectation of being treated with kindness from your staff, connecting with you as their surgeon, and having a positive surgical outcome. Those are all reasonable expectations, right? And you can meet every one of those expectations and still leave your patient with a generally *meh* experience.

Meeting the baseline expectation doesn't create a strong, positive feeling. It doesn't create a memorable experience. It barely even activates the memory center of the brain. If I had pulled up to the Taco Bell speaker and ordered a 7-Layer Burrito, and if they handed me a 7-Layer Burrito two minutes later, it would have been a perfectly fine interaction with their business. But I wouldn't remember it. What made the difference then is the same thing that makes all the difference with our patients: the surprise and delight that came along with the met need. If a $0.99 taco chain can get it right at 9:00 p.m., what excuse do we have as premium, professional medical practices?

Meet the need—*comma*—surprise and delight.

Make that part of your operational ethos, and your patients will rave about you to everyone they know.

Know Your Patient's Name

Jeremy: The surprise-and-delight factor cannot be overstated. And most of the time, it is the easiest thing in the world to do—as easy as greeting someone by name.

I'm sure I've eaten in a thousand different restaurants throughout my life. There's one experience, however, that stands out from the formless blob of restaurant memories all jumbled together in my brain. Years ago, my wife and I walked into a nice French restaurant to celebrate a special occasion. We'd made the reservation in advance, and we were excited to check out a new place. I was expecting good food, of course, but I was not expecting the actual chef of the restaurant to greet us *by name* as we walked through the front door. Sure, someone fed him our names in advance. The host staff, wait staff, and kitchen staff all played a big part in creating a wonderful experience for us. But it was that first impression, when the head chef and likely business owner personally welcomed us by name into his establishment, that set the tone for the entire night. Even if the food had been bad (it was the best I've ever had), I think it would still rate as my number one restaurant experience ever.

I couldn't get that simple, intentional act of courtesy out of my mind for days. So the next time I had a patient consultation in my office, I made a small change to our operational process for calling our patients back into my office. Borrowing and tweaking a practice I learned from Dr. Davis, I went into the waiting room, walked over to where she was seated, greeted her myself, and personally walked her back into my office for her consultation. Did my office staff give me her name and info that they'd already collected? Sure. Did the front-of-house person point her out to me before I walked through the waiting room door? Probably. Did any of that matter to the patient? Not at all. From her perspective, the actual surgeon who'd be performing her procedure, not to mention the owner of the business, was going out of his way to make her feel welcome, like an honored guest. Just like my experience at dinner that night, this small act of courtesy set the tone for her whole interaction with our practice.

Today, any patient who has a consult in any Amelia Aesthetics office is personally greeted by their surgeon. It required us to tweak some systems to set the surgeon up to win, but it was a small operational price to pay for making someone feel welcome in our practice—especially someone we know is already nervous to be there. Of course, a handful of patients won't care about this extra effort. Some may not even notice. Others, though, will be blown away. This will likely be the first thing they tell their loved ones when someone asks how the consultation went. It's such a small thing, but it says so much about your operational ethos. It says, right at the start of the relationship, that you value your patients as individuals—individuals who have a name—and that you're interested in developing a relationship with them, not just in taking their money.

I'll add one more practical note here since we're talking about getting to know your patients' names. Make sure your intake forms have a space for the patient to give their *preferred* name and make every effort use that name in all correspondence and personal interactions. A friend of mine goes by his middle name, and it's been an annoying issue his entire life. He told me, "My parents had three children, and they 'midd-named' us all. It's probably my most frustrating daily irritation." If your forms don't ask for the preferred name, you can never be sure what to call your patients. "William Robert Johnson" could be William, Will, Bill, Robert, Rob, Bob, Robbie, or Bobby, just to list a few. If you don't know what name they go by, even if you do greet them by name in your first meeting, you either put them in the mildly embarrassing position of having to correct you or in the annoying position of having to go by a different name in every interaction with your office. This could be easy to avoid by making that one tiny change to your intake form.

OPERATIONAL ETHOS ISSUE #3: STOP SOLVING ALL THE PROBLEMS

Robbie: When I first got involved in serving the business side of medical practices, I noticed a strange pattern I hadn't seen in any other industry. I was standing with the entire team at another medical practice, and someone asked a question about improving the arrangement of the patient waiting area. Every head in the room turned toward the surgeon, who gave their opinion. And that was it; the decision was made. On to the next issue. I sat there watching as the same thing happened in response to other questions about patient sales calls, a pay-per-click marketing campaign, and if checks should be entered manually or via a check reader. Maybe this sounds familiar to you, and maybe it doesn't. Either way, you need to understand something that may not be clear to you inside the bubble of medical private practice: no other industry in the world makes decisions this way. In every other business I've ever worked with, problems get pushed *down* into the organization to get solved rather than being pushed *up* to the most expensive, most important, and busiest person in the building.

This may sound crazy to you, but as the business owner, you should not be the person who is providing solutions to most of your practice's problems. Further, when someone brings you a problem, you probably don't have what it takes to provide the best solution. Not only do you, as the business owner, have the least amount of visibility into most of the problems that find their way into your practice, but you also have the least amount of context for understanding the root of the problem. You wouldn't expect the person at the front desk to be the best one to solve a surgical problem, would you? Then why would you expect the surgeon to be the best one to solve a front desk problem?

You may think that's a rather offensive position to take. I mean, it is *your* business, right? But it's not *my* position. Look at this priceless bit of guidance from four-time *New York Times* bestselling business author Joseph Grenny:

> *Anytime you become the hero by solving the problem, you risk teaching your team that without you, the situation is helpless. Over time, and with repetition, you collude with your team in creating a situation that isn't good for any of you. You surrender your bandwidth to low priority tasks and you reinforce weakness in your team.*[18]

Too often, we business leaders develop a "White Knight Syndrome" and feel like we have to rescue the team from every problem that crops up. Why? The best solutions typically come from those who are closest to the problem. If you're focused on the business owner's key responsibilities, which we discussed in chapter 2, that's almost *never* going to be you. Besides, if we train our team to depend on us to solve every problem, our decreasing availability will forever bottleneck the growth of the practice. Plus, we limit every single solution to our own incomplete context and distanced perspective.

Don't we all, as leaders, want to raise up high-capacity teams? Don't we want to give our team members the dignity of growing in their roles by facing and solving problems without us? Being seen as the one with all the answers may be fun for a while, but it's unfair to the business and to your team members. What's *really* fun is watching our team members take it upon themselves to wrestle a problem to the ground on their own—under the guidance of their immediate leader when needed—whenever an issue arises. That's a step that would help take your leadership from *good* to *great*.

You'll never put your practice on autopilot until you release the problem-solving function to the wonderful leaders and team members you've hired to help grow your business. Of course, that doesn't mean you should remain blissfully ignorant of what's going on in your business; they are still accountable to you, and sometimes their proposed solutions may need some additional context or guidance. This is something we'll cover in much more detail later in this section of the book.

DON'T DO FOR THEM WHAT THEY CAN DO FOR THEMSELVES

Jeremy: One of the most powerful business lessons I've ever received came from an unexpected source: my (then) two-year-old daughter's preschool teacher. When Eloise was two and ready for some socialization, my wife and I decided to enroll her in preschool. We interviewed several schools and decided on a Montessori school, which is a teaching framework that allows a child freedom to select which learning activities to do and when. It's the type of school I enjoyed as a kid, and I was excited about my children having that experience—but I was concerned about a two-year-old having so much say in her own education. It seemed like a recipe for chaos. What I found, though, is that the kids at her school were some of the most well-behaved, focused little people I'd ever seen in a group. Weird, right?

Near the end of my daughter's first week in preschool, our family was having dinner at our kitchen table. When Eloise was finished, without a word, she got up from her seat, took her plate to the garbage, scraped it clean, and carried it over to the counter. She was too small to reach the counter, but she tried. My wife, Meg, and I looked at each other, and I shot her a look that said, *What the hell was that?*

Meg asked the teacher about it the next day when she dropped Eloise off at school. Miss Wafa replied, "Of course she did that. She *could* do that." Miss Wafa went on to explain one of the tenets of Montessori education is, do not do for the child what the child can do for themselves.

Ouch.

If this is true for a two-year-old, how much truer is it for the grown, educated, experienced, professional men and women working on your team?

We doctors live in a high-stakes world. If we make a mistake or if our practice makes a mistake, a patient's health could suffer. That makes us hesitant to trust anyone else to make decisions that could impact our patients or our practice. And certainly, there are some decisions that need to be made either by you, the business owner, or by a small team of leaders who can provide the full, business-wide context. But ... that list of decisions is a lot shorter than most of us think.

It's been ten years since Miss Wafa gave us that little gem of wisdom, and it's affected not only how we raise our children but also how I operate my business. At least a few times a month, when I'm asked to make a decision I know I shouldn't be making, I stop and think, *What would Miss Wafa tell me to do?* More often than you'd think, the answer is to tell the employee bringing me the issue, "Well, what do *you* think we should do? Because I bet you can solve this without me."

My team members might read this and think, *I never hear him say that.* Truthfully, it's because I seldom *have* to say it anymore. I've been leading like this (or at least trying to) for several years now, so it's baked into the ethos of our business. As a result, I get a steady stream of happy surprises all the time. I might walk into the kitchen and find that all our plastic forks have been replaced with biodegradable silverware. Or I might walk through our waiting room and discover that our designer remade the space to feel more private and accommodating. These things happen without my involvement because we have built independence of thought into our core values.

It doesn't stop with cutlery and seating arrangements, either. This attitude permeates our business and all our decision-making, up to and including high-level practice operations that can and do impact our patients' care and our company's bottom line. Because the stakes are so high, we've had to develop an operational strategy for identifying issues and creating checklists for addressing them. That's what we'll discuss over the next few chapters.

CHAPTER 15
THE POWER OF CHECKLISTS

Robbie: If you travel frequently (or at all), you're probably preoccupied by the nuisances associated with air travel—getting to the airport hours early; being corralled through security like cattle; emptying your pockets, taking your belt and shoes off, taking your laptop out of your bag, and then frantically trying to get all your stuff off the table before you slow down the person behind you; hurrying to find the right gate but then sitting there for an hour before you're allowed to board; squeezing into the jet bridge, then into the tiny airplane door, and then into the even tinier airplane seat. It's like we have this mental checklist every time we fly, and we check off one irritating task after another until we exit the airport at our destination. The more we fly, the more we get used to it and run through this little program on autopilot, but we still usually do the same things in the same order, whether we're thinking about them or not.

That familiar, though annoying, routine may work well for us as passengers, but have you ever wondered what all is going on in the cockpit when you're on a commercial airplane? Believe it or not, it's not that dissimilar from what we're doing on the other side of the cockpit door. The entire operation of the aircraft—from takeoff, to flight, to landing, to emergencies—is governed by a time-tested set of checklists. A *lot* of checklists.

In Clint Eastwood's remarkable film *Sully*, Tom Hanks stars as Captain Chesley "Sully" Sullenberger, the legendary pilot who, in 2009, miraculously landed US Airways Flight 1549 in the Hudson River after both engines were incapacitated by a flock of geese. From a leadership perspective, what happens after the plane gets struck by birds is extraordinary. After trying to restart the engines, Tom Hanks's character, Sully, says, "Get out the QRH," referring to the Quick Reference Handbook—a step-by-step checklist pilots use to diagnose and solve problems mid-flight. Keeping their cool, Captain Sullenberger and his first officer start going through each item on the QRH checklist, trying desperately, yet methodically, to get the engines back online one step at a time. Ultimately, after exhausting all options, Sully brings the airplane down safely in the Hudson River, saving all 155 passengers and crewmembers aboard.

Captain Sullenberger was lauded for his levelheadedness and calm demeanor during and immediately after the incident, even earning the nickname "Captain Cool" from NYC Mayor Michael Bloomberg. But as terrifying as this moment was, it's important to note that airplane pilots don't use a checklist in only emergency situations. In fact, every flight crew uses over a dozen checklists for every flight, each of which is read aloud depending on the phase of flight; they include things such as,

- preflight and pushback
- engine start and takeoff
- landing and shutdown

You'd think the experienced pilot would eschew these basic procedural steps, trusting their gut over procedures and flying on instinct. However, professional and private pilots understand that too much is at stake every time they step onto an aircraft. They take these checklists *very* seriously. A friend of mine who teaches aviation classes calls these checklists *the pilot's cornerstone.*

While most of us may not have responsibilities as complex as flying an Airbus A320 like Captain Sullenberger, if checklists are good enough for ensuring that an airplane carrying hundreds of people leaves and returns to the ground safely, then checklists are certainly good enough to help our team members succeed, as well.

In our Amelia Aesthetics practices, we have seen the power and importance of checklists time and time again—from brand-new team members to our most seasoned leaders. In fact, I will go so far to say that checklists are the number one instrument that will allow you to create, track, improve, and scale the day-to-day operations of your private practice—both for your team and your patients. However, getting everyone on board with a new, standardized process for doing things may not be that easy.

PUSHING THROUGH THE PUSHBACK

Jeremy: "May not be that easy" is a massive understatement. The truth is, when Robbie and I implemented a series of checklists for different processes throughout our office, we came up against a mountain of resistance. Some of it was willful, as in team members didn't love the idea of having to follow a standardized checklist for tasks they were already used to doing their own way. Most of the resistance, though, wasn't intentional. It was simply the growing pains of implementing a new operational process into an already fast-moving business. As you start to implement what we'll unpack in this chapter, you're sure to face both types of pushback as well.

The Sullenberger illustration Robbie used to open the chapter is a great example of an industry that has long relied on checklists to get things done—everything from the mundane to the emergency situations. What do you think would have happened, though, if US Airways had just implemented their checklist system two weeks prior to the sudden "goose attack" of Flight 1549? My guess, based on my personal experience, is that the pilots would not have reached for the QRH in that moment. Instead, they probably would have tried to land the plane based on their gut or their vague memories of some emergency-training class they'd taken years earlier.

When Robbie and I originally presented our first collection of operational checklists to our clinical team—the team who flies the Amelia Aesthetics plane—the checklists were largely ignored. We even held the team accountable by providing a place for the team members to sign the checklists each day, indicating they'd followed the new procedures. The first week, the lists were signed every day. The second week was spotty. We got a couple of signatures the third week and then none the fourth. When I asked a team member to show me the checklist that fourth week so I could add something to it, she couldn't even find it.

In one month, our new checklist procedure had gone from implementation to decay to abject failure.

We kept pushing. Every time the team started slacking off on the checklists, we would reintroduce them. We were patient with them, but we were firm in reminding them that these new operational checklists were not going away. In time (a *lot* of time, to be honest), the checklists went from being seen as unnecessary, to annoying, to tolerable, to useful, to normal. It took time and persistence, but we changed the culture of the team regarding checklists.

Today it would seem wildly out of place *not* to use them—and we've added many more since that first implementation. When a new team member is being onboarded, there is a checklist to make sure everything is clear. When a patient is being prepared for surgery, there is a checklist to make sure everything is done correctly and in the proper order to ensure a smooth procedure. When the business director wraps up his work for the week, he refers to his checklist to make sure he's accounted for everything. When the marketing team is engaged on a project, they follow a checklist every step of the way. It's baked into the business now, and it keeps all of us—including me, the surgeon and business owner—on track and mindful of every detail we've decided is important to our business and our patients.

If your goal is to create a business that runs on autopilot *the way you want it* while you're personally busy doing other things, checklists are the surest way I know to make it happen. So let's spend some time discussing *why* they're so important both for our team members and our patients.

CHECKLISTS FOR YOUR TEAM

Robbie: As a leader, we are responsible for everything our team members do or don't do. And checklists are a great way to *inspect* what we *expect*. Not only do they give us a physical piece of accountability for our team members to turn in each week, but they also serve as an extraordinary training tool and reference guide. I'll briefly describe how we use them here, and hopefully you'll get some inspiration for how you can turn your daily and weekly routine tasks into actionable checklists.

We strongly encourage the business directors at each of our Amelia Aesthetics locations to implement checklists with just about every single team member. For example, we have opening and closing checklists for both the front-of-house and clinical teams, our patient care team has a checklist that covers the most important tasks of their day, and anyone who answers the phone has a checklist for how the sales process is designed to walk a patient through the call. Many of these checklists are organized by days of the week, and they include boxes for team members to *literally* check as they go along during their day and a signature line to add personal accountability.

Your business is forever evolving and that means different tasks come and go all the time. A checklist is perfect for making sure your people are doing things the way you want them done *now*, not like they did it five years ago. For example, in the wake of the COVID-19 pandemic, maybe you decided that your front-of-house team should start sanitizing each pen after a patient uses it. In the past, you would ask them to do so and *hope* they didn't forget the new task as they went about their other routine duties. The results would be mixed at best, causing you to become irritated by their oversight and your team to become irritated by your constant reminders. If you're operating with checklists, though, this becomes much easier. You simply add the item to the daily checklist—which they are dutifully following each day—and you're done. From that point on, the checklist carries the responsibility of reminding them to do it. They do the task, you don't have to remind them, and nobody gets unnecessarily frustrated with the other. Win-win.

Not only does this allow you to inspect what you expect every week, but you also get visibility into each item that they are being held responsible for. This is important, because oftentimes, due to the evolution of the business, some of their tasks should stop being done altogether. There is nothing worse than finding out you've been paying a team member to do something for the last six months that was a complete waste of their time. Checklists prevent this by giving you visibility into their daily tasks, allowing you to modify or remove outdated tasks as needed, and ensuring that the operational side of the business is running smoothly.

This concept of checklists is super-simple. But it's also very powerful. With everything going on, it's simply impossible for everyone to remember every single step, every single day. Our advice, then, is to turn everything you can into a checklist. Ask every part of your practice—your front-of-house, clinical team, patient coordinators, business office, and so forth—to carefully examine every task they do on a daily, weekly, and monthly basis. Have them document these tasks, and then work with them to group them into appropriate lists. For example, your patient coordinating team might have checklists for onboarding new patients or keeping up with their daily calls. Your front-of-house team would likely have checklists for opening and closing the business day. Your accounting team would have a checklist for closing out the month. Your clinical team would have a checklist for preparing the operating room for surgery. Again, anything any of your teams and/or team members do with any regularity should be accounted for. Have the team complete these checklists daily, weekly, and/or monthly as appropriate and turn them in to the business director. This keeps everyone doing the right things the right way every day, which ultimately keeps your practice running on autopilot without your having to micromanage everything everyone else is doing. Even better, these checklists help each of us double-check *ourselves* before any potential oversight becomes a problem.

CHECKLISTS FOR YOUR PATIENTS

Author Donald Miller, whom we've already mentioned once or twice in this book, introduced me to a phrase that I have drilled deep into the

PCC Checklist

WEEK OF	MON	TUE	WED	THU	FRI
Move all consults to the correct stage in Autopilot	☐	☐	☐	☐	☐
Fill out all required information in Autopilot • Name, Address, Provider, Procedure, Value, Email, Phone	☐	☐	☐	☐	☐
Fill out pre-op checklist for any booked surgeries • Add BMI and implants discussed to pre-op checklist sheet • Add BMI, implants and size to the surgery in Autopilot • Is surgery time correct in Autopilot? • Are correct procedures attached in Autopilot?	☐	☐	☐	☐	☐
6 months are moved to correct stage • Cons___ ___C or to be filed • S___ ___ew rep_	☐	☐	☐	☐	☐

hearts and minds of everyone who works in our practice. It's something I know our team is sick of hearing me say because it comes out of my mouth several times a week. That phrase is *the curse of knowledge*.

Anytime we become an expert on any topic—whether it's an academically trained expert or, frankly, an armchair expert—we instantly gain what Miller calls *the curse of knowledge*. That is, whenever we talk about that topic, we speak the language of experts. The problem is, in doing that, we forget that *we're* the weird ones. The people around us haven't spent those same endless hours poring through the stacks of information we have about a particular topic. They aren't "in the loop" when it comes to the acronyms, initials, inside lingo, concepts, and terms that we start throwing around without a second thought. And as a result, we're creating confusion and frustration left and right.

A perfect example of this was when Jeremy and I were going through our first tax season as a partnership. One afternoon, we were sitting in a meeting with our attorneys and CPAs after asking what we *thought* would be a fairly simple and straightforward question. It...was not. The attorney started answering first, and he didn't stop talking for about seven minutes. Then, as my head was still spinning from that barrage of legalese, the CPA jumped in and talked for another ten minutes. They were both using terms I'd never heard, giving examples that made no sense, and making strong arguments that had no impact on me—because I had no freaking clue what they were talking about. I *might* have understood three-quarters of the individual words they were using, but I couldn't for the life of me tell you what those words meant all strung together like that.

As embarrassed as I was, I had to tell them several times that I was lost in the conversation. I kept saying, "I'm sorry, but I don't understand. Can you please say it in a more simplistic way?" The problem was, they were speaking from their areas of expertise—with the curse of knowledge. They had no idea they were using words and terms that we, the "uninitiated," couldn't follow along with. It was a frustrating experience to say the least.

Now, here's where I have to step on your toes: There's a good chance your patients are just as confused and frustrated with you as I was in that meeting with my CPA and attorney. We talk the language of medicine all day, every day; it's become our native tongue. We forget that the patients coming in for consults, surgery, and exams don't speak our language. The curse of knowledge sneaks into our discussions with our patients, subtly (or not-so-subtly) driving a wedge between us and wrecking the personal connection we genuinely want to make. That's why we must be vigilant and intentional in creating *radical clarity* for the patients we serve by eliminating the curse of knowledge from the patient experience. The best way we've found to do that, without question, is with patient checklists.

Our team has thought through every aspect of the patient experience for each of the procedures we offer, and we've turned those insights into checklists, which we have printed and provide to every patient for every appointment. These checklists cover everything from how to prepare for the appointment, what to expect, when to arrive, and where to go. It's our way of taking them by the hand and guiding them from one step to the next without overwhelming them with any of the insider medical jargon that we take for granted. The patient has a printed guide to walk them through each step of the process, and our team members have a printed guide that reminds us to speak to our patients in plain English. By walking through the patient checklists with them, everyone stays on the same page, and we've eliminated an unbelievable amount of confusion, miscommunication, and frustration on both sides.

You may be reading this and thinking, *Isn't it kind of insulting to the patient to assume they won't be able to follow along with me as I explain the procedure?* If so, congratulations—you've proven my point. That attitude is exactly how you know you're suffering from the curse of knowledge. Whenever you feel like something is easy, try seeing it through the eyes of an already anxious patient:

- Would you think it's easy to find your office if you've never been there?
- Would you think it's easy to know what to wear to a consultation if you've never had one?
- Would you think it's easy to prepare for your first filler appointment?
- Would you think it's easy to know how to prepare and what to expect as you recover from surgery?

Whatever you think from your perspective as an experienced medical professional, let me set the record straight for you: your

THE POWER OF CHECKLISTS

Breast Augmentation Prep

2 Weeks Before Surgery
- ☐ Stop taking birth control pills, any product that contains aspirin, and all nutritional supplements. Also, get your prescriptions filled and picked up.

You will be prescribed:
- ☐ Celebrex/Celecoxib
- ☐ Gabapentin/Neurontin
- ☐ Zofran/Ondansetron
- ☐ Singular/Montelukast
- ☐ Phenergan/Promethazine
- ☐ Norco/Hydrocodone
- ☐ Oxycodone
- ☐ Tramadol
- ☐ Bactrim
- ☐ Cefadroxil
- ☐ Clindamycin
- ☐ Flagyl
- ☐ Skelaxin
- ☐ Scopolamine
- ☐ Colace
- ☐ Valium
- ☐ Xanax

2 Days Before Surgery
- ☐ Prevent constipation by taking Colace or eating two Activia yogurt cups a day.

1 Day Before Surgery
- ☐ Stop eating/drinking at midnight before surgery.

Morning of Surgery
- ☐ You may drink small amounts of water or sports drink up to four hours before your surgery. No coffee, tea, candy, or gum, but you can brush your teeth.
- ☐ Remove contacts and all piercings and leave at home. Wear loose, warm clothes. Zip-up tops and pajama pants are preferred. (No yoga pants.)

2 Hours Before Surgery
- ☐ Take three regular strength Tylenol (975mg total), one Celebrex and one Gabapentin with twelve oz. of sports drink (any flavor except red).

1 Hour Before Surgery
- ☐ Take four tablets of Zofran/Ondansetron with a small sip of water.

Arriving for Surgery
- ☐ If your surgery is prior to 9 a.m., go directly to our Surgical Suite (Suite 270) on the second floor. If after 9 a.m., check in on the third floor and we will walk you down to the Surgical Suite.

patients most certainly do not think any of that is easy. They're already doing something they've never done before. What's innately difficult for them will seem *impossible* if we—their guides—aren't speaking a language they can easily understand.

Patient and procedure checklists are the perfect way to put the cookies on the bottom shelf. We know this because we are constantly asking our patients for feedback, and our step-by-step patient checklists are consistently in the top three things our patients thank us for. Every week, we get several responses from patients thanking us for making their experience so much easier by providing them clear, easy-to-follow, easy-to-read checklists for what they need to do, what they need to know, and where they need to go.

We cannot change the fact that we all have the curse of knowledge when it comes to our practices—but we can be intentional about bridging the gap on behalf of our patients.

A CHECKLIST OF CHECKLISTS

Jeremy: As a plastic surgeon, I do a lot of breast procedures. That means I talk to at least a dozen women every week about their breasts, filling in the educational gaps in what they learned during their Research phase of the patient journey, explaining my approach to augmentation, and discussing their goals for their surgery. I learned a long time ago that how I talked to them—including the language I used—mattered a great deal more than I would have expected. Though it should be obvious to any normal person, it took a little while to realize that most people don't know what *inframammary fold* or *highly cohesive gel* mean. And unless they interrupted me to ask, they never would have known I was talking about the curved line at the bottom of the breast or "gummy bear consistency," respectively.

I was speaking with the curse of knowledge, and my patients were paying the price for it.

Getting around these little practice-to-patient misfires isn't difficult, but it does require a shift in your thought processes and probably a complete revamp in your patient experience. That's what it took for us to get better at it, and we're *still* identifying these sneaky little language and operational gremlins that are hiding in our operations. That's why Robbie and I run through a simple exercise every year or two that I'd like to introduce to you now. You can see this as a "checklist of checklists" that you should consider for your practice and patients.

I recommend setting aside several hours outside the office for this exercise; either a half- or full-day off-site meeting is best. I usually do it on a weekend so it doesn't interfere with my normal surgery and consultation schedule. You'll want to have a lot of space to write on, either whiteboards, poster paper, or projecting your computer or tablet onto a screen everyone can see. I'm weird in that I've painted an entire room of my house with whiteboard paint, meaning every wall surface is technically a whiteboard. It's fantastic for brainstorming, but I realize not everyone is quite as excited about scribbling on walls as I am.

Once you have your time and space set up, you and your business director should work through the following eleven questions very slowly and deliberately. If you've set aside six hours for this activity, which we recommend, you'll have about thirty minutes to thoroughly answer each question. I know that's a lot of time, but it is worth giving up a Saturday afternoon once a year to make this investment in your business and in your patients. For each of these questions, you'll answer as thoroughly as possible, accounting for everything you and your business director can think of, noting any red flags, breakdowns, and omissions—as well as any clear victories—in your existing processes for each area.

1. How does a person interact with your practice the first time (Internet or social media)? Is the customer experience in line with other successful businesses that are not medical in nature?
2. How does a person interact with your practice once they have decided to learn more? Does your site clearly point to educational resources in plain language?
3. How does a person reach out to your practice once they have decided to make contact with you? Is it easier or harder than scheduling an appointment at a nail salon? If so, how can you make it easier? (Hint: use a true online booking experience.)
4. What resources do you have to make sure the in-person visit has been stripped of the intimidating anxiety a person feels before a consult? *Consider:* Who have they talked to? What information have they been given? Do they know what your office looks like on the outside so they aren't anxious about finding it? Do they know how much time to allow? Do they know what they are going to be asked to do in your office?
5. Who is teaching your team how to avoid biases around the language you use in person? Have you refined your consultation conversation down to normal, human language?
6. Does the patient have a way to refer to what has been taught in the consultation, knowing that they are likely anxious and will certainly not remember everything you said? If not, what should they know and what should that resource look like?
7. What resources have you designed and distributed to help someone in the phase after a consultation when they are making the decision about whether surgery is right for them?

8. What tools do you have to help someone feel comfortable and informed about the weeks leading up to surgery (the most anxious time for many people)?
9. What tools are you going to give your patient's caretaker the day of surgery to make it easy for them, as a team, to get through the first week? *Consider:* All the goodwill you have garnered up to this point by making it easy to be a patient can be ruined immediately after surgery if you do not also make it easy to be a caretaker.
10. What resources have you collated to make recovery clearer and easier once at home? Does the patient know what to expect? Do they know an estimated time frame for reengaging in certain activities? Have you anticipated their most likely questions and provided clear answers on resources they can take home? Have you provided whatever garments, wound care, and bed pads they need, and if so, have you explained what all is in their take-home kit and why they need it?
11. Do you have a way of collecting feedback about your processes? What do you do with the information you've collected?

In general, all you're doing in this activity is mining each of these eleven areas for existing and potential checklists. Every one of these areas could be broken down into a checklist, and each one of those checklists could likely be broken down into multiple sub-checklists that account for every step of every process for every patient. Nailing down all those pesky details and putting some forethought and planning around each one guarantees a great experience for every patient, every time.

Now, to address the elephant in the room: I know most business owners who read this will not do this activity, or they at least will not devote as much time to it as we suggest. It's always surprising to me that surgeons are generally unwilling to spend a weekend afternoon creating checklist processes that will change the fundamentals of their practice and, as a result, their life.

Robbie and I have done this activity three separate times over the past several years. In one of those meetings, we revamped our entire approach to consultations, which we discussed at length in an earlier chapter. The changes we implemented came directly off the whiteboard walls of my home office, and they more than doubled our consultation conversion rate. As we discussed in chapters 12 and 13, a higher conversion rate means our surgeons have to do fewer consults to fill our surgery schedule. Fewer consults mean more surgery hours, and more surgery hours mean more revenue. In our case, we experienced an unbelievable 60 percent increase in revenue—and that was at a time when we thought we were *already* operating at maximum capacity!

Furthermore, that 60 percent increase in revenue didn't require us to hire a dozen new team members; it just required us to refine our processes and reframe how patients interact with our practice. And all that came from one weekend and two whiteboard walls. A few hours in front of a white board and a willingness to build better, clearer resources in the months that followed resulted in dramatically better experiences for our patients, fewer wasted hours for surgeons, and significantly more money for our practice (and our surgeons). The result? I spend fewer hours at the clinic, I serve my patients better, and I earn a better living. That can all be summarized as: *my life is better*. No exercise has ever been more valuable to me.

People think successful plastic surgery practices are made in the operating room, and it's true that we must do good work to succeed. But far more commonly, successful practices are made at a white board, creating checklists like these.

FROM PRIORITIES TO PROBLEMS

This exercise and the suggestions presented in this chapter will help you create a framework for managing priorities and responsibilities. That'll take you a long way, but all the new efficiencies you create on your team won't mean a thing if you don't also learn how to handle the problems that inevitably arise in every business. We'll talk about that next.

CHAPTER 16
FINDING, PRIORITIZING, AND ADDRESSING ISSUES

Jeremy: A big part of being a doctor is knowing how to distinguish between the things that need my immediate attention and the things that do not. When it comes to patient care, I'm pretty good at that. I don't hesitate to tell a post-op patient we need to wait a few months before making any decisions, when I know all they really need is more time for their results to settle in. However, when a team member comes to me with a business-related logistics concern, I feel overwhelmed by this strange need to solve it immediately. It took a while before I understood why I handled one situation so well and the other so poorly, especially since it comes down to the same core discipline: deciding which issues to act on and which to table for later.

When it comes to a patient, I realized I was comfortable with the process we had for making sure that patient came back for a follow-up. She'd raise an issue during an exam, and I suspected her body simply needed more time to heal. So I'd personally walk her to the check-out desk, ask the clinical team member to schedule a return visit for six or eight weeks out, and then say goodbye. I knew I wasn't leaving her in limbo, and I trusted that she actually would return for that next appointment. Experience had taught me that the process worked, so I didn't have to worry about "solving" her swelling issue then and there.

Business issues, though, have always been different. Up until a few years ago, I didn't have anywhere to "park" a business concern. When someone brought me an issue, I'd feel pressured to solve it on the spot because there was no process for me to set it aside with any assurance that I or another leader would get back to it. As Robbie and I rebuilt every business process from the ground up, it quickly became apparent that my tendency to jump headfirst into every issue as soon as it appeared was a problem. It led to a lot of bad, off-the-cuff decisions that either needed more time, more context, or someone else to solve. I can't tell you how many times Robbie had to come to me and say, "Uh, Jeremy, did you really tell Molly to do *this?*" or "Hey, you told Jess to do *that*, but you forgot about this other thing."

Old habits die hard...but this is one that *had* to die. And we killed it with what we call the Autopilot Issues List.

The issues list gives us a tool and process to record and then set aside issues that we know need to be addressed but aren't urgent enough to interrupt the flow of the day. It also ensures that items aren't forgotten (though sometimes, I wish a few *were* forgotten). Because we organize and act on the list in priority order, it also gives us a way to "blame" the list when an individual's primary concern (which may not bother anyone else) isn't acted on as quickly as they'd like. This also provides a built-in time buffer between an issue being raised and taking any action to solve it—and just like with my post-op patients, a little time is often all that's needed.

The Autopilot Issues List, which we'll discuss in this chapter, has been one of the most important additions to our practice's operational processes. It's given me, as the business owner, a way to overcome my tendency to solve problems immediately (even if they aren't important), and it allows our team members to use their time wisely by solving the most important issues first. It sounds so simple, but this was a game changer for our business, and I know it can be equally effective for you... that is, if you can break some old habits.

YOUR FAVORITE, MOST IMPORTANT NEW PHRASE

Robbie: In chapter 14, we discussed the need for you, the business owner, to stop trying to solve all the problems in the business yourself—not only because you don't have the full context needed to make the best decisions, but also because we want to empower and lead our team members to become great problem solvers themselves. If you're not the one who's jumping into every problem, though, how do we make sure all the issues are being properly captured, prioritized, and solved? That's where the Autopilot Issues List comes in. (That's what we call the tool that's built into the Autopilot software so we'll call it that in this chapter. As we'll discuss later in this chapter, though, the principles will work the same whether you use our software or something else.)

You and I both know how most problems enter our lives: as fires. It's as though every problem wants to be the most important problem, but we know it almost never is. One of the key characteristics of a great business leader is not allowing urgency and emotion to distract us from more important things. Jeremy admitted that he personally struggled with this for most of his career, and it's probably something you've struggled with yourself. It's one of those key business-leader traps that gets a lot of attention in the business world and almost no attention in the medical world. Physician/practice owners feel as if they have to solve every problem—and solve each one immediately—because *everything* feels urgent when you don't have a system in place. This is where the issues list will make an enormous difference not only in your business, but also in your quality of life.

This entire book is focused on one thing: putting your business on autopilot. One of the biggest obstacles to a medical practice running on autopilot is the self-imposed (and oftentimes *others-imposed*) pressure to solve every problem yourself as soon as it arises. So to make a huge, immediate change and to take a big step toward an autopilot business, you need to add a new phrase to your daily lexicon. Starting today, whenever a problem or an opportunity for improvement arises—whether it is something you notice yourself or something a team member brings you—you need to look to your business director and say, "Will you please add this to the list?" Then *stop talking*.

If you really embrace this, your team will start hearing you say this all the time. It will become one of the most important phrases for the success of your practice for several reasons. Most importantly, it will give you and your business director the opportunity to prioritize each issue in the context of every other issue, ensuring that you are always putting your time, effort, and resources toward the key tasks that can either drive your business forward or grind it to a halt.

In the rest of this chapter, we're going to unpack how to "mine" for issues in your business and how to solve the right ones at the right time. Before we go there, though, you've *got* to commit to this paradigm shift. No more fighting fires. No more jumping on top of the grenade someone throws in your practice. No more trying to be a knight in shining armor riding to the rescue. When an issue or opportunity arises, your response from today until the end of time must be, "Will you please add this to the list?" If you can't (or won't) do that, the rest of what we're about to discuss won't work for you.

FINDING, PRIORITIZING, AND ADDRESSING ISSUES

MINING FOR ISSUES

OK, but what about problems, opportunities, and issues that *no one* is bringing up? What about the ones hiding in the foundation of the business, the ones you only find by digging?

We call this discipline *mining for issues* because that's exactly what we're doing: we are putting intentional effort into discovering issues and opportunities that exist within our practice *before* they naturally or obviously present themselves. This gives us a head start on improving our practices and often allows us to stop a problem before it ever hits a patient's or team member's radar. The two resources we've found most helpful in mining for issues are *scorecards* and *anonymous patient feedback*.

Keeping Score with Scorecards

I mentioned in the "All Things Money" section of this book that I am not a fan of measuring anything we aren't going to use to make decisions. There's nothing more useless or distracting than "interesting data." That doesn't mean *all* data is useless, however. In fact, we have several scorecards throughout our practice that we look at every day. The key for us has been making sure we're tracking the right metrics, or the ones we know will help drive decisions.

Which metrics you track and act on is entirely up to you, and it's something the business owner and business director should always be reviewing and refining. Outside of the financial metrics we shared earlier, here are a few others we've found to be the most helpful:

- Surgical consultations booked over the next four weeks
- Surgeries booked over the next four weeks
- Consultation-to-Surgery CVR (Conversion rate)
- Medspa rebooking rate (returning patients)

- Retail sales per medspa provider
- Average procedure revenue per provider
- Number of five-star reviews

The numbers that show up on our scorecards are the metrics we believe show the overall well-being of our practice, and they help us visualize what's really happening in our business. Take the medspa rebooking rate metric, for example. Let's say our scorecards reveal our medspa team as a whole has a rebooking rate of 60 percent. However, we also see that one of our providers has a 93 percent rebooking rate while the others are lagging far behind. That's a big problem. It forces us to ask, "How is it that one of our providers has cracked the code on rebooking but we haven't taught that secret to the entire team?"

Listening to Patient Feedback

The second resource that helps us mine for issues is anonymous patient feedback. We have used our investment in technology to build a few custom solutions to capture this feedback, but there are many ways to do it without building your own. Whatever route you take—the tools built into the Autopilot software, a third-party survey and feedback service, Google reviews, email surveys, or even a paper feedback card—the goal is the same: every step of the way, get honest feedback from your patients about the best part of their experience and areas they felt could have been made easier for them.

If you don't ask the patients what they liked and didn't like, you may never notice a glaring hole in your business that every patient is falling through. Or you may mistakenly see problems that aren't there and change processes that are already a huge success. Knowing what they found helpful and confusing shines a spotlight on potential issues to address *and* cool, new opportunities to amplify what's already working well.

As painful as negative feedback can be, you can't sit back and wait for issues to arise. You'll get plenty of those without having to look for them, anyway. We've found that the biggest issues, the ones that were impacting patients every day, were usually the ones we never would have seen if we hadn't looked for them. For example, as our anonymous patient feedback started rolling in, we noticed several patients felt they weren't sure what was going to happen next whenever they were in our office. This is something none of us noticed because we were operating under the curse of knowledge. So we trained our team to say, "Hi, my name is <name>, and I'm going to <description of their specific task>. Once we're done with that, I'll hand you off to <next team member's name>, who will <description of the next person's task>." It was a simple solution but it made a huge difference in our patient's in-office experience.

The Downside of Customer/Patient Reviews

Jeremy: You know those Comedy Central "roasts" that are meant to honor a particular celebrity, but they "honor" the person by bringing in a lineup of friends and comedians who, one after another, publicly demolish the honoree? Some of the harshest, most vulgar jokes I've ever heard have been part of these roasts. I've never heard someone speak worse of another person than I have under the guise of this "ceremony." It's painful to watch.

This is how I view patient feedback.

I mentioned earlier that I took myself off the distribution list for our patient feedback. I don't read online reviews either. I did for a long time because, back then, online reviews were the only form of patient feedback we received. But it was extremely challenging for me emotionally. Several patient comments kept me up at night. I felt like I was being honored at a roast, but in this case, it wasn't my closest friends who were insulting me; it was my patients. Not every patient, mind you. Not even most of my patients. My typical patient back then was treated professionally, got the surgical result they wanted, had a good experience with our team, and went on their way. Of course, that's not the type of patient who leaves an online review. Online reviews, whether it's a basic Google review or on an industry-specific platform such as Healthgrades, represent extreme experiences—either incredibly positive or horribly negative. There is no middle ground.

Author Daniel Kahneman offers some excellent insights on this concept throughout his book *Thinking, Fast and Slow*.[19] He explains that simply meeting someone's expectations will almost never lead to them feeling as though they had a positive experience. Instead, a person's expectations must be met *and then some*. We will only get reviewed if we drastically *exceed* or *fall short* of the customer's expectations.

But what about the vast majority of your patients who left your care totally satisfied? They don't count in the world of online user reviews. Nobody is going to proactively go to a review site, give you five stars, and say, "It was pretty much what I expected." That's why it's so important to *pursue* their feedback; it encourages everyone to participate to provide a fuller, more reasonable, and complete picture of the typical patient's interaction with your practice.

Another problem with online reviews is that it gives every patient/customer a platform to air their complaints in public, usually without ever giving you the chance to make the situation right one-on-one. Patients with a quick Twitter trigger finger may not hesitate to drag your name through the mud over an issue that could have been easily and immediately resolved with a simple phone call. Or they may do both: call you *and* flog you in a review. The problem here is that it's unlikely they'll update their review with a happy ending even if you super-serve them privately (unless you ask them to).

This is another reason why it's important to formalize your system for gathering reviews and feedback: You don't want the public square to be the only place someone can tell you how you screwed up. There has to be an offline way to make it easy for patients to review your work at each step in their journey. There must also be a way for your practice to gather and filter these reviews. Patients' praise and their criticisms won't do a thing to move your business forward unless you put all that feedback to work by turning it into actionable issues. When it's accounted for on the list, and when you have a system in place for addressing every issue in its proper time, you'll be amazed at how the feedback you're receiving starts to change. Old problems will fade away, and new ones will start popping up. No matter how smoothly things are running, you'll *always* have new things to work on!

Gathering Feedback from Your Team

While patient feedback is important (and painful), it's not the *only* important feedback you need. If you aren't also mining for issues within your team, you're putting your entire operation at risk. The employee experience is just as important as the patient experience to the overall health of your organization.

The Ritz-Carlton, known for its world-class levels of service, coined a leadership attitude called "radar on, antenna up." The idea is that an organization's team members always need to be in a state of "radar on, antenna up," which refers to the Ritz-Carlton's persistent goal of anticipating its guests' *unexpressed* needs.[20] Essentially, the most important needs a guest, customer, or in our case, a patient may have will often go unspoken. If we aren't attuned to their needs, we'll never have the chance to meet them.

As business leaders, we owe that same level of attentiveness to our team members. These are the men and women who are living out the mission and vision we have for the organization. They've committed forty hours or more per week to helping us grow our businesses and serve our patients. These hardworking champions often spend more time with us than they do with their own families. Hopefully, we're paying them well for their commitment. In addition, we must also be striving to provide a better and better workplace for them to spend their days. A big part of that, in Ritz-Carlton parlance, is to continually be on the lookout for their unexpressed needs.

Mining for issues within your team cannot be simply setting a yearly schedule for reviews, bonuses, and vacations. You have to *surprise and delight* (chapter 14) your team just as much as you try to do for your patients. How you choose to do this will be specific to your business and team members. Some use 360° employee reviews. Some use suggestion boxes. Some use frequent one-on-one check-ins. The best businesses use some version of all these. However you choose to do it, though, remember that your efforts will never fully hit the mark unless you remember the key phrase: "Radar on, antenna up."

For example, in the first season of the popular AppleTV+ show *Ted Lasso*, an American football coach is brought in as the head coach for the English Premier League soccer team AFC Richmond. The players, of course, are irritated and confused by the fact that Coach Lasso has never coached soccer before and doesn't even seem to understand the fundamentals of the game. Knowing he needs some quick wins to earn the support of his players, Coach Lasso jumps in with a radar-on, antenna-up attitude. He installs a suggestion box that immediately becomes full of personal insults, but one suggestion seems legitimate: the clubhouse showers have "rubbish" water pressure. He tells his assistant coach to "make a note of that." In a later scene, Ted checks out the showers and confirms the problem. At the end of the episode, when the players hit the showers, you can hear the shouts of surprise (and pain?) as they each get hit with a surprisingly strong blast of hot water. Roy Kent, the team captain and Lasso's worst critic, is the first to realize what's happened. With a smirk, he turns to his fellow player and says, "Careful, son. The gaffer's fixed the water pressure."[21]

What's great about this tiny subplot running through the episode is that Ted never tells the players that he's even aware of the shower situation. He sees a three-word note in the suggestion box ("shower pressure's rubbish"), makes a note, checks it out, and gets it fixed. He doesn't make a grand display of it; instead, he subtly makes an improvement that instantly makes the life of each player a little bit better. He *surprises and delights* them. And that one small act of leadership becomes the first clear sign to the team that *something* has changed. They begin to realize they have a different kind of leader now—one who is paying attention and committed to taking excellent care of them.

Listen to your team, but don't forget to also keep your radar on and antenna up. What they tell you is important. What they *don't* tell you, though, might be more important.

SOLVING THE RIGHT ISSUES

Robbie: After you've gone through the work of mining for issues and curating a list, your business director should visually prioritize every item on the issues list and organize it from the most critical problem to the least critical problem in the business. We highly recommend utilizing what's called a Kanban workflow system to document and to track the progress of issues that have been raised. The Autopilot software makes this process super-simple. If you've downloaded and implemented Autopilot, you already have this tool baked into your office software. If you haven't, you can do this in another Kanban solution or, though we don't recommend it, even on a physical whiteboard, corkboard, or magnet board. We'll discuss it from a software perspective using Autopilot, but you can adapt as needed.

In the Autopilot Issues List within the Autopilot software, you'll see three columns labeled "DO," "DOING," and "DONE." Whenever the business director adds something to the list, it goes in the DO column, and it is prioritized in order of importance. Never prioritize something based only on how long the item has been on the list. Rather, every issue is considered individually and weighted by its importance to and impact on the business. Items at the top of the DO column will be done first so make sure the right items have been moved to the top of the list.

Next, as the business director or a designee begins to work on solving an issue, they drag it from the top of the DO column to the DOING column. This indicates someone is actively working on solving the issue. If you're using the Autopilot software, you'll see we've built an intentional limitation into the system: the software will not allow more than a certain number of issues in the DOING column at any one time. This may feel counterintuitive to you, but it's based on a workflow principle that favors *finishing* over *starting*. In the digital product world, this limitation is called a "Work in Progress" or WIP limit, and it prevents teams from trying to tackle too many projects at one time. Instead, by limiting the number of issues that are getting our attention, we increase our problem-solving velocity and feel a greater sense of accomplishment. In other words, it's better to have three *resolved* issues than thirteen *in progress* issues. No one is impressed by how many tasks we have open simultaneously; what matters is actually getting something done.

When an issue is resolved, the business director or designee will move that issue out of the DOING column and into the DONE column. At that point, the team member who successfully resolved that issue will pick the next issue off the top of the DO column and keep the process going.

A word of caution: One of the biggest temptations business directors fall prey to is the idea of solving the smallest or easiest problems first. This is a mistake for several reasons but here are the top two. First, there are almost zero issues that are actually easy to solve. If they were so simple, they would never have ended up on the issues list to begin with. Second, who cares if they're easy to solve if they aren't the most important issues in the practice? Would you rather have your business director spend five hours solving ten tiny issues that haven't made a huge negative impact on your business or have them spend five hours solving the single biggest identified issue in your entire practice? If it's really the most important issue, it will have the most significant impact. Those always deserve priority.

Now, you might be thinking, *The water pressure in the showers doesn't sound like AFC Richmond's biggest issue in Ted Lasso, Robbie!* And you'd be right. But do you know what *was* the team's biggest issue? Morale. None of the players liked or trusted their new coach. They weren't ready to receive any huge, sweeping changes from him yet, so he wisely keyed into a few smaller ways to accomplish the bigger goal of improving morale and building trust. You may need to do something similar—but do not use this as an excuse to waste time knocking out a dozen insignificant issues that won't move the needle in your business. If nothing needs your attention more than they do, and if they're really the most important issues on the board, then great; go ahead and knock them out. Otherwise, always keep your team's problem-solving eyes on the right issues in the right order.

Notice I said, "Keep your team's problem-solving eyes on the right issues." I said *your team* on purpose because nearly all the issues that go on the issues list will be solved by someone other than you. As we said in chapter 14, you, as the business owner, have to stop seeing yourself as the solution to every problem. You aren't. Once something is on the list, trust your business director to handle it. They should be keeping you in the loop on what's on the list and how things are progressing, though. In a weekly report, your weekly meeting, or however else you want them to inform you, have the business director update you regularly on what the biggest identified issues in your practice are and how the solutions are coming. This keeps your finger on the pulse of the business and your team members, and it gives you the opportunity to give your opinions and suggestions, as well as the chance to reprioritize the list if you feel something is out of order.

One last thing: Remember that the issues list doesn't just show you the issues and opportunities; it also shows you where the business director is dedicating their time and focus. This is your most valuable nonrevenue-generating team member so make sure they're spending their (expensive) time on the right things.

REAL SOLUTIONS

Jeremy: Every plastic surgery meeting, workshop, and industry event has some form of "business of medicine" track and/or a series of lectures on how to run your business. I've been to a lot of them, and I have one little complaint: they all suck.

These sessions are often led by people who are good at *doing* something but are terrible at *teaching* how to do that thing. It's always something like "Ten Reasons You Should Be on Social Media" or "Five Tips to a Happy Practice." But then, one of those "tips" is "Build a great team." Period. Full stop. Great, thanks for that pearl of wisdom. You going to tell me *how?* No? OK. We're done here.

Sometimes they prey on fear. An attorney may give a talk on how not to get sued and tell you a handful of malpractice horror stories that keep you up at night. Or an insurance guy may go on and on about malpractice insurance—and then set up a table in the back to sell you his products.

Whether they're peddling their services or honestly trying to communicate their tips for improving your practice, one thing is almost always true: the advice is vague, and it leaves you with no actionable recommendations. Without that, what was the point of listening?

If I were to make a Kanban board for the plastic surgery workshop industry, the issue at the top of the DO column would be, *Make the advice clear and actionable.* The reason we've done all this—developed the Autopilot software and made it available to you for free, produced the world's first online course on how to run a private practice from a business standpoint, and written this book—is because we looked at the business of private medicine and did for it what we've discussed in this chapter: we identified the biggest, highest-priority need (quality business instruction), and we moved it into the DOING column. Frankly, there's enough work to do to keep it in the DOING column forever, but that's OK. We're young.

As for your specific practice, we are happy to give you the Autopilot software and its built-in Autopilot Issues List because we want to come alongside you, help you improve your business, and provide real solutions to help you identify and solve your problems. If you don't use our software, that's cool; you can still use the problem-solving framework we discussed to come up with your own Kanban board. Whatever tool you use, though, it's going to require you to do something most of us in the medical world aren't great at: admit that we're probably not running our businesses well enough. Maybe you are. Maybe your practice is the exception. Maybe you don't have *any* issues to identify and solve. Maybe you've got the perfect, model practice we should all be emulating. But it's not likely. We all have room to improve.

If what you're doing is working, great! Let's hear about it. Robbie and I don't claim to have it all figured out yet. Our practice, and each of us as leaders, is a work in progress. We need what you know. The only way medicine gets out of the bottom of the business barrel is if we do with our business experience what we've always done with our medical experience: share the ups, the downs, and the new routes forward. Then maybe...*just maybe*...the business of medicine can begin to heal.

CHAPTER 17
KEYSTONE MEETINGS

Jeremy: For the first twenty years of my life, I ate what a typical American would consider to be a normal amount of pineapple. I thought I knew what pineapple really was. And it was...fine.

But then, I went on a trip to Costa Rica with my parents, and I discovered that I'd never *really* had pineapple in my life. Everywhere we went on that trip, we were served pineapple. Every meal, every activity...pineapple. It was literally everywhere we went, and I never got tired of it. I realized during that trip that fresh tropical pineapple is nothing like what I'd ever experienced from my local grocery store. Even now, twenty years later, North Carolina grocery-store pineapple is dead to me. Once you experience the best possible version, everything else tastes like trash.

The same is true for meetings. For most of my career, I thought I knew what meetings were. And just like grocery-store pineapple, they were...fine. Nothing special. Mostly filler. A lot of wasted time. No clear direction. Because I had only ever experienced meetings in the context of organized medicine, I didn't know meetings could be all that useful. I never really *minded* them, but I certainly didn't love them. I figured they were a necessary evil of the business side of medicine so I played along.

Then Robbie joined our practice and introduced me to what meetings *should* be. We started having good, even *great*, meetings, and suddenly I lost my taste for the old kind of meetings I'd always put up with. In fact, sitting through a typical healthcare industry meeting outside my practice has become insufferable. Nothing ever gets decided. Some people are afraid of hurting someone else's ego, so they don't say anything useful or remotely controversial. Other people seem convinced that their intellect is measured by how much they talk, so they dominate the conversation and drown out everyone else. Still others see every meeting as a performance, so they do their little song and dance in an attempt to get noticed and advance their careers. Frankly, I can't blame any of these people for how they act in meetings. Physicians only ever have meetings in the healthcare environment and, given how poorly that environment functions from a business standpoint, it's no surprise that we aren't good at them.

That's not as big of a problem as you might think, though. Our job is healthcare, not meetings. But if we want to cross over from being a business to *leading* a business, creating a customized schedule of high-quality meetings is critical. After all, many of the decisions that drive your practice will be made when you are not in the room. Most of the meetings we'll discuss in this chapter, in fact, happen without me. It's not that I'm not interested; it's that I have only so many hours in a day. I'm more valuable to the practice if I stay focused on generating revenue by keeping a full surgery schedule and trust my business director and team leaders to do their jobs the way they know I expect them to. So I'll hang back a bit in this chapter and let Robbie carry most of the discussion. He's excellent at leading meetings and the changes he's spearheaded have revolutionized the meeting culture at Amelia Aesthetics. It's put me in the strange position of actually *wishing* I was in some of these meetings more often—just like I wish I had a juicy slice of Costa Rican pineapple in front of me right now.

THE PURPOSE OF MEETINGS

Robbie: For most people in most businesses in most industries across the country, a calendar reminder of an upcoming meeting is met with a sad, wistful sigh rather than an excited gasp of expectancy. If you hate meetings, take heart—you're not alone. Citing a report from a Clarizen/Harris poll, Entreprenuer.com reported, "Almost 50 percent of respondents indicated they would rather do anything unpleasant—stand in line at the DMV or watch paint dry, for instance—than sit through another meeting of status updates."[22] Very few of us, especially in the medical industry, have ever had the privilege of being part of a well-run meeting. Every time the entire team gathers together, the business owner can often imagine all the lost productivity (not to mention payroll) floating away. And it's true: when done wrong, meetings are a drain on your time, energy, productivity, and resources; they seem like a waste of time—probably because they are. But when done right, a proper meeting can be one of the most powerful and underutilized resources available to business leaders.

That's the kind of meeting you're going to start having in your practice. Every time.

A proper, well-run meeting should be one of the most exciting parts of your day. It should be informative, create clarity, and leave people with things to do. If this doesn't sound like any meeting you've ever been a part of, let me assure you that there is a better way. And more importantly, great businesses hold a select number of very important meetings. So before we dive into the four meetings that will help put your private practice on autopilot, let's quickly cover the three specific reasons why healthy meetings are so important.

First, healthy meetings force communication. One of the most common elements of unhappy team members is a lack of communication between themselves and their leader and their immediate teammates. Regular meetings force communication by giving scheduled, structured time for leaders and team members to talk, collaborate, share updates, and remove the typical workplace confusion that so often derails our attempts to grow our businesses.

Second, healthy meetings set expectations. One of my favorite parts about meetings is that they give me the opportunity both to cast vision and to transfer my expectations to the team. This is much easier to do in person because I get the full benefit of body language, energy, enthusiasm, and all the other powerful communicators that are lost in an email. Personally, I have terrible luck communicating expectations via email. Something is always lost in translation and/or comes across as offensive or unclear. If you need to communicate an expectation to your team, there is no better place to do it than a healthy meeting, whether that's in person or via videoconferencing.

Third, healthy meetings create action. How many thirty- or sixty-minute meetings have you sat through that introduced an important topic, contained a lively discussion, and resulted in absolutely nothing being done afterward? That, my friend, is a worthless meeting. It doesn't matter how spirited the discussion was; if it doesn't result in clear actions that drive your business forward, the whole team would have been better off skipping that meeting entirely. Without clear action items, no one will know what's expected of them and everyone will ultimately forget the meeting within a few hours. That's why every healthy meeting ends with clearly assigned action items for all relevant participants.

Without question, productive meetings are one of the most beneficial uses of your team-member payroll. If that statement doesn't ring

true in your mind, I would challenge you to reconsider your paradigm as we unpack the four meetings we so strongly believe in:
1. Daily stand-up
2. Weekly check-in
3. Quarterly offsite
4. Annual retreat

If this seems like a lot, keep in mind that almost all your key decisions can be made within these four types of meetings. That means all those pesky pop-up meetings that eat away at everyone's time get cut down dramatically. You'll see why as we unpack each one.

THE DAILY STAND-UP MEETING

The first keystone meeting we encourage you to implement is the daily stand-up. This is a fifteen-minute meeting that should take place first thing in the morning, preferably before you unlock the doors and welcome your first patient of the day. It is an all-team meeting, meaning everyone who's working that day should be present (assuming they start their shift at the start of the day). Meetings like this were made famous by companies such as the Ritz-Carlton, where you aren't even allowed to begin your shift until you participate in your team's daily stand-up.

I realize that, if you're already predisposed to dislike meetings and you consider them a waste of time, coming right out of the gate with a proposed meeting that takes place every day of the workweek is a big ask. Hang with us. This dedicated time together every morning will more than make up for itself in time saved throughout the rest of the day.

The first three minutes of the daily stand-up is dedicated simply to giving each team member an opportunity to check in with one another about what's going on in their lives. We call this portion of the meeting *the good news*, where the team stands in a circle and each person shares what their high for the day is, what they're excited about, and generally what big thing is taking up space in their mind. Why would we ask team members to do this? Simple: because we want our team members to be as efficient and productive as possible, and team members who do not have a relationship with one another will never achieve this. Giving your team members space to share at least a glimpse of their work and personal lives on a daily basis has proven to be one of the easiest ways to see your team members genuinely grow to like and trust one another. They also demonstrate more understanding and patience with one another in times of conflict because they're able to see their teammate in the fuller context of what's going on in that person's life. It's hard not to cherish one another when we know what each other is struggling with. We work with people, not robots—and people have things they are excited and worried about. You can wish they'd keep their home lives out of their work lives all you want, but that's not how it works 99 percent of the time. If they're worried about something at home, you can be sure it'll show up in their effectiveness at work. If you don't make space for this fundamental fact of humanity, then you shouldn't be surprised when it creeps into your practice in other ways, whether it's gossip, long watercooler conversations, and/or distracted and inefficient employees.

Bestselling author Patrick Lencioni has made it his life's work to teach leaders how to build exceptional teams. In his landmark book *The Five Dysfunctions of a Team*, Lencioni calls this type of interpersonal sharing *vulnerability-based trust*, and he notes that your team will be terrified of holding one another accountable without it.[23] No one wants to be called out by someone who barely knows them. Taking just three minutes a day helps eliminate this fear because it sets the expectation that everyone in your business *will* get to know their coworkers in a personal way. They don't have to *like* one another, but they will *know* one another. That's often all you need.

While I understand the hesitation of giving your team the time to share what's going on in their lives (as much as they're comfortable doing so), and while it may appear at first glance to merely be sanctioned small talk, I have seen this practice pay off over and over. It's certainly not without risks (beware the oversharers!), but in my experience, the risks are far outweighed by the rewards. One huge benefit is the fact that giving your team this three-minute window every morning will eliminate an unbelievable amount of workplace gossip and one-on-one personal chatter throughout the day. If the whole team already knows something, hushed conversations in the corner aren't that fun.

The second part of the meeting is *the daily rundown*, a ten-minute window during which the team leader will fly through that day's schedule and the "need to know." In our practice, this could be reviewing the surgeons' schedules to identify challenging patients, reviewing the top items on the Autopilot Issues List (chapter 16), or identifying gaps in a medspa provider's schedule we might be able to fill at the last minute. This segment of the daily stand-up gives the team leader time to level-set with their team and get everyone's head into the game. Disney describes this as giving the team a place to get into character for the day.

The third and final part of the daily stand-up is a two-minute *inspirational push* from the team leader to encourage and inspire the team

> **Daily Stand-Up** — *15 min.*
> Led by: Team Leader or Business Director   *First thing in the morning*
> For: Entire Team
>
> The Good News .... *3 min.*
> The Daily Rundown .... *10 min.*
> Inspirational Push .... *2 min.*

members to have an exceptional day. That could be reading a patient testimony or positive feedback, unpacking a motivational quote, or telling a story about a team member who went above and beyond. These last two minutes serve as the "GO TEAM!" cheer that sends them into their day.

Of course, the team leader will need to be disciplined in controlling this meeting and heading off people who are dominating the high/low share time. Be firm in keeping time, cutting off the first part of the meeting at the thirteen-minute mark, and being sure to wrap the meeting at exactly fifteen minutes.

THE WEEKLY CHECK-IN

The second keystone meeting we strongly recommend is the weekly check-in. This is a weekly, thirty-minute, one-on-one meeting for leaders and *each* of their direct reports. As we saw in chapter 4, any one leader, including the business director, can only reasonably handle up to five direct reports. So if you're at max capacity, this should take up around two and a half hours of your week. If you have more than six direct reports, it will start to feel impossible to have the kind of personal, face-to-face interaction you need as a good leader.

The point of this meeting is simple: you want to spend this half-hour making sure that each person you directly lead is happy, challenged, and focused. If this sounds a bit too "fluffy" to you, please hear me out. This trifecta—happy, challenged, and focused—will be your best friend when it comes to team-member commitment and retention. If one or more of these three things is missing, you're almost certainly going to run into an HR issue sooner or later, and/or you'll have to go through the time and expense of replacing that person.

Let's take a moment to understand these three critical qualities better. Specifically, let's look at what happens when any one or two of these three qualities is missing. The result will be the appearance of one of the following six types of practice-wrecking team members.

Model Teammate Venn Diagram

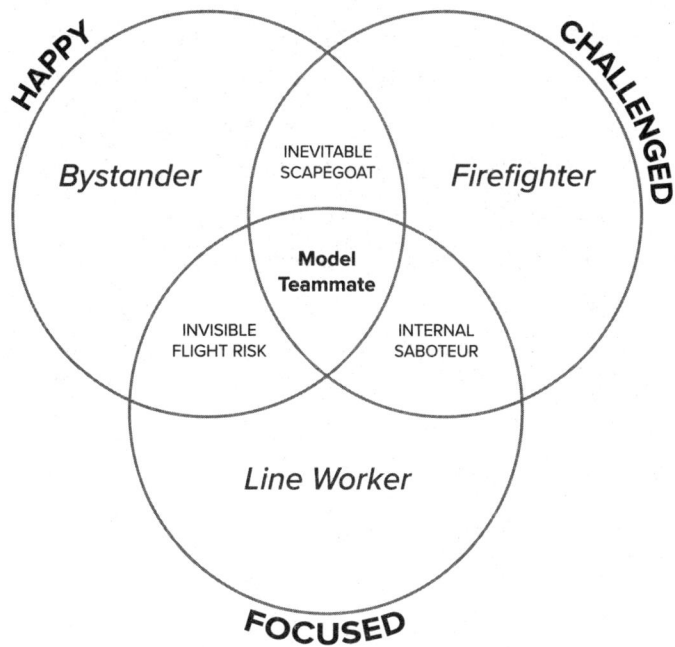

- **The Bystander:** A team member who is only happy but not challenged or focused is called a *bystander*. They are just wandering their way around the company, happy as a lark, but not accomplishing enough. Keeping this team member around may sound fun, but it is demoralizing to other employees who are working hard to accomplish the mission of the organization.
- **The Firefighter:** Someone who is only challenged but not happy or focused is called a *firefighter*. This person is running from one problem to the next, expending all their energy sideways, moving nothing forward, and growing more miserable by the day. This is the team member who only sees problems, so they can never stop complaining. No one wants to be around this person.
- **The Line Worker:** An employee who is only focused but not happy or challenged is called a *line worker*. They keep their head down and get their work done, but they find no joy in their work, remain disconnected from the mission of the organization, are obviously bored, and are clearly just there for a paycheck. This is a keeper of the status quo, not someone who will push your practice to new heights.
- **The Inevitable Scapegoat:** Someone who is happy and challenged but not focused is an *inevitable scapegoat*. This is the team member who will always get blamed for every problem that arises because for all their busyness, they never actually accomplish anything. This team member will eventually become cynical and disillusioned.
- **The Internal Saboteur:** A team member who is challenged and focused but not happy is an *internal saboteur*. Warning! This is the most disruptive and destructive person on your team

because they're getting their job done and probably bringing in revenue, but they are not happy. As a result, they are prone to gossip—often about the business owner or business director—and their vitriol spreads like a cancer throughout the practice. If you allow an internal saboteur to stay on the team for too long, the good team members end up leaving. Happy, challenged, and focused employees will not put up with this person for long.

- **The Invisible Flight Risk:** Someone who is happy and focused but not challenged is called the *invisible flight risk*. This team member is tricky; everything about their demeanor and work seems to be right on track, so it can be easy for a team leader to overlook the fact that they are not challenged by the work they're doing. This is the person who puts in their two-week notice seemingly out of the blue. They got bored while we weren't looking, and they're off to wherever they think the grass is greener.

I can almost guarantee that you have a mix of these six types of team members lurking in your office. The best way to find them, in my experience, is through the weekly check-in meeting. That's your time each week to dig in and get a feel for how happy, challenged, and focused each team member is.

So what do you actually *do* in this powerful half-hour? My advice is, don't overthink it, and don't worry if most of the time isn't spent on tasks. Just *talk* to them. Ask them how their family is doing and about their hobbies. Take notes and ask follow-up questions about whatever they told you the previous week. Don't let it turn into either mind-numbing chitchat *or* cold and clinical status updates on whatever's on their task list. Remember, these are *humans*, and this is your dedicated time to have *human interaction* with each of them. This meeting is your opportunity to build trust, influence, and context with your team members.

I will offer one tip on what *not* to do in the weekly check-in, though. Never reprimand a team member in their weekly check-in. That can be tempting since you already have this time on the schedule with them, but don't do it. Always strive to keep this meeting a safe space. If you need to have a hard conversation with them, schedule a separate one-off meeting that's dedicated only to *that* issue. You might even have that meeting in a different location than your weekly check-in just to safeguard the "sanctity" of your regular meeting spot. You want your team members to look forward to their weekly check-ins with you, and that won't happen if there's even a chance you're going to call them on the carpet for something. You'll inadvertently end up with some team members who are anxious about their weekly check-in every week. It's not fair to make them worry whether they're walking into a hard meeting every time they have their check-in with you.

Speaking as a business director, I can't tell you how beneficial weekly check-ins have been to me in getting to know my team members on a deeper level and in ensuring they stay happy, challenged, and

---

Weekly Check-In — *30 min.*

Led by: Team Leader — *Once a week*
For: Individual Team Member

— Loose, casual one-on-one conversation
— Don't overcomplicate or give reprimands
— Get a sense of how they are feeling

focused. One of the highlights of my week is almost always something that comes out of those meetings, and I'm always sharing those insights with Jeremy in our own one-on-one weekly check-in. We have found this type of meeting to be a foundational piece of putting and keeping our practice on autopilot.

THE QUARTERLY OFFSITE

Let's pull back for just a second. You may have noticed something about the first two types of meetings we've discussed: they are intentionally designed to create space for personal relationships in the workplace. This is considered uncouth—maybe even abrasive—within most of the medical industry. Our field isn't accustomed to this combination of relationship-building and accountability-holding meetings. But then, maybe that's why we are ranked as one of the worst-run industries in the nation.

Companies that rise to become industry leaders know the value this type of human connection creates in the workplace. The kinds of meetings we're describing aren't just *routine* for the highest-performing businesses; they're considered foundational to their teams' success. Yes, they take time. Yes, they require a payroll investment. Yes, they take emotional energy. And yes ... they are worth it.

Now, having dealt with the elephant in the room, let's dive into the third meeting that will be critical to your team's success: the quarterly offsite. That's right, I said *offsite*, as in *out of the office*. This one may be especially challenging for you but bear with me. This meeting can squeeze more focus and efficiency out of your team than you ever imagined.

In the first section of this book, we talked about four types of tasks:

1. Important and Urgent

2. Important but Not Urgent
3. Urgent but Not Important
4. Not Urgent and Not Important

The first type, important and urgent, seems to get most of our attention, but businesses are truly built on the second type, things that are *important* but not necessarily *urgent*. These are the big, slow-moving goals that make your long-term vision a reality. The problem is the lack of urgency causes us to lose focus on these issues and tasks over time. If we don't keep these far-off targets in our team members' sights, we'll fall into a pattern of firefighting, simply dealing with issues and opportunities as they arise rather than mapping out a course for where we want the business to go.

That's why we utilize the quarterly offsite meeting. Every ninety days, at the end of each quarter, we rent an affordable conference room at a local hotel, and I, as the business director, lead the team through the four exercises I'll discuss in the following section. Each of these exercises is designed to create a holistic look at your practice by answering three questions:

- Where were we?
- Where are we?
- Where do we want to go?

This meeting is your business director's responsibility, and the attendees vary depending on the size of your organization. If you have fewer than five people in the practice, I recommend your entire team attend. Once you have more than five, you'll start developing leadership roles within your team, as we've discussed previously. At that point, the quarterly offsite will include only you, the business director, and anyone in a leadership position. Don't overthink this, though. The goal is to get all your influencers in a room together to keep your company and goals aligned.

Exercise #1: Highs and Lows

The day should start around 8:30 a.m. The business director will kick things off with a welcome and a quick review of what you're going to do that day, and then they'll jump into the first exercise, Highs and Lows. This is a phrase we've seen before when we discussed the daily check-in. In the quarterly offsite, however, we're taking a broader look at things and asking the team to take five minutes to think through and write down their personal and professional highs and lows from the quarter that's just ended. Then, over the next twenty-five minutes, each team member will share their best and most difficult experiences from the previous ninety days.

If you've never done this type of exercise before, you may not yet see the point of asking everyone to take this moment of self-reflection and sharing. I get it; I've been there myself. After you go through this exercise once or twice, though, I promise you'll see the value. There is often laughter, expressions of sincere gratitude, surprising realizations, and even tears. All of these are great responses! This thirty-minute activity creates extraordinary alignment among the team, and it helps everyone buckle down and settle in for what will be an important day.

Exercise #2: Rock Review

In his book *Scaling Up: How a Few Companies Make It . . . and Why the Rest Don't*, Verne Harnish teaches leaders how to use a technique called "Rockefeller Habits" to identify and prioritize their mission-critical projects.[24] This model makes up the second exercise in your quarterly offsite.

The key phrase to know from the Rockefeller Habits model is *rocks*. A rock represents a key project you need to accomplish. I like the analogy for a few reasons. First, it's easy to imagine a rock as something standing in your way. If you want to move forward, you have to move that rock. Second, we can envision using rocks to build something. The fact is, we're building our business out of the rocks we carry. Third, and most importantly, a big rock is too heavy for any one person to carry alone. In order to successfully pick it up and move it where you want it, you need a team to come alongside you and lift in a coordinated manner.

At each quarterly offsite, you will select a *small* handful of mission-critical projects that must be completed by the end of the quarter. We call these ninety-day projects *rocks*, and we'll discuss how to create them below. In your first quarterly offsite, you'll need to start off by explaining what rocks are and why you're going to start using them as a goal-setting model. I strongly suggest checking out Harnish's book *Scaling Up* for the complete details; however, you'll be able to get by with the information below. For every other quarterly offsite, once your team is familiar with the rocks concept, the first part of this exercise will be a presentation from your business director on how the previous quarter's rocks went.

And when I say *presentation*, I mean *presentation*. If something is important enough to spend an entire quarter working on, it is certainly worth the time it takes to present a clear, informative presentation to show your team how effective they were at getting that key task done. Leave space in the presentation for the team to join the discussion. They should be asking questions such as:

- Was this rock completely finished?
- Are there loose ends?

- What differences are we already seeing because of the work we've done?
- Do we need to put time on the calendar in the future to re-evaluate whether we've made the right decisions?

Encourage your team to think strategically. Lead the way. Ask questions. Ask specific team members if *they* have any questions. This is the business director's presentation, but it should include the whole team.

Exercise #3: Team Review

After the Rock Review, it's time to shift gears into one of our leadership team's favorite exercises. We call it the Team Review. During this exercise, you're going to specifically give your focus to each team member, one at a time, as you all meet together as a group. The goal here is to make sure every single person is winning in their role and is still a great fit for your organization. After all, part of putting your practice on autopilot is not burying your head in the sand when it comes to the health and effectiveness of your entire team.

To make this exercise visual, I like to create a simple chart ahead of time. I list team members' names down the left-hand side to create rows and write these three questions across the top to create columns:

1. **Is this team member happy, challenged, and focused**
   You should be able to answer this easily if you've been conducting appropriate weekly check-ins, as we discussed.
2. **Is this team member a culture fit?**
   That is, do they feel like part of the team? Do they model the organization's core values most of the time? Even if someone is happy, challenged, and focused, keeping someone who is

clearly not a culture fit can be disruptive and demotivating for everyone else.

3. **Would we rehire this person?**

In my favorite business book, *Good to Great*, business growth and leadership expert Jim Collins asks, "Would you hire this person again?"[25] That is, if you could go back in time, knowing what you know now, would you still hire this person? If you cannot enthusiastically say yes, there is a good chance you should replace that team member.

For each question, I suggest a three-point rating scale:
- Green + indicates an excellent rating.
- Yellow +/- indicates there are some things to work on.
- Red - indicates severe deficiencies in an area.

Walk through each question with the team member, get their feedback on where they think they are, and then reveal where you think they really are.

This is a great exercise for us as leaders because it gives us a clear visual of where the entire team stands. You'll often discover an outlier who is clearly struggling or needs to be replaced. After you complete the Team Review, you may need to have some conversations about how you can improve or replace those struggling team members.

The thought of giving this level of honest critique and review of each team member in front of their coworkers may sound shocking to you. If so, don't worry. We'll cover this concept in much greater detail in chapter 20.

Exercise #4: The Four Helpfuls

The fourth and final exercise of the quarterly offsite is called the Four Helpfuls, and it's taken from Tom Paterson's excellent StratOp materials (www.patersoncenter.com). This is a simple, yet powerful tool to help you clearly identify what needs your attention over the next ninety days.

Start by putting two huge sticky notes side by side on the wall and making four columns labeled RIGHT, WRONG, MISSING, and CONFUSED. Ask your team to spend five minutes silently writing down their thoughts on the following:

- What they feel is *right* about your practice
- What they feel is *wrong* with your practice
- What they feel is *missing* from your practice
- What they feel is *confused* within your practice

After five minutes, ask your team to start sharing what they feel like is right, wrong, missing, and confused. Capture their responses on the sticky notes on the wall. Your business director should allow a bit of conversation during these exercises, but they need to make sure the discussion doesn't get away from them. Capture the idea, make sure everyone understands it, and move on.

Once the feedback starts to dry up, it's time for the leadership team to decide which three to five issues deserve the most attention over the next quarter. That is, what three to five big projects, or *rocks*, are you going to tackle over the next three months? If you were to spend the next ninety days focusing on a handful of large projects, which of the issues identified in the Four Helpfuls exercise would most benefit your practice? If there is no clear consensus, you might choose to leave it up to a vote. Give everyone a marker and tell them they each have five votes. Have them go to the sticky notes and place a checkmark next to the five items they believe should be addressed this quarter.

Once you've captured your new rocks, circle them, identify a project owner for each, and write that person's initials next to the item. The owner will be responsible for making sure that rock gets well-defined and addressed over the next ninety days. Of course, if you have a small team, your business director may be responsible for all of them. As the team grows, however, you can begin delegating these projects to others so everything doesn't always fall squarely on the business director's shoulders.

At this point, you have your practice's three to five big initiatives for the next few months. As the quarter moves along, your business director should update you, the business owner, each week on how each of the rocks is going.

That's the quarterly offsite, and you'll use the same agenda every time. Trust the process and embrace these tools, and you'll discover new clarity and focus that will drive your business into the future.

Quarterly Offsite *All Day*

Led by: Business Director
For: Entire Team (5 or fewer) or Team Leaders

At the end of each quarter

Exercise 1 .... *Highs and Lows*
Exercise 2 .... *Rock Review*
Exercise 3 .... *Team Review*
Exercise 4 .... *The Four Helpfuls*

THE ANNUAL RETREAT

The fourth and final keystone meeting we recommend is the annual retreat. This is a two-day retreat that includes the same group of people who regularly attend the quarterly offsite, and this retreat replaces the stand-alone quarterly offsite for that quarter. The goal of this meeting is to unplug from the day-to-day operations of the business and zoom way out—as far as you can—to ensure that the trajectory of your culture and your priorities are clear, on track, and moving forward. This type of far-off vision casting is an entirely different kind of mental activity than the daily grind of the office and the short-term planning of the quarterly offsite. For this reason, we find our annual retreats are most effective when we pack up and leave town for a couple of days. No, I'm not suggesting you take your leaders to Aspen every winter (although once or twice wouldn't hurt). Instead, I'm talking about driving an hour or two out of town to a cabin, beach condo, lake, retreat center, or some other scenic place that's outside your normal atmosphere.

Day One

You'll break the first day into three parts. You'll need to hit the ground running early on day one, so it's probably best to drive and settle in the evening before. The first portion of the day will depend on you, the business owner. Your top priority to get things started well is to come prepared to create an inspirational experience for your team. That could be a speech, a presentation, a team-building exercise, or anything else—as long as you drive home the *why* behind your business. You, the owner, should have the clearest understanding of your *why*—why you do what you do every day, why it's important, why people trust you to serve them, and so on. Your team needs to hear that *why*, and they need to hear it from you. This is a critical time to transfer a piece of your heart to your leaders, to inspire them and remind them all why what you do matters in the world.

I know that sounds like a heavy burden to bear, but do not let it intimidate you. Figure out what format works best for you, even if it's just sharing the story of your business. Fill it with your heart and passion for what you do, be vulnerable and open, and your team will love it.

When you're done with that, your business director will join you for the second portion of the first day. Everyone looks to the two of you for their direction, so take plenty of time to reiterate the long-term strategy of your practice. If there are foundational parts of your organization that need major changes, this could be a great time to open that can of worms.

The goal of this portion of the meeting is to set a strategic direction for the next twelve months. There are several great tools on the market to help you develop a long-term strategic vision, and it's more than we can get into in this book. If this is a new exercise for you, I suggest starting with the *Vision/Traction Organizer* (V/TO) that was created by Gino Wickman and offered through his Entrepreneurial Operating System business (www.eosworldwide.com). Our larger Amelia Aesthetics practices have used this tool to create a visual reference for our core values; core focus; ten-, three-, and one-year goals; and more.

For the third and final (organized) activity of the first day, do something fun as a group. Have your business director plan something the team can do to create fun memories together. Options might be an escape room, a tour of a local brewery, an inspiring movie, or a concert. Again, *what* you do doesn't matter as much as the fact that you're doing it together, deepening the important relationships of the team members who most affect the future of your entire practice.

Day Two

On the second day of your annual retreat, you will hold that quarter's quarterly offsite meeting. The format is exactly the same here as it is every other quarter. That means, of course, leaving the annual retreat with your "big rocks" for the next ninety days, ready to tackle the most important issues facing your business.

Annual Retreat — *2 Days*

Led by: Business Owner and Business Director   *Annually; replaces one Quarterly Offsite*
For: Leadership Team (same as offsite)

Day 1
— Business Director teaching session on the "Why"
— Business Owner and Business Director review an in-depth look at the strategic vision of the organization
— Do something fun as a team

Day 2
— Same as the Quarterly Offsite

FROM ONE BUSINESS OWNER TO ANOTHER

Jeremy: Robbie unpacked a lot of information in this chapter, and frankly, I know it seems like we're making a huge—possibly unreasonable—ask by suggesting you and your leaders tie up so much time in meetings. Fifteen minutes at the start of every day; thirty minutes per direct report per week; one entire day per quarter; two entire days (plus travel expenses) once a year. I get it. It's a lot. And if you're anything like I was when Robbie first brought this suggestion to the table, you've probably said "no way" a dozen times already as you've read through this chapter. That's why I want to close this discussion on meetings by telling you what I, as the business owner, thought when Robbie first suggested this. Maybe it will help you put this whole meeting paradigm in perspective.

It was the summer of 2017. Robbie had only been with the practice full time for a few months. At that time, Robbie and I still had our Friday morning meetings just like we had done the previous year when he was acting as a consultant, and the only other regular meeting our team had was a leadership meeting every Wednesday morning. This was when we dealt with everything in the practice, and the agenda was always full. In one of those 6:30 a.m. meetings, Robbie put our issues list on the screen and asked if anyone had anything new they wanted to add. No one did. Except for Robbie.

Full of his trademark confidence and authority, Robbie said, "I'd like to add that we need to create a quarterly and yearly meeting schedule. These meetings will be about building strategy and ensuring that we are completing our large-scale objectives in a thorough and timely way."

Dr. Glenn Davis, whom I've mentioned a few times, was my partner at the time. He and I shot each other a look that communicated, clear as a bell, *No, we're not doing that.* So he and I voted that issue down, and we moved on to the next issue on the list.

Robbie stopped us and asked us to reconsider.

Glenn and I had sixty years of combined medical experience and, at the time, were the only owners and only people in the room with any veto power. Robbie had been with our team for three months. This made the strength of his pushback noteworthy. It was becoming clear that Robbie was ready to take a stand on this issue. We trusted him and, remembering that this was the kind of thing we brought him on board to help us with in the first place, we allowed discussion on his suggestion.

By the end of that conversation, Glenn and I had agreed, somewhat reluctantly, to spend one day a quarter working on strategy and long-range goals at an offsite meeting. I agreed, but I still wasn't comfortable. Ready to move on, I brought up the next issue on the list.

"Hey man, we're not done," Robbie interjected. "We need to choose the dates for the next year's meetings and go ahead and lock them on the calendar."

That caused a knot in my gut. Committing actual days to this took it out of theoretical and into real life—and my real life was a bit of a mess at the time. I was working way too many hours. My wife—who is also a busy physician, mind you—was making it clear that she and my kids needed me home more, and I knew she was right. The thought of giving away four more Saturdays to offsite meetings almost caused me to call the whole thing off.

Robbie, knowing my concern about losing more weekends, suggested we hold the quarterly offsite on the last Friday of each quarter and make the yearly offsite a two-day retreat. I felt like this was getting out of hand. First of all, Glenn and I didn't even think we needed quarterly meetings at all. And second, he and I both operated on Fridays. It was a huge revenue-producing day, and we couldn't imagine giving it up once a quarter.

Robbie pushed through our resistance. Never one to use hyperbole, he argued, "I guarantee that if we will commit to spending five days a year on strategy, it will pay for itself *tenfold*."

Well, now it felt like a bet. Almost to prove Robbie wrong, we agreed to try it for six months. Then we would decide at our first annual retreat in January whether these meetings, which we knew would be ridiculous and unnecessary, should continue. In the meantime, we changed one clinical day each quarter to a surgical day (one of the many advantages of having your own operating room), so we wouldn't lose that Friday's surgical revenue. Finally, Robbie was satisfied, we moved on to the next issue on the list for that day's meeting, and he started planning our first quarterly offsite meeting.

It is no understatement to say that what started out as a six-month experiment I "knew" would fail became something that fundamentally changed the direction of our practice and, as a result, my life. We've met every quarter since then without fail. Robbie was wrong about one thing, though. He promised us a tenfold return on the days we spent discussing strategy. He vastly *underestimated* how valuable this investment of time would be to the business. I'm not even sure I could calculate the return we've gotten on an investment that, in retrospect, seems minuscule compared to what we've gained from it.

The two-day annual retreat in particular has become my favorite two workdays of the year. They are the heaviest days for me in terms of brain power, but they are invigorating. It's the one time per year when we can take our nose off the grindstone, take a breath, and look around. That's where we calculate our yearly wins and shortfalls and where we get to introduce exciting new projects we know will take a year or longer to complete. And that's OK. We've got time, and now we have a system in place to ensure those long-term projects are being properly led instead of being left to languish with no ownership or oversight.

I wanted to give you this admittedly long-winded background in the hope that it helps you avoid the mistake I *almost* made, which was nearly blowing off what ultimately became one of Robbie's greatest value-adds to our practice. Even if you don't think you need it. Even if you don't think you have the time. Even if it feels like too much of a gamble…give it one year. Just try it. Three one-day offsites and one two-day retreat. Five days to fundamentally transform your business and your life. If it doesn't work, you can always send us a nasty email. But it's far more likely you'll be sending us a box of cigars and a thank-you card instead.

SECTION 5
ALL THINGS LEADERSHIP

CHAPTER 18

ALIGNING YOUR TEAM

Robbie: Jeremy opened the introduction to this book by describing the *accidental leader*. I love that phrase. Most of the best, highest-quality leaders I know fall into that category—including me. Growing up, most of us have these big ideas of *what* we want to *do*, not *who* we want to *be*. You probably dreamed of becoming a physician. Others dream about being an astronaut, scientist, fireman, police officer, or movie star. As I write this, my seven-year-old daughter dreams of becoming a nail artist and hairstylist. Those are things we *do*. But leadership... that's different. A leader is something we *are*, either by nature of our personalities or our positions. It usually just *happens*. And then, we have to figure out what kind of leader we want to be.

When I was in high school, I outright refused to get a minimum-wage job flipping burgers like most of my friends. No offense to anyone who started out that way; it just wasn't for me. Even then, I had a huge entrepreneurial drive that pushed me to get more creative. I was also in a punk band, which gave me a solid familiarity with the different amps, cables, pedals, and other pieces of gear musicians rely on. I put those two interests together in a surprisingly profitable way. I noticed that a lot of music gear was being listed on eBay with misspelled listing titles. This was before search engines autocorrected things like that so those listings barely got any views. So I started winning auctions for $100 equipment for around ten bucks. Then I'd immediately relist the item with the correct spelling on a twenty-four-hour auction and have no trouble getting buyers at the full $100. Even better, I (covertly) gave my winning bidder's address to the person I bought the item from, so the person I bought it from for $10 shipped it directly to the person I sold it to for $100! I never even had to handle the merchandise! I did stuff like this all the time and ended up making ten times what my friends were making while working one-tenth the amount of time.

A couple of months before graduating from high school, I took a job at a print shop in Atlanta where I taught myself print and web design and a bit of coding. I eventually moved on to a $100 million company in Nashville, where I grew into the role of Creative Director and then Product Owner, leading an entire team of designers, developers, writers, and marketers. I had never planned on becoming a leader, but that's where my drive and career choices led me, whether I wanted it or not. My guess is you've got a similar story. The work we do has been different, but it's led us to the same place: leadership.

I've only met a small handful of physicians who've dreamed their whole lives about running their own private practice. For the vast majority, it's something that just happened. Maybe they joined someone else's practice and eventually took over when their partner retired. Maybe there wasn't an existing practice in the town they wanted to live in, so they opened their own. Whatever the reason, they found themselves not only in the role of a physician but also a business owner. Becoming a leader was a byproduct, not their primary goal.

So what do all of us *accidental leaders* do with the new responsibilities and opportunities we've been given? If everything really does rise and fall on leadership, as John C. Maxwell says, then we've got to face the fact that the success of everything and everyone around us depends on our ability to *own* our role as leaders. We don't get a free pass simply because we never *chose* to become a leader. Being an accidental leader doesn't remove our responsibility to grow as leaders; it amplifies it! We set the pace for the whole company and each team member. If we coast, they coast. If our personal growth stagnates, the practice will stagnate. If we give mediocre effort, we'll have a mediocre business full of mediocre clock-punchers.

Accidental or not, there are business-leadership principles we all must work to master. There's no way we could produce a resource called *The Private Practice MBA* without touching on the topic of leadership. However, this is a huge area, and it would be impossible to cover everything all at once. John Maxwell has written more than *seventy* books on leadership and sold more than 24 million copies, and he still hasn't covered everything yet! So, we're intentionally limiting the discussion in this section to three areas of leadership we've found most foundational for running a private practice:

- Aligning our teams
- Growing our teams
- Leading our teams

We'll just scratch the surface here, but it should give you enough to both significantly improve your leadership skills and (hopefully) encourage you to continue your leadership development with other resources beyond *The Private Practice MBA*.

Now, let's dig into the first area of leadership we'll cover, which is team alignment. Getting your team to *look*, *act*, and *feel* like a team isn't easy or immediate, and it starts with teaching them your vision for the organization.

THE VISION: TEACHING YOUR TEAM "THE WHY"

Jeremy: For all but two years of my career, I've had the pleasure (and sometimes the pain) of training residents. We get residents from the nearby University of North Carolina, who spend a chunk of time in our office, as well as residents from all over the country, who visit to get a feel for what we do. Residents are great because they aren't yet as jaded as the rest of us can get after several years of running a practice. They haven't been fooled by marketing companies. They haven't been abandoned by reps who acted like their best friend until they switched jobs. They haven't been sent strange and aggressive messages through social media from other plastic surgeons. They haven't faced the wrath of challenging patients or felt the weight of leading a team of people. They're still full of the stuff that keeps dreams floating above their heads instead of weighing them down into the ground.

And then...

A few years later, those same bright-eyed doctors are out in the world of private practice, and every one of those things and more start happening. A lot. You'll get a $20,000 bill for an EMR that was *supposed* to be $10,000 and realize you've got to read every word of every agreement before you sign anything. Then another sales rep will tell you that you're getting the best rate in the country and will ask you not to tell anyone ... only to find out you're paying the full retail price, and the reason they didn't want you talking to anyone about it was to keep you from finding out they were lying. Then you walk into a post-op exam with a patient who clearly has a phenomenal result, but she's irate that when she bends forward, twists 30 degrees, and raises her arm *just so*, she can see a wrinkle on the side of her breast—and she is certain her life is ruined as a result.

Sometimes all that stuff happens on the same day, and you really feel it. Your team feels it too. The office manager will wonder if she screwed up the EMR purchase. The person who orders implants will beat herself up for falling for a crooked sales rep's lies. The patient care coordinator and clinical team member who worked with the patient whose life is "ruined" will feel defeated and deflated by the patient's disappointment and horrible attitude. We all need a soft place to land when that happens, and it can be hard to remember why we're even doing this at all.

As doctors and practice owners, it's a safe bet that we'll get over it. We take the bad day like a punch in the gut, go home sad, get some sleep, and then feel better in time. Sure, there are nights when we toss and turn, and too many of these days will definitely put some gray in our hair, but we don't bail out because we know where we're heading. We have a vision in mind of where we want our practice to go, and we know there will be plenty of rough days in between here and there.

As we go, we cannot forget that our job as a leader—even an accidental leader—is to help the people around us also see the vision of where we're going. That means helping the office manager see that $10,000 overage in the greater context of a well-run business. It's an expensive learning opportunity, but it's not going to break the bank. It also means helping the patient care coordinator and clinical team member know one angry patient isn't going to derail our business and doesn't mean they or anyone else did anything wrong. Some people, and therefore some patients, just suck. They can be mean, petty, impatient, and ungrateful. We may not get many of these people, but they're out there. We see them out in the world all the time. And sometimes, one will walk into our office, and we have to deal with them. In other words, when your ship is in a storm, your team needs you to stand strong and remind them that you're still on course and that, together, you'll get where you want to go.

The operative phrase here is "where you want to go." Does your team know where that is? If you don't have a vision statement for your organization, they almost certainly don't.

Robbie is about to explain why and how to create a vision statement for your business, and I strongly encourage you, owner to owner, to take it seriously. This statement, and certainly the discussions around it, give your team the much-needed context for seeing *where you all are* by clearly pointing out *where you're going*.

Are You Pulling or Pushing Your Team?

Robbie: One of the most overlooked areas of running a practice is intentionally and continually aligning the hearts, minds, and perspectives of your entire team. Of course, it makes perfect sense why this area is so often undervalued. As leaders, we like to see immediate progress in what we put our efforts toward. And yet, working on things such as vision, mission, and culture doesn't naturally feel like it will have much payoff, at least in the short term. As a result, we set these things aside and spend our energy on more "quick-fix" issues. Even if we have a nagging sense that these higher-level issues are important, we keep them at the bottom of our ever-growing issues list. This is a perfect example of what we've discussed earlier: ignoring the *important* for the sake of the *urgent*. We can only do this for so long, though, before those long-neglected important issues suddenly turn into raging fires within our practice. When it comes to defining your vision, mission, and culture, that "fire" will most likely be a practice that no longer reflects who you are and what you wanted your business to be.

One of my favorite books of the past decade is Walter Isaacson's excellent biography of Apple cofounder and CEO, Steve Jobs.[26]

ALIGNING YOUR TEAM

Love him or hate him, you can't deny that Steve Jobs was a master of casting a clear, compelling vision for his company and his team. Jobs is widely quoted as saying, "If you are working on something exciting that you really care about, you don't have to be pushed. The vision pulls you."

Can you honestly say your vision is *pulling* your team members in your practice, or do you constantly feel like you're *pushing* them to do things you feel are important but they don't seem to care about? Can you imagine how powerful it would be if your entire team was so excited about the vision of your organization that they rarely had to be motivated? If they so clearly understood the life-changing nature of your business that they continually went above and beyond what was asked of them? If they woke up every Monday morning excited to get back to the office and were exceedingly proud to tell their friends what they did for a living?

We all want that for our businesses, and just as important, we want that for our team members. Why, then, do so many of us undervalue the very thing that makes this possible?

Having a clear, inspirational vision is indescribably powerful. It supercharges the engine of your practice, driving you all further, faster. If you truly want to create a practice that runs on autopilot and that reflects the heart of the owner, you cannot afford to ignore clarifying your vision and mission any longer. It's time to finally bring it up from the bottom of the issues list and make it a priority. But how?

State Your Vision

Of course, all this begs the question, *What is vision?* How do you create one that's compelling? And then, how do you align the hearts, minds, and perspectives of your entire team with that vision?

A vision is simply a mental picture of what *could* be, fueled by a passion that it *should* be. A vision statement is the *why* of your organization, and it almost always carries some sort of burden with it—a burden of what should be different in the world. Some of my favorite vision statement examples include the following:

- Netflix: "Becoming the best global entertainment distribution service."[27]
- Southwest Airlines: "To be the world's most loved, most efficient, and most profitable airline."[28]
- Nike: "We aim to bring inspiration to every athlete in the world and to make sport a daily habit."[29]
- Apple: "To make the best products on earth, and to leave the world better than we found it."[30]
- Amelia: "Our vision is to take plastic surgery to the masses."

Do you see a theme here? Your vision statement should make everyone on your team feel a fire burning in them. Again, it should show them what *could* be and inspire a passion for what *should* be. Airlines should be loved. Athletes should be inspired. We should leave the world better than we found it. Plastic surgery should be available and simply explained to everyone.

Now, how do you turn your big, grand, motivating vision into a clear and compelling vision statement? The best advice I can offer is to make it short and memorable. That is, don't even attempt to make it "complete" or try to answer every question about how you'll pull it off or who's involved. Just state clearly and quickly what is driving you and your business to do what you do—or, as ancient Hebrew wisdom puts it, "State the vision and make it *plain*."

Take Southwest's vision statement, for example. They want to be "the world's most loved airline." Talk about incomplete! *How will we do that? What does "loved" even mean? How do we measure how loved we are? How do we make people in Australia, where Southwest doesn't even fly, love us?* These are all great questions . . . and none of them matter—at least not when it comes to the vision statement. Southwest team members get it. The vision statement doesn't have to provide all the details to fuel the fire they have inside. It just needs to be short and memorable.

Then, once you've created your vision statement, you've got to get it into the hearts and minds of your team. This is far more difficult than it seems, but not for obvious reasons. As leaders, we often fall into the trap of believing we only have to communicate something one time to get people on board, but that isn't how vision works. As bestselling author Andy Stanley teaches in his great book *Making Vision Stick*: "Vision doesn't stick. It leaks."[31] So as leaders, we have to find ways to *recast* our vision, over and over, in new and different ways. For example, I suggest using every company-wide communication—whether it's an all-team email or a staff meeting—as an opportunity to recast your vision. If you've actually taken "short and memorable" to heart, this won't feel like a burden to you or your team. Beyond these team-wide communications, though, I would argue that communicating vision should be something we as leaders do every day in as many interactions as possible.

Let's say I'm looking at a page of the Amelia Aesthetics website that our Amelia Agency product designer is working on. Instead of saying, "I don't like the picture you've chosen," I could fall back on our vision statement of taking plastic surgery to the masses and say, "I feel like the photo you've chosen doesn't represent a reasonable body type for a typical person. Let's pick a photo that will help destigmatize plastic surgery for the masses instead of making it look like something only for supermodels."

Whatever the situation, there's almost always a way to reinforce your vision statement in your regular, day-to-day interactions with your team. When our leaders send emails, write thank-you notes, or end a daily stand-up, we'll usually say something like, "Let's take plastic surgery to the masses." It may sound simplistic or even a bit corny but hearing that same message every day from the top leaders of the company drives the vision into the hearts of our team members—and it will do the same for yours. Remember, vision doesn't stick; it leaks. If you're not constantly refilling your team's inspiration bucket, you'll be left with a dry, unmotivated team who doesn't know why your practice even exists. So state your vision, cast your vision, and then recast your vision over and over again. Your team may tease you if they hear it all the time, but hey, at least they'll know your vision.

THE MISSION: GIVING YOUR TEAM A TRUE NORTH

Jeremy: Our mission is to make it easy to be a patient.

You cannot imagine how important this clear, simple mission statement is for us. Literally every decision we make passes through this filter. Those eleven words drive every decision we make every day, and every team member knows they share the responsibility of throwing whatever flag they need to throw to make sure we're *all* making is easy to be a patient—even when *I'm* the one making things more difficult than they need to be.

For example, I used to personally see all my early post-op patients. It felt important, and I was reluctant to give up that one-on-one level of care with people I had recently operated on. However, as our demand increased, my available time slots for post-op visits became painfully scarce. Eventually we stopped *asking* patients when they were available for a follow-up and instead started *telling* them when they'd return. This made it easier for me but much harder for them. After fielding one or two (perfectly reasonable) patient complaints, a team member approached me and said, "Dr. Pyle, is there any reason we couldn't have someone else see your short-term post-op patients and only involve you when you're needed?"

My answer was short, quick, and clear: *no*. It wasn't even an option in my head ... at first. But when Molly, the nurse who had seen all my early post-op patients with me for years, agreed to fill the role, I was tempted. Unsure of what to do, I ran it through the filter we all used: Would this change make it easier to be a patient? Of course it would. Everyone else already knew that; it just took me a little longer to come around.

It's worth noting that, in this example, the transition was neither quick nor easy. We spent dozens of hours building out a schedule for Molly, creating resources to make sure our patients knew I wasn't abandoning them, and making sure every patient had my cell phone number and felt empowered to call me if needed. Very few ever do. It turns out that Molly is better at post-op visits than I am. She has more time, she's developed clearer language for the short-term expectations and patient instructions, and she has eight available hours every day to accommodate any schedule. This change has absolutely made our practice better. More importantly, it's made it easier to be a patient. My team fought for our mission ... even when I was the one they had to convince. I couldn't be prouder of them for that.

Pushing the Organization Forward

Robbie: If your vision statement helps communicate the *why* to your team, your mission statement is going to communicate the *how.* Both pieces are important. Having only a vision statement isn't useful if you don't also give your team a quick and easy way to understand how they can help push the organization toward the vision. That's where your mission statement will come into play.

One of my absolute favorite things about a well-crafted mission statement is that it gives your team the ability to self-lead and self-decide in almost every situation they find themselves in. Without a clear mission statement, your team is going to feel helpless if they encounter a new challenge they've never faced before. But if they have the guidance of a mission statement, they will be much better prepared to make decisions that reflect you and your practice, even in the most unpredictable of moments.

Take a look at these examples:

- Netflix: "To entertain the world."[32]
- Southwest: "Connect people to what's important in their lives through friendly, reliable, and low-cost air travel."[33]
- Nike: "Bring inspiration and innovation to every athlete in the world."[34]
- Apple: "To bring the best personal computing products and support to students, educators, designers, scientists, engineers, businesspersons and consumers in over 140 countries around the world."[35]
- Tesla: "Accelerating the world's transition to sustainable energy."[36]
- Amelia: "Our mission is to make plastic surgery an easy choice."

In each of these, you'll see the same operating principle at play that we had with vision statements: keep it short and memorable. If you try to make your vision or mission statement "complete," you're going to end up with three paragraphs that no one will ever remember or use when making decisions. If your mission statement is too wordy and complex to be of any practical value or for people to even remember, why bother? A clear mission statement is the best filter that could ever exist for your team's (and your) day-to-day decision-making.

Several years ago, for example, we noticed how frustrating it was for patients to have to call our practice or have a consultation to find out the cost of a procedure. We could have made two dozen different arguments for why publishing our prices online might hurt us. Isn't that why no other practice puts their pricing out there for the world to see? Instead, we looked to our mission statement and realized the answer was obvious. If the mission of Amelia Agency, which handles the sales and marketing of our Amelia Aesthetics practice, is to make plastic surgery an easy choice, and if that choice depended on knowing the price of a procedure, then the only option was to post our pricing online.

Did publishing our prices online create a lot of business problems for us to solve? Absolutely. Was it expensive to build our own pricing application? Yep. But those were necessary complications if we wanted to be true to who we've said we are. Accomplishing our mission (to make plastic surgery an easy choice) enables us to fulfill our vision (take plastic surgery to the masses).

In the same way, your mission statement will give your team members a True North in all their decision-making. Whenever they are unsure of what to do, they simply ask themselves, *What does our mission demand that I do?* A team member at Southwest would ask themselves, *What must I do to connect this person to what's most important in their lives?* A person working at the Genius Bar at an Apple Store would ask, *What must I do to give the best support to this person?* And at Amelia Agency, our team asks, *What must I do to make plastic surgery an easier choice for this patient?*

Too often, we view vision and mission statements as worthless corporate jargon that looks nice posted on the wall but ultimately means nothing and has no effect on how a company does business. That's a shame. Companies that do this literally have the answer to most questions hanging on the wall, and yet their team members still don't know what to do in many situations. Don't do that. Don't be the business that goes to the trouble of creating short and memorable vision and mission statements and yet doesn't take the crucial step of driving them down into the organization. If you put these things into the hearts and minds of your people, you're going to get a return on your investment that you never would have expected. Plus, you'll give every one of your team members yet another tool for making decisions without you, bringing you a giant leap closer to putting your practice on autopilot.

THE TENSION: DEFINING YOUR CORE VALUES

We've mentioned the term *culture* a few times throughout this book. That's a word that's used all the time to describe what an organization is like on the inside, but it's also a term that can feel impossible to define. How do you tell someone who's unfamiliar with your practice what your *culture* is? More importantly, how do you define it for the team of people who are already there working alongside you?

Earlier we argued that if you, as the business owner, don't set the overall tone or culture of the practice, someone else will. That's how many physician owners ultimately find themselves in a practice that no longer feels like home. They've allowed others to set the tone while they put 100 percent of their focus on practicing medicine, and as a result, they start to feel like an employee in their own company. If you want your business to reflect your values, you've got to lead the charge in determining your practice's core values—the backbone of your culture.

If our vision statement is *why* we're doing what we're doing, and our mission statement is *how* we believe we're going to accomplish the vision, then our core values are simply the agreements we're making between each other along the way. Our core values represent the fundamental core of who we strive to be as individuals and as an organization.

It's also worth saying that, whether you take the time to name and define them or not, your company's core values do and will still exist. Anytime you see a team member do something that just feels weird—not necessarily unethical, but something that feels *off* from who you are as a team—they have probably stepped outside of one of your team's core values, even if you've never properly defined them.

For example, one of Amelia Aesthetics's core values is, "We believe in change." So our team members expect change and generally have a good attitude about it. Newer team members who haven't fully *caught* the core values yet are slower to come around to something new. They may struggle to accept a revised process or a new piece of software, frustrated that we're changing a system they just learned. However, because everyone knows that change is central to who we are as an organization, the team members who've been here a while won't put up with their complaints. Even if their tendency is also to resist change, someone who has worked with this awareness long enough knows resistance is futile. That message then gets relayed to newer team members.

In this way, your core values, *when properly defined and communicated*, give your team a clear filter for knowing how to act and how to make decisions in different situations. They are guideposts, which create clarity around how we win and who we want to be.

Now, how do we go about defining our core values? Again, there are many great resources in the leadership field (my favorite is *Making Vision Stick* by Andy Stanley), but here are a few tips to get you started.

First, start by thinking through what's already important to how you and your team operate within your practice. What sayings are often repeated? What do team members sometimes need to remind each other of? Think through what is important to you as a physician and business owner and use that to identify at least three to five things (but no more than seven) that could become core values.

Second, turn these concepts into statements. You want to make them short and memorable, just like you did with your vision and mission statements. But then you want to take your core value statements one step further by making them *actionable*. For example, if you value profits (and who wouldn't?), it's not enough to say, "We want to be profitable." You need to put some action behind that conviction, such as, "We *protect* our profits." That gives your team a guideline. If your IT person is about to spend $1,000 on some piece of software with questionable benefit, they'll be forced to stop and ask, "Does this purchase help me protect our profits? If not, is there another similar product to explore?"

Third, communicate these value statements to your team, get their agreement, and continually remind them of and reinforce these values every chance you get. These things should represent who you are and how you act in nearly every situation. You can't just shove these in a drawer and forget about them.

One word of warning: Great core values always create some sort of tension because a core value will always cost you something.

That is, to honor the agreement, we are personally going to have to stretch ourselves a bit. It's much easier *not* to protect profits, to gossip and gripe to whomever's sitting beside us, or to maintain the status quo instead of getting excited about change. But if we as leaders help our team members lean into the tensions our core values create, we will not only create a well-defined culture, but we will also create a team whose hearts, minds, and perceptions are aligned with each other and with us as their leaders. When that happens, your efforts to put your practice on autopilot will shift into overdrive because you can trust your team to think, act, and make decisions just as you would.

Core Values Help Us Direct Behavior

Jeremy: *Core values ... what a bunch of crap.*

If you'd been inside my head the first time Robbie suggested articulating our practice's core values, that's what you would have heard. Loudly.

We were prepping for a rare all-team, all-day offsite meeting, and Robbie suggested spending an hour getting everyone's input on what they *thought* our core values were (we had never articulated them). I pushed back for a couple of reasons. First, we're talking about thirty-five people. Spending an hour on *anything* represented thousands of dollars in payroll. Second, I thought discussing core values in general was a waste of time. I figured everyone in the room knew the values that determined who we were, what we believed, what drove our decisions, and how we acted. Why bother spending so much time and money writing down what everyone in the company already knew? I finally gave in to Robbie's suggestion, but I knew it would be a total waste.

It ... wasn't.

Robbie opened that part of the meeting by asking the whole team to write down what they believed our core values were, and then he read each response out loud. Their responses were all over the place. Very few were similar or even remotely related. Even worse, most of the answers were things that I, the business owner, did not believe in. The values my team thought the business represented didn't look, sound, or feel anything like me at all. I went into that meeting assuming everyone knew what mattered, and I came out of it realizing no one did. I thought our core values were obvious, but it turns out we didn't have any.

Correcting that glaring oversight has made a huge difference in shifting our practice into autopilot because it has clarified the values I, the owner, think are most important to growing the business, serving our patients, and working alongside the men and women we spend nine or ten hours a day with. That's not to say I personally came up with all our core values; the ideas came from everyone on the team. I just get to select the ones that are most aligned with our mission and vision.

Beyond that, defining our core values has fundamentally changed how I direct behaviors in my practice every single day, in every key interaction. And *directing behaviors* is the one thing that enables me to work effectively as both a surgeon *and* a CEO. Anytime I can spend a few hours developing something that then allows my team to function better whenever I'm in the operating room is a win. Few things have done that as powerfully as defining and communicating our core values because everyone on the team now knows what I think is important to us. It's hard for someone to go wildly off course as long as they use our core values as a filter in their decision-making. I usually don't even mind if they make the wrong choice, as long as they erred on the side of our core values.

While the core values primarily help everyone know what to do when I'm *not* around, I also use them as a tool when I *am*. Specifically, I use them in three ways. First, whenever we have an all-team meeting, I spend the first five minutes talking about some aspect of one of our values. I take this time seriously and usually spend a couple of hours the night before planning what I want to say, coming up with real-life examples of how I've seen that value at work in our practice, and putting it all in an entertaining format (as opposed to a crappy PowerPoint presentation with a thousand words per slide). The goal with these mini talks is to create some enthusiasm around the core value while reminding everyone that it is a piece of our identity.

Second, whenever I notice a team member doing something I'm proud of or exhibiting a behavior I'd like to see more often, I attach a core value to the praise. In my years playing sports as a kid and now as my son's soccer coach, I've learned that *specific* praise is much more powerful than general praise. That is, saying "Great work today" doesn't go very far. However, imagine you have a core value about not gossiping, and your business director told you about a team member bringing a reasonable concern directly to their leader. You could say, "Hey, I heard about <this situation>. I'm going to trust your leaders to solve it, but I wanted to tell you how grateful I am for how you handled it. You went straight to your leader with the problem instead of griping about it to everyone else, and that was a perfect example of living up to our core values. That's awesome to see. Thank you for representing our practice so well."

Third, when I notice a team member do something I'm *not* proud of and want to see less of, I attach a core value to the correction. That helps me focus on the *behavior* as the problem rather than the *person* being the problem. For example, if a team member is upset about having to cover another employee's responsibilities for an unexpected absence, you might say, "Listen, I know your job is a lot more difficult whenever she's out of the office. I can see it in your face, and I can hear it in how you're talking to everyone else. But we've all agreed that 'we take care of each other' is one of our core values. It's who we are, and it's what we're going to do. You know she would do the same for you."

I love how core values give me a framework for having both encouraging and intimidating conversations. I shudder to think about how I used to handle these situations before we had them, especially since everyone on my team apparently had a different idea about who we were and how we were supposed to act as a team. Articulating our core values got us all on the same page and speaking the same language, and I can't imagine ever going back.

THESE THINGS WORK

Robbie: Vision, mission, and core values. So many people think these three things are fluffy, feel-good, do-nothing niceties that have no concrete bearing on the business. Even if leaders do take the time to articulate them and write them out, they may still end up being shoved in a drawer and forgotten. This is insane to me. These are fundamental elements of the business. They are filters to be used in evaluating opportunities. They are accelerators to increase the speed of quality decision-making. They are true norths that provide much-needed clarity in moments of confusion and distraction. I would go so far as to say that nothing can take more credit for our team's consistent track record of quality decision-making than the combined power of our vision statement, mission statement, and core values—not Jeremy's charisma, not my obsession with planning, not our leadership structure, and not even our preoccupation with world-class patient care. These three items have our cultural DNA baked into them, and all of us trust their ability to lead us in the right direction.

If you doubt the power of vision, mission, and core values, I challenge you to take another look. Do the things we discussed in this chapter. Take this stuff seriously. Put it to work for your business and see for yourself how powerfully they can affect your team's alignment and growth—while taking your leadership prowess to the next level.

CHAPTER 19

GROWING YOUR TEAM

Jeremy: My friend Dr. Rafi Fredman opened his Amelia Aesthetics practice in St. Louis in 2020—five months into a global pandemic. I've mentioned Rafi a few times in this book because, frankly, he is freaking brilliant as a surgeon and a business owner. I was fortunate to join and then buy an existing practice that Dr. Glenn Davis already had up and running with an office, operating room, phone systems, IT support, and staff. While I've certainly had my share of tough lessons as a business owner, I've never had to face the bootstrapped pressures of being essentially a one-man show. Rafi, though, had to start from scratch, and I've learned a lot by watching how he has grown his business. One of the most useful things I've learned from him is how small of a team someone can get by with if they're willing to be creative.

My guess is that you're like me in that you can look around your office right now and see at least a dozen different people taking care of different parts of the practice. You probably have people at the front desk, someone doing scheduling, one or more patient care coordinators, nurses, PAs, and a bookkeeper at a minimum. If that's where you are, great. I'm right there with you. We have around forty team members across our Amelia Aesthetics and Amelia Agency businesses, and I'm grateful for each one of them.

Can you guess how many people Rafi employed for the first year or more of his business? Two—a patient care coordinator and a clinical assistant. Two people. That's it.

You'll notice there was no one to answer the phone. Why? Because he structured his business to eliminate the need for patients to call to ask basic questions. He used an online pricing tool to post all his prices on his website, eliminating the need for patients to call for a price. He implemented an online scheduling tool that enabled patients to schedule their own appointments, which eliminated the need to call for scheduling—which, by the way, also made things much easier for patients. He signed an agreement with a large technology company for basic computing infrastructure, which included HIPAA–compliant email. This enabled him and his small team to help patients with nonurgent concerns on their own schedule. Of course, he made sure his existing patients could reach him directly with any emergencies, but those rarely happened because he carefully planned from day one how to run his business as lean as possible.

So for a year, Rafi had a busy practice that generated $2 million in revenue, and he did it with almost no phone calls, extremely low overhead, and only two full-time salaries on his books. That's what a new practice running on autopilot can look like.

If Rafi had gone the traditional route and *assumed* he needed someone to answer the phones, he would have paid about $42,000 in the 2020 economy. Add about 20 percent in other employee-related business expenses, and that one person would have cost him roughly $50,000. And we cannot forget the other major expense this would have cost him—his time. It would have taken dozens of hours for him to find, interview, and hire someone. Then he would have had to train them how to do the job and, of course, spend a few hours per week actively *leading* that person. This would have cost him revenue because it would have kept him out of the operating room, meaning he'd be *paying* money in salary and *losing* money in lost revenue at the same time—a double whammy. Some days, this team member would be out sick. Some days, they'd be out on vacation. Some days, they'd be at work but not very productive. Some days, they'd butt heads with other employees. That's all normal and to be expected whenever you're dealing with people.

What's *not* normal is to do what Rafi did, to stop assuming every task requires a new team member. Employees cost both money and time. Rafi chose to rely on systems and technology wherever possible and only hire when absolutely needed. By watching him, I learned that knowing when to hire is important, but knowing when *not* to hire might be even more important. In medicine, we embrace progress in clinical care. We love the newest and best technologies in our personal lives. Why, then, do we ignore these things in our businesses?

This chapter is a short introduction to growing your team, but I thought it would be worthwhile to start by challenging your assumptions about when you *need* to grow your team. If you've put as much of your practice on autopilot as we've discussed and still need help, then go for it! If there are ways you can automate a few processes and systems to eliminate the need for another fixed cost in the form of a new salary, start there. As business owners, we've got to get past the mindset that we *have* to have these particular roles on our team simply because that's how we've always done it. Instead, I want to challenge you to view each salary on your payroll as an investment. Like any investment, a salary should ultimately *make* you more than it costs you. If it doesn't, then each new hire will take you one step backward.

Now, all that said, let's get into the issue of when to hire, how to interview, and when and how to let a team member go when necessary.

"FULLY STAFFED" IS A MYTH

Robbie: Before we run through the prequalifying questions that I suggest you ask yourself before making a hiring decision, I want to ask you a broader question about your preferences when it comes to the size of your team. Will you be more comfortable being *overstaffed* or *understaffed*? That's a key question that almost no business owner ever asks themselves, but it's important for one reason: the idea of being *fully staffed* is a myth. There's no such thing as being fully staffed because there is no "perfect" number of people for your organization. Workloads fluctuate, people take vacations, they get sick, your practice is always evolving, you have more patients some months than others. These and many other factors influence the number of people you need on any given day. As a result, the staff-to-work scales will never balance. It will always lean toward *too many* people or *too few* people. So you need to ask yourself which you prefer.

If you are a bit overstaffed, you are always going to have enough people to run your practice without having to consistently scramble when someone is unexpectedly out sick or when patient demand suddenly increases. On the other hand, it takes more leadership investment, and it's more expensive to be a little overstaffed than it is to be understaffed. There's no universally right or wrong answer here; there's only the answer that works best for you.

When you can settle this in your mind once and for all, you can enjoy greater peace of mind when the unexpected workflow fluctuations hit. If you choose to stay lean and things get tight one month, you can say with confidence, "That's OK. We expected and prepared for this." If you prefer more margin on the size of your team and business slows down, you can say, "It's OK that everyone's getting a little break this month. I'm just glad they were here last month when business was booming." Again, neither is right or wrong as long as you visualize which position you'd rather be in and commit to making hiring decisions that reflect that preference.

FIVE QUESTIONS FOR KNOWING WHEN TO HIRE

One of the most common questions we get from private practice owners is, "When do I know it's time to hire a new team member?" It can definitely be confusing, especially if you're in the middle of a wild fluctuation in your business. To help clarify things in your mind, I want you to ask yourself the following five questions before pulling the trigger and posting a job opening:

1. **Will this hire create more financial value than it would cost?** Jeremy mentioned this earlier, but let's dig in a bit more. In the business world, leaders always look for the ROI—return on investment—on every expense. The same should be true for your private practice. Except for intentional charitable donations, every dollar you spend should come back to you—and then some. If a new $80,000 medspa provider can generate $200,000 in profit, that's a great ROI. If a $10,000 part-time bookkeeper can save you $20,000 in CPA fees, you literally doubled your money but on a much smaller scale. The idea is to think through not only what this person will *cost* you but also what this person will *make* you.

2. **Can a technology resource, instead of a human resource, meet this need?**

   There are obvious pros and cons both to technology resources and human resources, but I've found the medical industry tends to overly favor human resources. If we can stop assuming that a new task means a new hire, like Jeremy said earlier, we free ourselves to new and emerging technology solutions that are cheaper and more efficient and create better experiences for our patients.

3. **Can we afford the additional fixed cost on our payroll?**

   Do not post a position until you are absolutely sure you can afford the added expense. This is such an obvious point, but it's shocking how often a business—especially a private practice—jumps straight to posting a position before ever considering the budget. You have to factor in the salary plus benefits and payroll taxes. This is a good time to pull out the Revenue versus Expenses chart we discussed in chapter 8 to get a clear picture of the margin you have in your finances.

4. **Do we have the leadership in place to support a new hire?**

   Every hire includes *hard costs* such as salary and benefits and *soft costs* such as a leader's time to hire, train, and lead the new team member. And of course, there's the mental and emotional cost of having another person around to support and coach. In my experience, business owners typically underestimate the soft costs around new hires, so do not move forward without discussing this with your business director, who should be much closer to the day-to-day demands of the practice's leadership team.

5. **Am I committed to waiting for the right candidate?**

    The only thing worse than having too *few* team members in place is having the *wrong* team members in place. Never hire in a panic, and never rush through the interview process we'll discuss in the next section. No matter what you're experiencing, you do not want to commit your money, time, and emotional energy into someone who's a bad fit for your practice. If all you need is a warm body to help with a short-term busy season, avoid the long-term commitment to a potential bad hire by getting a temp from a service for a few weeks. Anyone you hire into a full-time position will become part of your culture whether you like them or not. Take the time to make sure you do.

Once you've settled in your mind whether you want to be overstaffed or understaffed *and* you've taken a breath and asked yourself these five questions, it's time to post the position and start interviewing.

HOW TO INTERVIEW

I'm going to start with the assumption that you have some candidates. Maybe you put a job posting on Indeed.com, emailed your newsletter list, or have some internal referrals from your current team members. Wherever these candidates are coming from, it's time to begin the interviewing process.

I strongly recommend not jumping right into bringing someone into your practice for an in-person interview. That's a time-consuming process for everyone involved. Instead, start by having your business director ask the candidate to send a cover letter explaining why they want to join your team. You can tell a lot about someone by reading two or three paragraphs they have written.

If you're happy with what you see in the cover letter, have your business director conduct a simple phone or video-call interview. This is an appropriate next step after a cover letter, which gives you a chance to interact one-on-on without making the candidate get all dressed up and drive across town to meet you. It also saves you the trouble of "hosting" a candidate at your office while still giving you the opportunity to engage enough to see if the person would be a good team, culture, and skill set fit.

Only once you've gone through these two initial steps should you consider bringing a candidate into your practice in person. And when you do, make sure you have a plan. I like each candidate to do two to three one-on-one interviews as well as a team interview; these can be all in one day or split up across a couple of days. I'll find two or three team members who I know "get the practice" the most, and I will have them interview the candidate. Even if these team members don't know the particulars of the position we're filling, they will be able to determine if this candidate would be a good fit for our team and culture.

Finally, we have the candidate do a team interview with the people they will be working most closely with. This gives you the ability to see how they are going to interact with their potential future team. A word of warning with this group interview, though: Be sure to stay in control of the meeting, and don't let your team members view this as a time to joke around too much. It's fine to keep it casual but remind your team beforehand that this is still a professional job interview. They should keep inside jokes and certainly any good-natured jokes about the business leaders to a bare minimum. This interview should stay focused on the candidate; it should not seem like a fun break in the day for the team members involved.

After the interviews are over, I thank the candidate and send them home, letting them know the ball is in their court. This is a really important point. I make sure to tell them to let me know if they are interested in continuing the pursuit of the role. This creates a unique moment in which I get to see them make a judgment call. Do they send a thank-you note? Do they send a well-written email thanking us for our time? Many times, the way they respond is a make-or-break moment because it shows me how they handle a high-stakes decision and interaction.

Last, I like to connect with everyone who interviewed the candidate, usually in a short meeting, and I ask them three specific questions:

- Do they understand the job?
- Do we believe they can grow past the current responsibilities?
- Are they hungry, humble, and people-smart?

That last question, which I've adapted from Patrick Lencioni's excellent book *The Ideal Team Player*, is especially important. I'm careful to listen intently to my team members' responses, paying close attention to what they say *and* their nonverbal cues. I let them speak first, and I wait until the end to give them my personal feedback so as not to unnecessarily influence them.

If all goes well, we send an offer letter. If not, we send a very short, simple, and clear rejection letter. An employer never owes the candidate a detailed explanation why they did not get the job, and offering such an explanation can lead to unexpected legal complications. Sometimes a candidate will follow up to ask if they could have done anything differently or better and responding to them with some coaching might seem like the kind thing to do. Do not do it. All they need to know is that you decided to go with another candidate or continue your search. Any information you give them beyond that could come back to bite you. It sucks, but you know ... lawyers.

The Business Owner's Role in Interviewing

Jeremy: For my first five years of running the practice, I was heavily involved in every step of the hiring process for each new team member. That included the decision to hire, creating the job posting, the interviews, salary negotiations, the offer letter, and the onboarding and training. I didn't do it all alone, of course, but I was neck-deep in every phase. That meant taking stacks of resumes home with me at night, doing interviews late in the afternoons or early evenings instead of going home after a busy day, and stealing several other pockets of time from my family to get the hiring done the way I wanted it done.

Then Robbie and I developed *The Private Practice MBA* principles and changed how we run the practice, which included the hiring process. I was confident in the things we had planned and put in motion, but some days I was still surprised to walk into the office and see the process working without me. For example, I'll tell you about one of my all-time favorite days at work. When I walked through the door first thing one morning, I saw an unfamiliar face sitting behind our front desk. Frankly, it was weird. That had never happened before; it was one of those moments that makes you think for half a second that you walked into the wrong office. I found Robbie and asked who she was.

He replied, "Oh, that's Sarah. Today is her first day. I hired her to replace Katie, who's moving in a few weeks. The salary's the same so there's no impact on revenue, and Katie will train her over the next three weeks before she leaves. Let me introduce you."

Admittedly, this knocked me back a bit. I had a rush of thoughts and feelings that were new to me as a business owner. I felt guilty that this person was already an employee of my company (though only for an hour at that point), but I hadn't met her yet. I was worried that I wasn't involved in this important decision. I wondered what type of person Robbie had brought into the business without me weighing in. All those thoughts swirled around my head for maybe an hour before it dawned on me what had happened. The system had worked. From my perspective, the practice had hired an awesome new team member on autopilot.

I also realized what the autopilot system had given me. In the weeks prior, instead of wondering what the job posting should say, reviewing resumes, and interviewing a half-dozen people, I was busy doing other things—things that were more important to me and my family. I had spent those weeks eating dinner with my family, coaching my son's soccer team, going on dates with my wife, and generally living my life.

The front desk is a high-turnover position in our business. That's not good or bad; it's just a fact. People come into that role and either advance in the company or happily stay there for a year or two before moving on. If I was still personally involved in every phase of the hiring process for every position, I'd be spending a few weeks every year or two dealing with that one vacant position. Frankly, I don't want to do that every time the person at the front desk leaves. Because we've committed to the simple hiring process Robbie has outlined, I don't have to. I can trust my business director and key leaders to fill the practice with amazing people while I'm off living the life I want to live.

The point I want to make crystal clear is this: Robbie laid out a clear system for hiring excellent team members—but that system does not (and often *should not*) be implemented by you. In fact, the faster you can find someone to do it for you, the better your life will be. Your goal as the owner, then, should be to set the tone and help create the steps and rules for how to hire, find someone you trust to implement them, and then get out of the way.

When the Business Owner Needs to Be Involved

Now, there are times when it's not appropriate for you to get out of the way—such as when you're hiring a key position that will directly impact your day-to-day work. For me, this is usually either a high-level business and/or leadership role or a position that impacts my work as a surgeon, such as a surgical tech. For these roles, I let the system play out as we've explained, but I personally conduct a short interview where I cover four specific questions. I've honed these questions after more than a decade of hiring these positions, and I always phrase them exactly the same way each time I interview a candidate. Those questions are:

1. Imagine you're driving home from work, windows down and music blaring, and you're feeling great about how work went that day. What is likely to have made the day a good one?
2. Imagine you're driving home from work with the radio off, and you get home without even remembering the drive because you were so distracted by the challenges of your workday. What causes those kinds of days for you?
3. No one works perfectly with every personality type. We all struggle with some people. What are the personality types you struggle with?
4. What are the personality types you really gel with?

Depending on how chatty the person is, it only takes fifteen to thirty minutes to cover all four of these questions, but I've found the answers tell me what I need to know from job candidates. And it's not only about what they *say*. That's important, but I'm just as focused on their body language and nonverbal cues. I'm looking for how comfortable they are, whether they're simply putting on a show, if they're making eye contact, and whether they can confidently describe the type of people they do and don't like working with. All those things matter.

A coach once told me, "Jeremy, people will tell you who they really are. You just have to be willing to listen when they do." A big part of someone telling you who they are is what they say *without* saying it. The words coming out of their mouth are only half the message. Be sure to listen to both halves when interviewing.

WHEN AND HOW TO FIRE A TEAM MEMBER

Robbie: Now we need to discuss one of the most uncomfortable responsibilities every leader will face at one point or another: firing a member of your team. Letting a team member go is obviously emotional and difficult to do well, but there are a few guidelines you can follow to ensure that you protect your practice and make this conversation the least painful as possible for you and your exiting team member.

Before we get into the *how* of the discussion, we should examine our expectations as business owners when it comes to our team. Hopefully, you like every member of your team and would love for them to stick with you for the long haul. It can be easy to get so comfortable with the people you spend so much time with that you can't picture your practice without them. We can forget, though, that the people we've hired don't have the same connection to the business as owners do. They may love their job... but it's still their *job*. The fact is there are very few (if any) team members who will be "lifers" inside your organization. As the owner, you will likely outlast most of them—and that's OK. It doesn't mean you or they did anything wrong; it's just how life is. So as we shift our mindsets into how to let someone go, give yourself a break. Too often, when we think about firing someone, we feel like we're destroying their life. Sure, it's a tough situation for everyone, but it's unlikely that person would have stayed in that role for the next twenty years. They probably would have left eventually; you're simply expediting the process for them.

Now, how can we go about letting someone go in the most professional way possible? We start by giving them every opportunity to keep their job. Especially if you're dealing with an attitude or competency issue, it's best not to jump to removing the employee too quickly. Instead, we put the team member on a ninety-day improvement plan with a clear growth plan, which includes specific requirements and milestones. We tell them exactly how their performance will be evaluated, leave no room for ambiguity, and give the person full ownership of reaching the goals we've set for them. Then we check in with them often throughout the process and sit down with them every thirty days to review their growth plan and their progress. Our goal whenever possible is for them to make the changes needed and remain on the team. If they succeed, we both win. If they cannot make the necessary changes, we recognize that it's probably time for them to leave the company. Those situations still suck, but we at least know we did everything we could to help them before letting them go.

Even if you go through a formal process of reprimanding someone for behavioral issues or walk someone through a ninety-day growth plan with clear expectations and consequences, there's something that's almost universally true when you sit someone down to fire them: it's a surprise. They'll be shocked. Sometimes they'll act like they have no idea what you're talking about. I've often heard leaders say that no team member should ever be surprised the day they get fired. That's a fine goal, but despite my best efforts, it's never been true for me.

I've seen team members who haven't completed a single item on their ninety-day plan react with complete shock when they're ultimately fired. I've looked team members in the eye as I've read them written reprimands that effectively said, "If you ever do this again, you will lose your job." Then they do it again. And get fired. And are stunned. "What?! How could you do this? Why didn't you warn me? I had no idea you would do this to me!" Despite everything you do to make this an obvious outcome, prepare yourself for a reaction of shock and betrayal. It's weird, but it happens. A lot.

Few people react well to being fired, which is understandable. You cannot let this endanger your practice, however. Work with your corporate counsel to create a proper process for removing a team member from the company. Have the paperwork ready and be prepared to walk them all the way out the door that day, making sure you get their keys, key cards, and security codes to prevent them from accessing the building. You also want to revoke their access to your computer network and email immediately. You might even have your IT person do this while you're still meeting with the team member. Even the nicest person in the world can surprise you with a final vindictive act when they're reacting out of anger, shock, and fear. Be kind to them . . . but protect yourself. Once they're gone, inform the team that the person is no longer a part of the company, but do not go into detail. Again, consult your attorney for what is best to say (and not say).

While it's certainly difficult to *be* fired, most employees don't recognize how hard it is for us, as business owners, to be the one firing a team member regardless of the reason. If you struggle with this, I want to remind you that, if you are letting someone go for all the right reasons, you are doing that team member a tremendous service by letting them go. Although this is a difficult moment, you are setting them free to go find a career or a different company where they will be able to thrive. There have been a couple of people I've fired and then run into a year or two later who have literally thanked me for letting them go. They told me that once they calmed down, they realized they hadn't been happy in that position for a long time. When they were forced to find a new job, they found a renewed passion and sense of purpose that made them happier than they had been in years.

It takes a lot of humility to thank your former employer for firing you, and it won't happen every time, but we can still do our best to act in the best interests of both the practice and the team member who's being asked to leave. Even if they don't come back to thank you, you can at least sleep at night knowing you did the right thing for everyone involved.

MORE MONSTERS

When my daughter was four or five years old, I used to read her a book called *The More Monster*. No matter how many good things the More Monster had, it would always roar for more. If it had three cookies, it wanted four. If it had five balloons, it wanted six. The More Monster was never satisfied. The lesson for kids was clear: be grateful for and strive to be content with the good things you already have, and don't worry so much about the things you don't. It's one of the most difficult lessons for a parent to teach a child.

Sadly, some people don't learn this as children. They grow up into real-life, adult-sized More Monsters... and sometimes, they come to work for you. You might even be thinking of some More Monsters you've led or worked with in the past. No matter how many benefits they have, no matter how many times you ask their opinion, no matter how much paid time off they have, no matter how much you pay them, no matter how much grace you show them... it's never enough to keep them happy. They always want more. The result is misery for everyone around them. They're frustrated because they think they're undervalued. You're frustrated because you're already going above and beyond to make them happy. Their teammates are frustrated because they know the "squeaky wheel" is getting all the grease—and because they're sick and tired of listening to the More Monster's constant complaints.

Once you identify a More Monster on your team (and it's usually easy to spot them), you have to decide whether to *keep* them on your team. Having a More Monster stomp around your practice is destructive in many ways. They demand much more of your time, attention, and resources than anyone else, even if their position doesn't warrant much of your direct interaction. And if you're not careful, you end up giving the More Monsters way more of everything—including your time and energy—than they deserve. These people are also extremely demoralizing to those around them. They constantly complain, they gossip, and their actions make it crystal clear that they are in this for themselves.

At first, this may not seem like a big deal. After all, we all believe in investing in our team. But that's my point: an investment into a More Monster isn't *really* an investment at all because there is no ROI.

Investments are supposed to produce a return, but when you invest into a More Monster, you're playing a zero-sum game. You already know there will be no return. Instead, that "investment" will just get lost in the black hole of the *more* the monster demands.

To be clear, More Monsters aren't necessarily bad people; they're just bad team members. One of the most important jobs we have as leaders is to cultivate a team of grateful, excited, and passionate individuals. The old adage is absolutely true: one bad apple really can ruin the whole bunch. There is nothing you can do to satisfy a More Monster, but you can give the rest of your team the gift of helping the More Monster find somewhere else to work. So I challenge you to decide right now, as harsh as it might seem, to commit to a More Monster exorcism in your practice. If you discover one, your best and only option is to defend the health and integrity of your team by showing the ungrateful individual out the door.

Are More Monsters Worth Their Productivity?

Jeremy: Robbie didn't mention one thing that might make you hesitate to fire a More Monster. Because they're never satisfied, they are usually highly competitive, aspirational, and *uncomfortably* productive. By "uncomfortably," I mean your constant annoyance at their attitude is slightly offset by the value they're bringing into the practice. The More Monster could be the salesperson with the highest close rate, or it might be an extremely efficient provider who's able to see 20 percent more patients than the other providers. You can tell they aren't only pushing *you* for more; they expect more from themselves, as well. As a result, the thought of firing a productive More Monster could seem like a big hit to your bottom line.

And...you might be right. At least in the short term.

But here's the rest of the story you might not be able see through your understandable fear: Removing a More Monster—even if it's your top revenue producer—will likely impact your revenue for a little while, but it will set your practice up for even greater success in the future.

What Robbie and I call More Monsters is close to something I've heard Dr. Brad Calobrace, one of plastic surgery's most inspiring voices, describe as an Energy Vampire. This is a person who is high capacity and super-productive... but also narcissistic and a challenge to be around. Their high volume gives them an inflated sense of their value, and as a result, they don't hesitate to suck up all the resources, energy, kindness, and tools around them if they believe doing so will benefit them.

An interesting thing happens, though, when you remove an Energy Vampire from the room. As Dr. Calobrace explains, Energy Vampires create a vacuum wherever they go that sucks in all the resources around them. When you remove one, then, it's not just their productivity that leaves; the vacuum disappears with them too. That's why it's common to experience what feels like a sudden rush of oxygen flooding the room whenever an Energy Vampire is removed. Everyone else can finally breathe again. The energy that was sucked up by one person is now available for everyone else to share. The result is more energy and resources that the rest of the team can use to boost their own productivity.

In the same way, when you remove a More Monster, you free up more of *everything* for the rest of your team. In my experience, that trade-off has paid off in spades. You suddenly have a team of people growing and evolving in new, unexpected ways because they're finally getting the time, energy, attention, and resources they needed to thrive. I have, in Robbie's words, helped More Monsters "find somewhere else to work" many times throughout my career, and we have ended up in a better place because of it literally every time.

DON'T TAKE IT PERSONALLY

Something I've learned over time and with maturity is that we all tend to take our jobs way too personally. This causes us, as business owners, to hold on to people too tightly, and it causes team members to react in surprising ways when we ask them to leave. That's a dangerous combination, especially in our overly litigious culture in which recording devices are ubiquitous. Every word you say when you're letting someone go is important. One careless word could cost you years of stress and hundreds of thousands of dollars from a lawsuit. If the person you're firing has an outburst that you respond to in kind, and if that causes you to say careless things yourself, *and if that person is recording the conversation*, then you, my friend, are screwed. Keep your cool at all costs. Give them the information they need and not one word more, and then escort them out of the building. You have to keep your focus on your practice. Don't endanger it by trying to be too kind (or getting too hotheaded) with the person you're removing. And please, stop taking every departure so personally.

Early in my career as a business owner, I felt like a failure every time a team member left our practice. If someone chose to leave for another job, I lost sleep wondering why they weren't happy in our business and what I could have or should have done differently to make them want to stay. If someone had to be let go, I felt guilty for not being a better leader who could have helped them turn things around before it got to that point. I took it personally every single time, even if it was someone I didn't interact with much on a regular basis.

With time and experience, though, I've matured as a leader. Part of that maturity is accepting the fact that very few people will stick with me all the way until I retire. Looking around my office right now, I can see and hear people I absolutely love working with, but I know most, if not all, of them will exit the practice long before I do. That's not because I'll fail them in any way; it's because that's how life is. Most people work a job for a while and then they move on. And oftentimes, they're moving on to something better. Stepping forward in their career might require them to step out of our business. Stepping forward in their personal lives might mean moving on to something that gives them more time for their families or side projects. Those aren't failures; that's how people grow.

We might like to point to someone in our practice and say, "This person is absolutely irreplaceable. We couldn't survive without her!" But that's simply not true. You *could* replace her. You *would* survive without her. It may be a bumpy ride for a while, but your practice will fall into a new normal soon enough, and then you'll find someone else you'll start viewing as irreplaceable. Of course, that person won't be irreplaceable either. The hard truth is that we can *all* be replaced. Who knows? A year from now, it's possible everyone on my team will still be here but I'll the one who'll be gone! I have zero plans for that but anything could happen. And if it did, I'm sure Robbie and the new business owner would carry on just fine.

Now we've spent two chapters talking about how to *align* our teams with a vision, a mission, and a handful of core values and how to *grow* our teams by hiring the right people and removing the wrong people. Next we'll dig into how to *lead* this group of people we've assembled into the success we've always dreamed of for our practice.

CHAPTER 20
LEADING YOUR TEAM

Jeremy: Ego is like oxygen in the medical field. We breathe it in. It feeds us. It nourishes every cell in our bodies. We suffocate without it. I'm sure ego has *some* positive role in the world and in medicine specifically. There has to be some good that comes from it *sometimes*. But it is so unreasonably powerful. So many relationships are ruined by it. So much effort is wasted trying to satisfy inflated egos, and so many mistakes are made when our egos blind us to the realities of life. We don't know everything. We can't perform every procedure. We can't diagnose every ailment. We can't avoid every bad result. We can't guarantee perfect results. None of us can.

If I had to pick one characteristic to grow in every human—and especially in every physician—it would be the opposite of ego. I'd choose humility.

Humility feels so uncommon in our world—*our world* in general, but especially in *our world* of practicing medicine. Humility doesn't get much attention. It's not great for marketing. It doesn't fuel as many flashy Instagram pictures or ad campaigns. It stays in the shadows, mainly in the context of one-on-one relationships. But don't let humility fool you. It's every bit as powerful as ego. It's just not as loud.

As physicians—and this is especially true for those of us who are plastic surgeons—we tend to shout our greatness to the world. Every one of our websites and social media accounts feels like they are designed for one purpose: to feed our egos. We shout into the void, "Look at me! Look how great I am! Look at my artistry! Look what I did for this patient! Look at this gift basket a patient sent me to say thanks for the awesome work I did!"

I get it. Marketing is weird. Even those of us who aren't comfortable in the heat of the spotlight have to put *something* out there to drive business. We definitely don't want to come across as ashamed of our talent and embarrassed by our good work. I'm not sure how we could come up with a marketing campaign centered around how *humble* we are anyway. What would "humble" before-and-after pictures even look like? Maybe we'd post a photo of our most average patient result on Instagram and say, "We did this for her. Maybe we can do it for you too. Give us a shot." That's not very compelling. So instead, we select the best "after" picture we took that week and say something like, "Wow! Look at this fantastic result! We can do this for you too if you call now!" Again, marketing is weird. It *needs* ego. But we cannot allow the fluff we use to drive business to become our whole world. We've got to keep it in perspective by balancing the ego with humility.

Imagine how much better we would all be if, instead of creating yet *another* environment in which to strut around like a ridiculous peacock, we created safe spaces to talk about what isn't going right.

Imagine if the pictures we showed at meetings weren't the same five patients, talk after talk, year after year, but were instead the things we can't quite get right.

Imagine if we had national meetings where the luminaries didn't stand before the crowd and say, "Look how great I am. Don't you want to be this great?" and instead say, "Hey guys, this is where I'm struggling. I know you look to me as an expert, but I could really use some help on this one thing I can't quite figure out either. Maybe together, we can."

Of course, we can't do that on a national scale. It's too scary and given the overly litigious climate we're all working in, it's not safe. But I believe we can do this on a small scale. We can choose to lead our businesses with the safety that comes from pushing ego aside and replacing it with the humility that says, "I can be better—a better doctor and a better leader. I can do *more.*"

When I say *more* here, I mean squeezing every last drop of *potential* and *production* from ourselves and our team members. Very, very few of us are working at peak efficiency. There's always room for growth and improvement if we as leaders are open to looking for it within ourselves and doing the often-uncomfortable work of drawing it out of our teams. That's what leaders are called to do, so we better learn some strategies for making it happen.

INCREASE PRODUCTION BY COMPARING PERFORMANCE

Robbie: You'll remember from previous chapters that we are big fans of using scorecards to gauge performance. Now I want to suggest implementing a different type of scorecard in your business—but this one is going to be extremely uncomfortable for both you and your team at first. However, it's something I've seen pay off time and time again. It's the practice of comparing your team members' performances with one another . . . in front of them.

Your gut may scream, *That's the worst piece of leadership advice I've ever heard!* That's a fair reaction, so let me explain.

Early in my career, I had recently joined an in-house creative team for a nationally known brand. I was one of twelve graphic designers at the time, and part of my job was to create graphics for web ads and email newsletters. After our designs were approved, these marketing pieces were sent out into the world with the hope that our designs were compelling enough to make someone click on the ad. The company had several different product lines so most of us were creating ads for different things ranging from established, enormously successful products to brand-new, untested offerings. I loved my job and the company, and we all believed our products could change someone's life for the better. It wasn't just about making money; it was about helping people—and we were all highly motivated to help as many people as we could. So each designer shared a strong desire to create the most effective ads possible.

Enter Daniel Bell.

Daniel joined the company as a designer and quickly rose through the ranks to become a leader in the creative team. He was a great guy and strong young leader. He was also a big fan of taking risks other people wouldn't take. That often made the people working under him . . . uncomfortable.

One day, Daniel printed several copies of a line graph that clearly showed how many people had clicked each designer's ads, week by week, over the past three months. He hung these all over the room where we all worked, showing each of us, for the first time, how each of our work compared to everyone else's. A quick look at the chart revealed three things:

- Three designers' ads were far more effective than everyone else's.
- The results were flat across the twelve-week window, showing that none of us were steadily improving.
- My ads were the least effective. I came in twelfth out of twelve.

Having these charts taped to the walls of our workspace stripped all the politeness out of the discussion, and our effectiveness was laid bare for everyone to see. And it sucked.

I sat and stewed about it for a little while before sticking my head in Daniel's office. "Dude, what the heck? Maybe a little head's-up next time?"

Daniel grinned back at me and said, in his perfectly deadpan tone, "Why? Because it hurt your ego?"

Of course, that was why. And of course, I didn't admit it.

"No, it's just that I'm the newest designer in the room," I argued. "It's not fair to compare me to people with five or ten years' more experience!"

"Why?" he replied. "Because it hurts your ego?"

Again, that was definitely the reason, but I wouldn't admit it.

I pushed back again, this time with a new excuse. "But part of the team is working on a more popular product. Of course their ads will get more clicks. Shouldn't you at least compare apples to apples?"

"Why? Because it hurts your ego?"

I walked out.

That was a bad day for me. It was painful to see how my work compared to the work everyone else was doing—especially since I was falling so far behind the others. I fumed. I grumbled. I whined. But then, over the next two years, something amazing happened—something that made me *love* being publicly compared to my peers.

I know this will be somewhat controversial so let me continue this story as I run through five reasons why I'm such a strong advocate for publicly comparing team member performance.

1. **Public comparison forces us to decide what kind of team member we are going to be.**

   Daniel was right. The only reason I didn't like to be publicly compared to my teammates was because of my toxic ego. Conversely, some of the higher-performing team members worried the comparison would hurt the feelings of those who weren't as effective. Their success made them feel responsible for their teammates' emotions—which is just as toxic as ego.

   Even amid all the pushback, Daniel went to great lengths to ensure we all saw those charts on a regular basis. He even put them up on a huge screen in our team meetings every single week. After a few weeks, something beautiful started happening: Every time we saw those lines, we had to make the conscious decision to be humble team members who didn't hold ourselves responsible for other people's emotions. It took some time, but each of us found ourselves becoming healthier adults with healthier perspectives.

2. **Public comparison forces us to decide what kind of team we are going to be.**

   The first reason is all about who we are as individuals; the second reason is about who we are as a team.

   Simple charts and direct patient feedback are so powerful because they remove noise and reveal an accurate view of reality. If we don't have a clear picture of reality, it's nearly impossible to know how we can improve as a team. Daniel helped us realize that we can't just care about our own, individual line on the chart because none of us is working in isolation. We work as a team, and strong teams care about each person's results because those things collectively represent how much life-change we are creating *together*.

So let's stop being afraid to admit that some team members simply are not as effective as others. Instead, let's look at reality from our patients' perspectives and use it as motivation to increase the impact our whole team collectively is making in those patients' lives.

3. **Public comparison leads to intentional collaboration.**

Once we got our humility in check, a bunch of us designers at the bottom of the chart started having more conversations with the designers at the top. Similarly, many of the designers at the top of the chart started proactively reaching out to the ones at the bottom to offer whatever help and support they could. We started collaborating more as a team than we ever had.

The most effective designer in the room was Chris Sandlin. I hadn't interacted with Chris much because he was quieter and more reserved than most of us. But he was so excited and helpful when I started sending him my designs to get his feedback. Soon after, Chris started hosting a type of design camp once a week for thirty minutes before our typical day started. It wasn't mandatory, and he didn't ask anyone's permission. He just started doing it. And he didn't just show up and talk off the cuff; he always had something prepared to teach us. During one of his training sessions, someone asked him why he spent so much of his own time preparing for the group. He replied, "Because I've decided that if all of us aren't improving, then I am personally failing." We all immediately adopted the mantra for ourselves as well.

4. **Public comparison increases personal and collective effectiveness.**

As you can imagine, collaboration within our team spread quickly. But you know what else started happening? Genuine celebration. There was one week—I'll never forget it—when I had somehow squeaked out the most effective ad group of the prior week. It was the only time anyone had ever topped Chris head-to-head.

The funny thing was, I felt a dichotomy of emotions. I was excited, but I was also nervous. I thought, "Who am I to unseat the master, even for just a week? He's been teaching me so much. What's he going to think and feel knowing that I beat him?" And yet Chris was the first one to stand up in the group, start clapping, and congratulate me from across the room.

Do you think it stung Chris that someone had finally beaten him? Maybe. It would certainly be a natural reaction. Whether it did or didn't, though, Chris set his ego aside because he was committed to the idea that *great teams trade personal comfort for collective impact.*

5. **Public comparison keeps the top performers hungry.**

As memorable as (finally) beating Chris was, I think what happened the following week stands out even more in my mind as I sit here reflecting.

By this point, our team had grown to about fifty designers, and Daniel was sending out the line chart via email. It was obvious when it hit our inboxes because a wave of endearing heckling and clapping would erupt throughout our area. But not that week.

That week, as we all read the email and examined the chart, everyone was mostly silent except for occasional whispered comments such as, "Whoa. Is this right? No way." The confusion was understandable because there was a spike on the chart that was higher than any of us had ever seen.

Not only had Chris reclaimed his spot on top, but he'd completely crushed his previous record. In fact, he crushed *all* the records from every area. It was incredible. Later that day, Daniel sent out an email that contained a single sentence: "Last week, Chris's ads received more clicks than our entire team got the first week we compared our effectiveness."

Our team had grown so much, which in turn pushed Chris so much, that he alone created more life-changing opportunity for our customers than all of us had created during our first week of being measured against one another.

Over a period of just a couple years, I watched our entire team go from a group of designers working in silos, focused only on our own success, to a legitimate team that was deeply invested in one another's success. Not only were we healthier and more effective as individuals, but our team was doing dramatically more to accomplish our shared mission of changing lives through the products and services we offered.

Those two years fundamentally changed my view of public, one-to-one comparisons between team members. Sure, it can be awkward at first, but no leadership strategy, exercise, or technique has done a better job of making me more effective personally *and* more effective as a leader. As a result, I've made public comparisons a part of how we evaluate team members at Amelia Aesthetics and Amelia

Agency—whether it's from feedback we receive from a patient (both good and bad) or through the Team Review scorecards we use to track specific metrics for each employee, which we discuss as a group at our quarterly offsite (see chapter 17). Once the team members got used to the idea, they quickly came together to support one another just like my old team of designers did, and we've had equally outstanding results. I challenge you to try it for yourself and see how much more production and collaboration you can squeeze from your team by comparing them *to* one another *in front* of one another.

RAISING UP NEW TEAM MEMBERS

I used to think building a great team was easy: hire great people and you get a great team. Boom. Done.

I wish I was kidding, but it's true. I put most of my effort into the hiring process, and then part of me felt like my job was done. The new team member would start, I'd give them a high five, pass them the baton, and wish them luck. That was the extent of my training and "leadership." You'd be surprised by how many massive failures I endured before I figured out that the problem with my team ... was me. I realized that the only way to build a great team was not only to hire excellent people but also to lead them through a process from *new* team member to *great* team member. I don't just owe that to my business; I owe it to the team members themselves. How can I expect them to be successful if I'm not setting them up and building them up for success?

I've come to view my role as a leader less like passing a baton and more like holding on to a rope. Dave Ramsey often uses the analogy of a rope when talking about raising children, but I think it applies to raising up team members as well. You can picture it like this: On a team member's first day, imagine yourself clipping a rope to their waist, just like you'd do if you were "tying in" a mountain climber. The other end of the rope is in your hands. As the team member proves himself and you gain more confidence in their ability, you let out the rope and give them more slack. That "slack" means more freedom, autonomy, and the ability to make more important decisions. When the team member makes a poor decision or you can tell they haven't fully caught on to your way of doing business, you might pull back on the rope a bit, bringing them closer and limiting their ability to run too far on their own.

How do we know when to lengthen or shorten the rope? For that, I rely on a four-phase model I learned from leadership guru Ken Blanchard.[37] He originally presented it as a leadership development tool, but I've found it works just as well for raising up quality team members in general. As someone advances through the four phases, I'm comfortable giving them more rope. If they stumble and fall back into a previous phase, I pull the rope back in. Let's dig into what these four phases look like and how we can tell if someone's ready to move from one to the next.

1. **Phase 1: Directing**

    The first phase (bottom right of the chart) is called *Directing*. During this phase, your new team members simply don't know what they don't know. Having been part of your business for as long as you have, you know how to navigate the landscape and avoid the land mines, but they don't. If or when they step on one, you're the one who's going to have to clean up the mess.

    During this phase, as you'll see on the chart, you've got to be *high direction* and *low collaboration*. How often have you seen a leader give a new team member what he or she thought was a simple task, only for that leader to have to spend the next hour or two cleaning up a hot mess? Invariably, it's because the team leader didn't give *high direction*, and they trusted their new team member to make important judgement calls.

Sorry, but it doesn't work like that. You can't just tell your new team members to get to work; you have to show them how.

2. Phase 2: Coaching

After spending some time working with your new team member, you'll enter the second phase, *Coaching*. This phase is still *high direction*, but now it's *high collaboration*. They should know the basics of their job and your business, and they should even be able to spot many of the land mines in

The Four Phases of Intentional Leadership

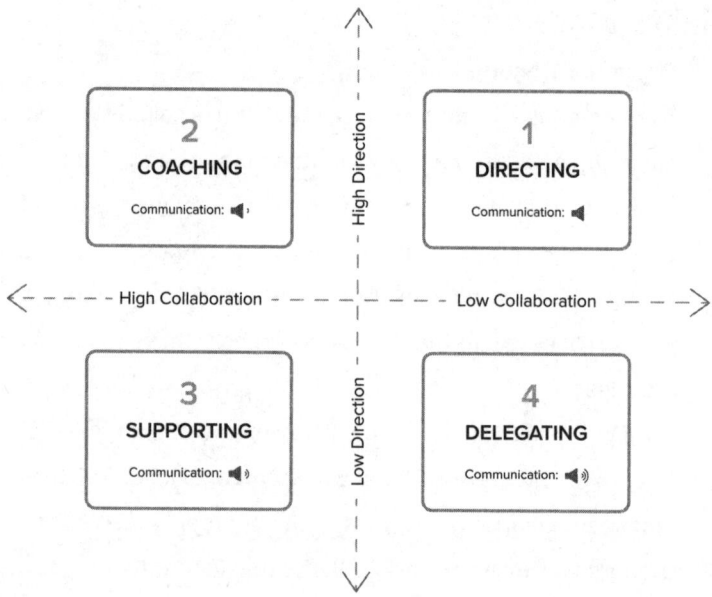

their path. However, they aren't sure how to *avoid* them yet. They still need your direction for that. So you can start to let out the rope a bit and give them some freedom to walk around, but don't let them run too far ahead of you.

Phase 2 is one of my favorites because I love teaching people how to navigate organizations, which is a key piece of *Coaching*. Here you are still telling your new team members exactly what to do, but you should also begin asking them a very important question in the process: "What do *you* think we should do?"

Expect your new team member's answer to be a little shortsighted, incomplete, and quite possibly incorrect. But don't let that discourage you because their answers will reveal three things:

- How well they understand the situation or problem
- Where you need to focus your efforts in coaching them
- How close they are to being given even more rope

You can then respond to their suggestion by telling them how they are right, why they are wrong, and/or why their proposed solution is incomplete. In this, you are teaching them how to make decisions in your business without risking any negative consequences.

3. **Phase 3: Supporting**

Phase 3, *Supporting*, represents an important shift in the team member's development. For the first time, you can downshift into *low direction*, meaning you start to pull back on the hand-holding. You also move into *high collaboration*, which gives the team member more authority to do their job. This is where you're more confident in giving the rope more slack so you can see what they do with it.

During this phase, your new team member starts to anticipate what they don't know. That is, they know the land mines are out there, but they still need some periodic guidance in how to avoid them. During Phase 3, your primary question is no longer "What do you think we should do?" Instead, the question evolves into "What do you *plan* to do?"

It's a nuanced difference, but it communicates that you are gaining a significant amount of trust in their decision-making (while still giving you a strategic moment to course-correct). It also sets the expectation that they shouldn't take action without consulting with you first—not yet anyway.

I love Phase 3 because it's where every new team member starts taking ownership of their decision-making. It's where they start innovating and coming up with unique (and actually good!) ideas.

4. **Phase 4: Delegating**

Finally, there's Phase 4, *Delegating*, which is *low direction* and *low collaboration*. During this phase, your team member "knows and goes." They see land mines, rarely step on them, and they have begun helping others to do the same.

During Phase 4, instead of basing your relationship on planning and coaching, your conversations turn into getting caught up on the decisions they've *already* made. Your main question during this stage is, "What decisions have you made that I should know about?"

One warning here: Just because they are making decisions on their own doesn't mean you, as their leader, aren't still accountable for everything they are doing, so it's critical that you keep a pulse on what they are up to. Remember, even your strongest team member will never have the visibility you have, and they will always need some slight course corrections.

Before we move on, I want to talk about "communication volume." One of the more dangerous misconceptions about raising up new team members is that the more rope you let out, the lower the level of communication needs to be. This is not only incorrect, it is exactly the opposite of what you should be doing.

The more rope you give them, the more distance you'll have between you and your new team member. When someone is in Phase 1, they are glued to your hip, so all they have to do is whisper for you to hear them. But once someone is in Phase 4, they're several miles away from you. They are going to have to yell as loud as they can to ensure you are in the loop on everything they are doing. For that reason, you have to be even more intentional about your communication as you give them more rope.

We've all been in new career situations, whether it's a new job, new role, or transfer to a new team. What would have happened if the leader of that team had just looked at you and said, "OK, you're on the team now! There are a ton of land mines out there; have fun figuring them out!"?

Please don't put your new team members through that kind of pain. After all, if you don't help them learn about land mines and how to avoid them, you will only find yourself spending more time than ever on things you thought you hired someone else to do.

It Can't Be You

Jeremy: Robbie did a great job unpacking how we get new team members up and running, by directing, coaching, supporting, and collaborating. But there's one important point I need to add here: you, the business owner, cannot be the one doing these things most of the time.

The whole point of *The Private Practice MBA* is to help you put your practice on autopilot, meaning your business keeps moving full steam ahead even when you aren't around to make all the decisions. What we're talking about in this chapter (and especially in this four-phase system we've adapted from Ken Blanchard) gives you a way to lead without being present. You do that by training your business director to do these things first, and then releasing them to develop your team members the same way.

Even if you aspire to maintain a small, no-frills practice with only a handful of employees, you cannot be the one to direct, coach, support, and collaborate with everyone on your team. You just can't. Your time is worth far more than anyone else's in your business—literally thousands of dollars per hour. Spending even a couple of hours getting a new patient care coordinator up to speed on the basics of the business can cost your practice $10,000 or more in opportunity cost from lost revenue. That time isn't free; it's coming from somewhere. You're either taking it away from a paying patient or taking it away from your family who'd rather have you home for dinner. Neither option is worth the sacrifice—not when there are others who could do just as good of a job—if not better—developing a new team member.

I know that sounds cold, but I'm not saying you shouldn't interact with your new employees. All I'm saying is that you should reserve your time for the things no one else can do. In this case, that means spending whatever time you have developing a personal relationship with the employee while others do the heavy lifting of training them. Fortunately, if you're structuring your practice the way we've discussed, you already have a strong system in place for making this happen. It starts, of course, with your business director.

Your job is to run your business director through the four phases we've discussed here. *Direct* your business director that your team is going to start being very intentional in onboarding and developing new team members. *Coach* them through what an onboarding checklist might include for the position being filled. *Support* them during the process with encouragement and gentle redirection when needed. Then, in time, back off and fall into your role as *Delegator* with them as they take the reins in leading your team-member development experience for new hires.

That's when onboarding becomes fun for you because it is happening—and happening effectively—without you. Because you invested time in building the infrastructure, you don't have to have entire weeks and months derailed every time your practice needs to fill a position. Instead, you can spend your one-on-one time with each team member, making a personal, human connection, while trusting your leaders to teach them how to be effective in their roles.

YOU NEED A COACH TOO

Jeremy: Throughout this section—and really, throughout this entire book—we have talked about ways to be a better leader and coach to our team members. As the business owner, we have a huge responsibility to the people who work with us to make sure they are being cared for, trained, led, corrected, encouraged, and properly coached throughout their tenure with our practice. But…what about us? If we're at the top of the org chart, who's looking after us?

Life in our twenties is absolutely insane for every physician. That's when we get out of college, go to medical school, and then go straight into residency. All our time is spent studying or working twelve-hour shifts in the hospital. Some of us get married and start families during those years, which adds a whole new level of insanity to an already crazy existence. It reminds me of a video I saw of Jordan Peterson, one of the most influential psychologists of our time, who described that season of life like this:

> You should push yourself beyond your limits of tolerance in your twenties to find out where it is. How much can you work? How disciplined can you become? Can you work twelve hours a day? Can you work eight hours a day? Can you work three hours a day, like flat out? Where's your limit? How much work can you do and how much socialization? You should find out, push yourself past, and then back off to that point where it's optimally sustainable.[38]

For doctors, getting to the edge of how hard you can work is both easy and necessary. It's not a choice we make; it's part of our training.

Now, even if you think all of this is worth it—if you can keep your eyes on the goal and trust that this whirlwind of activity is actually taking you somewhere—you most likely hit your thirties with a sense that something was missing. You're right. I think what's missing is what Peterson calls "socialization." Most of our friends during that season of life are right there next to us, doing the same thing we're doing as students and residents. They live the same life we're living. They have the same struggles and the same victories. That's great in that it gives us a built-in support network of people who truly understand the unique pressures of residency, but it's also a big limitation in that it limits us from being exposed to a variety of different people who represent the fullness of life outside the hospital. The result is that we don't have what we need to build a full library of skills. If everyone we know is just like us and doing the same things as we are, we miss out on the key lessons young professionals in other industries get—chief among them, perhaps, is the ability to understand anyone who's *not* a doctor. And frankly, this doesn't get much better when we complete our residency and enter private practice. At that point, we usually join another older, more experienced doctor's practice—but they have had the same experience we've had. We might be excited to have a new mentor and new perspective when, in reality, what we get is more of the same.

Here and there throughout this book, I've bemoaned how seldom these important "soft skills" are taught during our medical training. This may not be a big deal to you. You may only be interested in the more practical and tactical teaching that Robbie's provided than the softer-skilled, more self-care and others-focused perspective that I've brought in. If that's you, great. I understand. If you don't think something is missing in your life, if you feel *complete* in your medical practice, your business, your relationships, and your family, it's fine. You should just ignore what I'm about to say ... although I don't understand why you'd want to.

I firmly believe that a healthy, well-rounded physician needs a few coaches actively speaking into their life. First, we need a professional guide. Physicians are professionals. In the same way professional athletes need trainers, professional writers need editors, and professional musicians need conductors, we need a trusted medical professional who's further down the road than we are to bounce ideas off of, vent to about our patient-related stress, and consult for medical opinions. Our training doesn't end when we complete our residency; instead, that's usually when we are thrust into a whole world of new things we don't know. We need a guide to help us navigate safely through all the new land mines in our path if we hope to have a long, happy, successful career in medicine.

Second, we need an executive coach. In many ways, Robbie has been this coach for me, as he brought in a whole new world of leadership, operational, financial, and sales and marketing expertise that I didn't even know I was missing. Doctors are not taught how to run a business or lead people. We're taught medicine. For those of us who go on to own and run a practice, that means we have a huge gap in our training that we need to fill. I encourage you to find a trusted individual to come alongside you and help you become a better, more well-rounded businessperson. And while this coach is ideally a *person*, you can get much (if not most) of these benefits through books, videos, workshops, mastermind groups, and online training courses.

Third, we need an emotional health coach. I'm talking about a licensed mental health professional like a psychologist or licensed counselor. While your medical coach focuses on making you a better doctor and your executive coach focuses on making you a better executive, your emotional health coach focuses on making you a better *you*. My therapist has helped me with everything from integrating my family life into my professional ambitions to understanding the pathology and tactical tools I need to deal with some of the more challenging personality types I either work with or treat in my practice. She's made my life and my work richer and much calmer. In short, she's made my life—and me—better.

Why bring this up here and now, as we are right at the finish line of this book? Because your *The Private Practice MBA* will never be complete if you aren't doing as good a job at taking care of *yourself* as you are at taking care of your patients and your business. That brings us to the final word Robbie and I want to leave you with, which is how to navigate the space between efficiency and effectiveness—where tasks, people, and self-care collide. We'll cover that in the next and final chapter.

CHAPTER 21

THE PRIVATE PRACTICE MBA METHOD IN REAL LIFE

Jeremy: Robbie and I want to end this book with a real-life example of what everything we've discussed looks like... but we need to start with a confession.

We believe in everything we've written in this book. Every process. Every principle. This really is the playbook for how we transformed our practice, from a successful-yet-sloppy business that ate up every minute of every day and stole my nights and weekends from my family, into a smooth, process-driven business that runs on autopilot—a practice our patients and team members love and that doesn't keep me up at night. This is the plan that's enabled me and my whole team to earn a much better living by working half as much. It may sound like I'm overselling the benefits here, but I'm not. Every principle and process we've unpacked in this book has contributed to the freedom I now enjoy.

However, I must admit that even we do not do every single thing we've discussed in this book—not anymore, anyway. To be clear, we have done it all throughout the years, but we are now many years into this, and our business has evolved past a few of the things we've talked about here. If you ever visit our office or see us at a conference, ask us about which things we've changed to accommodate our growing business. Based on how the past decade has gone, there is a 100 percent chance we will have found a better way to do some of these things by then, and we'd love to share it. Heck, maybe we'll even write a follow-up book titled *Private Practice Ph.D.* some day!

Of course, we believe everything we've presented here is worth considering, and most things (if not all) are necessary at the beginning of the process. But every business is different, every situation is unique, and it's unlikely that any business—private medicine or otherwise—will ever use every tool in this book at the same time and in exactly the same way that we've done. That doesn't mean I support someone randomly picking and choosing which handful of things they want to implement in their business. Chances are, the things that are least attractive to you are probably the things you need the most. Your initial discomfort at those ideas might indicate a potential blind spot for you as the business owner.

Beyond that, though, none of these techniques exist in a vacuum. To maximize your business and set your practice up to run on autopilot, you need a thoughtful, intentional strategy for each of the four wheels we introduced in the beginning of this book: Money, Sales and Marketing, Operations, and Leadership. And you need to build those areas on the firm foundation of the key Autopilot People we discussed in section 1: the business owner, business director, and team leaders. The right people doing the right things in the right areas will take your practice further and faster than you could imagine. And that brings us to the example we want to leave you with.

I have been struggling for months to figure out how to conclude this book. Just last week, the universe dropped the answer in my lap with a real-life example of how all the tools we've discussed here worked together to solve a practice's problems, relieve the pressure of the business owner, and make life better for their staff and patients alike. As soon as it happened, I realized it would be the perfect way to wrap things up.

An Amelia Aesthetics location recently opened in Charlotte, North Carolina. As we've explained, I do not own the other Amelia locations around the country; we have a licensing deal with these practice owners, which simply gives them access to our brand name and, of course, our Amelia Agency for sales and marketing support. One week ago, as I write this, I had a Sunday-night, check-in phone call with the surgeon who owns that practice. They'd been open six weeks, and I was excited to hear how it was going.

How it was going ... was poorly. Since they'd opened, their team had only had a handful of consultations, which had resulted in an even smaller handful of surgeries scheduled. I wanted to be reassuring, but I was careful to fight back my instinct to blame the economy, the time of year, the newness of his practice, or any other excuse. The truth is, this doctor had a problem, and that problem needed a solution fast. Ignoring it or excusing it wasn't going to help anyone. As we wrapped up that check-in phone call, I assured the business owner that I'd take his concerns to our Amelia Agency team, and we'd be back in touch ASAP with a plan.

I called Robbie immediately, explained the situation, and started brainstorming solutions. Even several years into this, and as much as I've tried to remove myself from the day-to-day problem-solving of our business, I still secretly love finding a reason every now and then to jump into "Situation Room Mode." Helping this fellow surgeon and business owner was a perfect opportunity. Robbie did some background work to gather issues and information, and he presented everything to the team in the Agency's Monday morning meeting the next day. Together, they got to work creating a plan alongside the Charlotte team.

The first step was to create interest in the location's offerings in the Charlotte and surrounding areas. Surely there were plenty of potential patients who had already changed lanes from Awareness to Consideration and then into the Research phase of the patient journey, so how could we let them know an awesome surgeon had just opened a new practice near them? Jenny, the face of the Bustmob online community with whom we've spent several years developing a trust-based relationship, was tasked with making a post in the group highlighting the new location. Other team members worked with the Charlotte office's owner to develop a sales script to help transition new interested patients from the Research phase into Intent to Buy. The web team triple-checked the location's website to make sure their pricing information was clearly visible and that their online booking system was ready for a new influx of patients. And then everyone held their breath as Jenny's community post went live.

Over the next twenty-four hours, the practice booked nearly one hundred new consultations, which created literally months of work. While the Charlotte team was prepared to answer a higher volume of phone calls than normal that day, the phones were mostly quiet. Instead, interested patients did what they were meant to do: they used the freely available tools and information for their research and then scheduled an in-person consult for themselves online. And remember, every one of these new patients scheduled their consult already knowing how much the procedure they were interested in would cost. So as chaotic as you'd think it would be around the office to go from practically zero consult bookings to nearly a hundred in one day, it was relatively quiet. The system was working—the way it was supposed to: on autopilot.

The patients were having an excellent experience too. When someone signed up for a consult, she was immediately and automatically directed to a screen where she signed up for an onboarding call. This call ensured that there were no surprises for her on the day of her consultation and that she was signing up for the correct procedure, whether it was a lift, reduction, tummy tuck, lipo, or whatever else she thought she needed. Patients often aren't sure which procedure they need at that point so it helps to have them talk with an educated member of the practice's team on these onboarding calls before the consult. As we discussed earlier, the consult is a terrible time to conduct research.

The power of having all the preliminary work happen online cannot be overstated. Think about what the office would have been like on this day if every patient had to call to schedule a consult. If the average call took about six minutes, booking one hundred consults would have required ten hours of nonstop phone conversations. Because the team wasn't tied up on the phone all day, they were able to start gathering the right data for the consultations to make sure these patients were super-served. And because the onboarding calls had a pre-written script and checklist, the team members knew exactly what to ask and how to ask it.

Let's review how all this happened so (apparently) effortlessly:

- The business owner started by making the right financial investments in setting up his practice and, of course, hiring the right people in the right positions.
- This one-day turnaround began with good marketing, through a community built on trust.
- It evolved into a trusted sales process, with online scheduling for consultations, freely available information online, and clear and up-front pricing on the website.
- This led to an opportunity for operations to excel by ensuring the automated tech solutions were up and running and by arranging the schedule to accommodate the increased demand.

- The whole thing was overseen by the business owner as the emotional/visionary leader and the business director as the tactical business leader.

There it is, the four wheels of Money, Sales and Marketing, Operations, and Leadership working together on the foundation of the right team of people in the right positions. This is a picture of everything we've been talking about working seamlessly together to build the business and serve the patients—without throwing anyone into a panic or causing the business owner to tear his hair out worrying about how to handle the dramatic increase in demand.

In fact—and this is my favorite part of this story—the surgeon did the unthinkable the very next day after this incredible day of bookings. He went on vacation. He actually left the country for a week. He had carefully built a team he could trust and a system that could operate without him, so he did exactly the right thing: he got the hell out of the way and let his team and systems do their jobs. The team did not disappoint either. They spent the week he was gone creating a bulletproof plan for how to manage the extraordinary demand, and they executed that plan just as they had been trained to do. The big takeaway here is how effective this new practice owner was at doing his two most important jobs:

1. Assembling a team and system capable of winning.
2. Trusting them to win.

The result of this one campaign was mind-blowing. In just under two days, this practice booked one hundred and twenty-three consults that turned into $600,000 in revenue; much of the work was done on autopilot while the business owner was on vacation; and it all came

THE PRIVATE PRACTICE MBA METHOD IN REAL LIFE

from a single message to a community that had been built on trust over several years.

Of course, every surgeon knows this only represents half the story. The practice in Charlotte still has to be exceptional in providing services, in taking care of these patients, and in earning the trust that made all of this possible in the first place. I have no doubt they will do just that. These leaders have done the work to set up their practice, and these team members have shown they have the passion and commitment to follow through just as they've been trained to do.

If you thought the time and effort required to build a practice that runs on autopilot isn't worth it, I know a surgeon in Charlotte who'd disagree. And he's not alone. Every one of us who works in the medical system knows, as I said at the start of this book, that the business of medicine is sick. It's sick from a patient perspective, sick from a physician perspective, sick from a business owner perspective, and sick from a team member perspective. It's been infected by mismanagement, ego, bureaucracy, bad hires, sloppy finances, disorganization, poor systems, and red tape—and if we want it to get better for all of us and our patients, we've got to root out these inherent problems and replace them with healthy, intentional, patient-focused systems. No government body or medical board is going to swoop in and save the day. It's up to us.

Nelson Mandela once said, "Education is the most powerful weapon which you can use to change the world." I know you didn't get this education in medical school. I didn't either. But you have it now. The question for you, then, is how will you use this education—your new *The Private Practice MBA*—to change your world?

Because if we each change our own small part of the business of medicine, we can change it all.

RECOMMENDED READING

If *The Private Practice MBA* has inspired you to invest even more into developing your skills and knowledge as a leader, we suggest starting with some of our favorite business books. Here are five suggestions for each of the four key areas we've discussed.

Money

The Total Money Makeover by Dave Ramsey
The Psychology of Money by Morgan Housel
Think and Grow Rich by Napoleon Hill
The Goal by Eliyahu Goldratt
Tax-Free Wealth by Tom Wheelwright

Sales and Marketing

This Is Marketing by Seth Godin
Building a StoryBrand by Donald Miller
Shoe Dog by Phil Knight
Getting to Yes by Roger Fisher
The Thank You Economy by Gary Vaynerchuk

Operations

Rework by Jason Fried
Radical Candor by Kim Scott
Better by Atul Gawande

The Power of Habit by Charles Duhigg
The Five Dysfunctions of a Team by Patrick Lencioni

Leadership

EntreLeadership by Dave Ramsey
The 21 Irrefutable Laws of Leadership by John Maxwell
Making Vision Stick by Andy Stanley
Linchpin by Seth Godin
Dare to Lead by Brené Brown

ACKNOWLEDGMENTS

Jeremy: The least comfortable part of writing a book is that it requires me to take the collected influences of many and, without credit, make these ideas seem like they are mine. Thank you to all who show up in this book but who are not credited.

Meghan: Thank you for making this a part of your life as well as mine. Thank you for covering for me on weekends so that I could write. Thank you for allowing this to happen in the middle of our family time and space rather than outside it. Also, thank you for everything else, especially for making me laugh when I'm taking myself too seriously.

Eloise: Thank you for being my biggest cheerleader and the most honest guide in the world. I'm so thankful and proud and full of love for you.

Samuel: Thanks for always inviting me to play soccer when I was tired of writing. Someday I hope you get to learn how important those moments are to a dad. I love you for them ... and for a bunch more.

William: I cherish those early mornings writing with you, and I hope you never stop wanting to wake up early to be together. Even when you do, I'll be with you always. I love you to the moon and back.

Mom and Dad: I won the family lottery. Thank you for never making me feel like my ridiculous plans are ridiculous.

Allen: I hear your voice when I'm not sure what to do. I hope you always knew that.

ACKNOWLEDGMENTS

To the team at Amelia Raleigh: You make me proud to work together. We laugh every day and we do good things. That's the most a person could ask of their workplace. Many of you, and you know who you are, have become cherished friends, and I am so thankful for you.

To the team at Amelia HQ: I'm so tremendously proud to be one of you. You are a ragtag group of crazy—stupidly crazy—talented, rock star, legendary freaks. You can do anything digitally. And you are so cool.

Robbie: There's only one Robbie Poe. I've never met anyone who's more able to create, design, and lead a team and company. Thank you for pushing when I pull and pulling when I push. Here's to whatever is next.

Dr. Argenta: Thanks for convincing me to wait on this until I had the time and mental space.

Dr. Marks: Thanks for planting the seed of a book long before we knew the topic.

Dr. David: Thank you for being such a thoughtful and skilled leader; your measure of excellence being so absurdly high is a tremendous gift.

Forefront Books: Thank you for being willing to work with us and for letting us push when you were tired of it. We are already looking forward to the next one.

Robbie: Books don't happen because of the people whose names are on the cover. They happen because some really good people cheered us on, gave us some material worthy to share, and allowed us to unplug from our normal day-to-day responsibilities for way too long. I can't possibly thank everyone, but here's my short list:

ACKNOWLEDGMENTS

Amanda—This book was born during a season when I least believed in my ability to lead—much less to teach others about leadership. Over and over, you stood in the gap and quieted the megaphone of self-doubt that had taken up residence in my mind. Thank you for reminding me who I am.

Jeremy—Holy shit, we did it! I know you know this, but you are one of the few Level 5 Leaders who I've ever met, and being your business partner has been one of the greatest honors of my life. What a ride.

Mom, Dad, Grom, Daddy Bob, Corey, and the rest of the Jones Family—If my life is an airplane, you are my runway. Thank you for *always* providing this frenetic, strong-willed kid with an absolutely endless amount of love, grace, and acceptance.

Amelia Agency—I was out of pocket for an ungodly number of hours while writing this book, and you ensured that extraordinary work continued happening. I'm so proud of you and the revolutionary work you do each and every day.

The Amelia Aesthetics Team—All of you are amazing human beings. Working at an Amelia practice is one of the most medical-rebel things you could do, and I am so proud to be a part of doing what you do.

Dave Ramsey + Ramsey Solutions—I would never have believed in myself to write a book like this if it hadn't been for the ten years y'all tolerated me.

Michael Reddish—The only reason I have anything to say about leadership is because you took a chance on me. And not only that, you continually chose to have my back through every land mine I stepped on.

Allen Harris—Let's be honest: If you hadn't agreed to be our developmental editor, this book would have *really* sucked!

ACKNOWLEDGMENTS

Nancy and Dave Keener—Why in the world did you hire a kid with a green mohawk and zero self-awareness?! I'll never understand, but I'm grateful beyond words that you were the very first business leaders who I had the privilege to be inspired by.

Dr. Glenn Davis—Your legacy will live on forever. Without Davis Plastic Surgery, there would have been no Amelia Aesthetics. Thank you for paving the way for all of us.

Endnotes

1 Eric C. Schneider, Dana O. Sarnak, David Squires, Arnav Shah, and Michelle M. Doty, "Mirror, Mirror 2017: International Comparison Reflects Flaws and Opportunities for Better U.S. Health Care," *The Commonwealth Fund*, (July 2017): 5, https://www.commonwealthfund.org/sites/default/files/documents/___media_files_publications_fund_report_2017_jul_schneider_mirror_mirror_2017.pdf.
2 "The Eisenhower Matrix: How to prioritize your to-do list," Asana.com, June 1, 2022, https://asana.com/resources/eisenhower-matrix.
3 To learn more about our Autopilot software solution, visit AutopilotOnline.com.
4 Michael Hyatt, *Free to Focus* (Grand Rapids: Baker Books, 2019), 95.
5 Lori Boyer, "5 Tips for Dealing with Medical Practice Employee Turnover," *SolutionReach*, July 14, 2020, https://www.solutionreach.com/blog/5-tips-for-dealing-with-medical-practice-employee-turnover.
6 "Why People Quit Their Jobs," *Harvard Business Review*, September 2016, https://hbr.org/2016/09/why-people-quit-their-jobs.
7 "Understand Team Effectiveness," ReWork with Google, https://rework.withgoogle.com/guides/understanding-team-effectiveness/steps/introduction.
8 Ian O'Connor, *Coach K: The Rise and Reign of Mike Krzyzewski* (Boston: Mariner Books, 2022)
9 Emily Weller, "Top-10 IRS Audit Triggers," *Houston Chronicle*, https://smallbusiness.chron.com/top10-irs-audit-triggers-24366.html.
10 Viktor E. Frankl, *Man's Search for Meaning* (Boston: Beacon Press, 2006), originally published 1946.
11 Rabbi Daniel Lapin, *Thou Shall Prosper: Ten Commandments for Making Money* (Hoboken: Wiley and Sons, 2002, 2009).
12 Kerry Jones, "The Most Desirable Employee Benefits," *Harvard Business Review*, February 15, 2017, https://hbr.org/2017/02/the-most-

desirable-employee-benefits.

13 Andrew Chamberlain, "What Matters More to Your Workforce than Money," *Harvard Business Review*, January 17, 2017, https://hbr.org/2017/01/what-matters-more-to-your-workforce-than-money.

14 Information taken from keynote presentation offered by silicone breast implant manufacturer Sientra at their national sales conference.

15 "Cosmetic & Plastic Surgery Marketing," *Agency H*, https://agencyh.com/industries/medical-marketing/cosmetic-plastic-surgery-marketing.

16 Ben Lovejoy, "Can You Guess What Percentage of Macs, iPads & iPhones Are Bought Direct from Apple?" 9to5Mac, October 19, 2017, https://9to5-mac.com/2017/10/19/apple-store-sales-cirp.

17 Amy Gallo, "The Value of Keeping the Right Customers," *Harvard Business Review*, October 29, 2014, https://hbr.org/2014/10/the-value-of-keeping-the-right-customers.

18 Joseph Grenny, "When to Solve Your Team's Problems, and When to Let Them Sort It Out," *Harvard Business Review*, July 20, 2017, https://hbr.org/2017/07/when-to-solve-your-teams-problems-and-when-to-let-them-sort-it-out.

19 Daniel Kahnemann, *Thinking, Fast and Slow* (New York: Farrar, Straus and Giroux, 2013).

20 "The Best Customer Service Uses Ritz-Carlton Radar On, Antenna Up Model," *Chief Outsiders*, November 25, 2012, https://www.chiefoutsiders.com/blog/bid/92733/the-ritz-carlton-radar-on-antenna-up-customer-service-style.

21 *Ted Lasso*. 2020, Season 1, Episode 2, "Biscuits." AppleTV+, Directed by Zach Braff.

22 Avinoam Nowogrodski, "Would Your Teammates Rather Watch Paint Dry Than Attend Your Status Meeting?" Entrepreneur.com, May 18, 2015, https://www.entrepreneur.com/article/246170.

23 Patrick Lencioni, *The Five Dysfunctions of a Team* (San Francisco: Jossey-Bass, 2002).

24 Verne Harnish, *Scaling Up: How a Few Companies Make It ... and Why the Rest Don't* (Ashburn: Gazelles, Inc., 2014).

25 Jim Collins, *Good to Great* (New York: HarperCollins, 2001), 58.

26 Walter Isaacson, *Steve Jobs* (New York: Simon & Schuster, 2011).

27 "Netflix Mission and Vision Statement Analysis," https://mission-

ENDNOTES

statement.com/netflix/#:~:text=Netflix's%20vision%20statement%20is%20%E2%80%9CBecoming,of%20on%2Ddemand%20video%20services.

28 Southwest Airlines corporate website, https://www.southwestairlinesinvestorrelations.com/our-company/purpose-vision-and-the-southwest-way.

29 "Nike Mission, Vision and Values," Comparably.com, https://www.comparably.com/companies/nike/mission.

30 Christine Rowland, "Apple Inc.'s Mission Statement and Vision Statement (An Analysis)," Panmore Institute, May 9, 2022, https://panmore.com/apple-mission-statement-vision-statement.

31 Andy Stanley, *Making Vision Stick* (Grand Rapids: Zondervan, 2007).

32 Anthony Rivera, "Netflix's Mission Statement & Vision Statement: A Strategic Analysis," Rancord Society, November 10, 2019, https://www.rancord.org/netflix-corporate-vision-statement-mission-statement-strategic-analysis#:~:text=Netflix%20Inc.'s%20corporate%20mission,on-demand%20movie%20streaming%20services.

33 Southwest Airlines corporate website, https://www.southwestairlinesinvestorrelations.com/our-company/purpose-vision-and-the-southwest-way.

34 "Nike Mission, Vision and Values,"

35 Christine Rowland, "Apple Inc.'s Mission Statement and Vision Statement (An Analysis)."

36 "About Tesla," Tesla.com, https://www.tesla.com/about#:~:text=Tesla's%20mission%20is%20to%20accelerate,to%20drive%20than%20gasoline%20cars.

37 Ken Blanchard, "A Situational Approach to Effective Leadership," Ken Blanchard Companies, August 22, 2019, https://resources.kenblanchard.com/blanchard-leaderchat/a-situational-approach-to-effective-leadership.

38 Joe Rogan and Jordan Peterson, Episode 1,208, *The Joe Rogan Experience* (podcast), Time Stamp 2:04:37, November 29, 2018, https://open.spotify.com/episode/3wmETCtL54gUbDJS4LfxLy.